Also by Tilly Rose

A Spirit Called Alcohol

Going to California

A Prayer for Veterans
from Every War

By

Tilly Rose

Going to California

Copyright © Tilly Rose, May 2015

All Rights Reserved

For more information visit:

A Spirit Called Alcohol on Facebook

aspiritcalledalcohol@gmail.com

DEDICATION

WARRIORS OF BATTLES PAST

To the Warriors of battles past
May you find Peace at last
For those imprisoned, who starved to death
May Joy accompany your last breath

For those, who a cruel hand stole life away
May the Spirit of Justice guide your days
For those whose inner demons took them to the gates of hell
May you be forever loved, with stories left to tell

For those tortured souls of endless wars
Now knocking on death's door
May the Light of Heaven guide your way
Out of hell, may you stay

May the inner wounds of battles lost
Be forever healed, no matter what the cost
With blood-stained hands and tattered hearts
May Creator bless you with a new start

May the howling fears of yesteryear
Be washed away with your sacred tears
May the Sacred Fire purify your soul
And allow your heart to be forever whole

For battles won and battles lost
Leave a soldier inwardly tossed

From rage to madness and back again
May the need for battles forever end

TABLE OF CONTENTS

CHAPTER ONE: I HAD NO CHOICE.........................2
CHAPTER TWO: GOING TO CALIFORNIA............17
CHAPTER THREE: FREE AT LAST........................55
CHAPTER FOUR: NATURE'S LAWS......................81
CHAPTER FIVE: TO BE OR NOT TO BE..............107
CHAPTER SIX: A HERSHEY'S KISS.....................134
CHAPTER SEVEN: SPIRIT FOLLOWS SPIRIT....146
CHAPTER EIGHT: WELCOME HOME................160
CHAPTER NINE: A POWERFUL PRAYER...........177
AUTHOR'S NOTE...238

CHAPTER ONE: I HAD NO CHOICE

Scarlet

"I'm not a harlot anymore,"
Screamed Scarlet standing by the door
I have dignity and I am proud
And this I can say out loud

"I'm not a harlot anymore,
It's a life for me that's lost
I AM a new woman now
It doesn't matter what the cost."

She looked back upon the brothel
That fed and clothed her all these years
With her chin held high, she wouldn't cry
And reveal the pain with all her tears

A new world, now it beckoned
And she mustered up some grace
It would only be by Creator's blessing
That she would find her place

The road, at times, was slippery
Sometimes she lost resolve
But Grace again would find her
With Love, the problem's solved

Make peace with your journey
Especially when you slip and fall
These are but the best of times
And Creator will grace us all

"OH YEAH!" Rhoda's lightly freckled, alabaster face grew beet red as the venomous words flew out of her mouth. "YOUR MOTHER LOVED YOU SO MUCH SHE COMMITTED SUICIDE!" Her lion's mane of fiery red curls shook wildly. Being a hell-raiser from the Eastern Seaboard, her balled up fist slammed down on the metal table The cheap tin cutlery jumped. All the eyes around the table got wide, as these two hellcats squared off.

Like murderous vultures, dozens of dark shadows peered down from the steel girders snickering. To keep themselves amused, their sharp black talons violently stirred the stale air inside the prison's gray cinder block walls until it boiled like a black, menacing thunderhead. Fight was in the air. Its looming, stormy, crackling energy caused the air to quake while Rhoda's fighting words echoed off the concrete. That was it. With her eyes spitting fire, Rhoda threw her verbal lance and knocked Mirabelle, the tarnished Southern princess, right off her high horse.

Sparks of fury flashed from her eyes as Mirabelle slid gracefully off the steel table. "Well, at least I had a mother," her sweet, but lethal Southern voice was quiet and contained. "Your mother loved you so much that she died in childbirth. Your devilish horns probably tore her up from the inside. Making you nothing but a ward."

Sharper than ice cycles, Mirabelle's words slashed through Rhoda's thick tortoise skin. Like BB's in a tin garbage can, they bounced around the cell block. With currents of hot fury crackling in the air, the other women in the quad gathered round. Seeing this high voltage trouble brewing, two of Rhoda's friends grabbed her arms before she launched at Mirabelle's throat. "She ain't worth it," Jesse whispered. "You're getting out in a week. You know she hates you enough to get you thrown in the hole for fighting."

One of the shadowy war-hawks leapt from his perch, his leathery black wings enfolded his charge, making sure she heard every whisper he planted in her smoldering mind. Gathering her composure, Rhoda willed herself to calm down, calculating her next shot. "Yeah, I read about you in that daily rag, a newspaper," Rhoda smirked. "Nanny from Hell! That's what they called you!"

"I worked for the stars," the ice queen smiled coyly. "Some of them were just falling stars. With all their lipo-suction, drug addictions and face lifts. They were hardly fit to be parents. Somebody had to tell their story. It might as well have been me." Slowly, she walked around the quad, sizing Rhoda up with her calculating, ruthless eyes of cold steel. "I'm sure the toilet bowls you scrubbed for a living weren't much cleaner than your mouth. And since your words come from your heart, it must be black as coal."

Watching from above in the observation deck, two guards had the mike in the quad turned on the whole time, listening to these two cougars go at it. "Ya think we better break it up?" asked Roger.

"Naw, I'd let them work it out for a while," said Clyde. "It's better than day time TV. Rhoda's getting out in a week. I doubt she'll throw that away for that Southern tramp."

"I'm not too sure, Clyde. Rhoda's got a bad temper. I've watched that girl crack under pressure," Roger observed. Roger flipped on the loud speaker. "You girls better settle down in there before I put y'all in lock down."

If someone gifted with spiritual sight were watching this prison shrouded in razor-wire from afar, they'd see a boiling black thunderhead, a fiery electrical storm, hovering over the entire concrete and steel complex. This barely perceptible swirling cloud of angry, hate-laden spirits and thought-forms clashed their blood-stained sickles and blades through the hearts and bodies of the living. Though these hulking war-hawks were unseen by the human eye, their hateful influence was definitely felt and oftentimes their whispers were carried out in great detail.

"Come on, Rhoda," Jesse grabbed her arm. "That bitch ain't worth it. Remember you got your little girl out there waiting for you. You been away from her for 4 years. You don't want to mess that up now."

With a flaming ball of rage searing in her heart, Rhoda couldn't let it drop. So she hurled one more poisoned dagger. "Why don't you try eating your make-up from now on," Rhoda snarled. But the ice queen cut her off.

"Why? Pray tell, would I do that?" her Southern drawl trailed on.

With her hands on her hips, Rhoda's fiery eyes stared Mirabelle up and down. "Then at least you'd be pretty on the inside, ya ol' bitch!" Gloating, she finally struck pay dirt. Unheard and unseen, the dark shadows snickered and jeered, furiously stirring an unseen cauldron bubbling over with fury and fright.

"ZZZZHHHH!" the ice queen hissed, a thousand angry voices screaming in her mind. With her fingernails pointed in Rhoda's direction, her poisonous glare sent sizzling, invisible sparks of wrath. Dusting her hands off, Rhoda threw Mirabelle a spiteful look and went back to her bunk.

As cat fights go, this one was just heating up. Smoldering inside, Rhoda walked into her cell and flopped down on her bunk. She took the school picture out of her daughter Clarissa and stared into her big brown eyes. The last four years had inched by. Clarissa was just a baby, when Rhoda got locked up. What she did was stupid. Of course, she thought she could get away with it. But her thinking wasn't straight. She was desperate at time. By the time she changed her mind, and tried to pull out of the deal, it was too late. The cat was out of the bag. There was no turning back. It wasn't her first time in front of Judge McGroeder, which didn't help her cause any. No matter how she tried to explain her hard luck story to him, he didn't see it that way.

Sitting on a chair inside her cell, Mirabelle furiously filed her fingernails. Nothing jolted her so hard as reliving the image of her mother's dead body. Seeing its lifeless shape draped over the steering wheel of the family car, stole away her young life. The image rarely left her mind. Every Mother's day, Christmas, Easter and holiday, brought that sour taste back into her mouth. It was inescapable. How could anyone expect her to function, let alone get good grades in high school when she was haunted by something so gruesome?

With nothing but time to think, Mirabelle stared at the ceiling. The mind is a cruel, hard place. Especially when it came to remembering all those horrible things. Slowly she felt her mind drowning in the endless seas of hopelessness and despair. Down deep in the secret caverns of her soul, Mirabelle always felt that she embarrassed her mother. Though she wasn't stupid, doing time in these cold cinder block walls, she gained an understanding about herself through the wrong choices that she made. Even so, she knew she couldn't help her ancestry.

On those long, restless nights, it was as if a plow mercilessly churned up the soil of her soul. Lurking deep in her memories were all the ugly, hidden things of her childhood, which came flooding to the surface on these endlessly cold, lonely nights. Within, she felt the unspoken, deep seated roots of worthlessness. Her inner self was like a barren field of hard, flinty rock where no corn could grow. Living in this gray world, she was tired and had forgotten how to dream. Her life had been a firestorm, making up of good reasons to do bad things. No matter how hard she worked to prove she was valuable in society's eyes, it all ended with a rash of desperate, stupid mistakes.

After her mother's suicide, the church refused to let her be buried in the graveyard, because it was consecrated ground. It was far too holy for someone who'd committed such an act of faithlessness. After years of devout service, this was the ultimate disgrace. The church deemed her mother's self-annihilation to be an unforgivable mortal sin. Since she was considered "eternally damned," no resident of hell would be allowed to rest in peace in their cemetery.

Then, as a young girl, Mirabelle fell into a spirit-breaking depression. In those years, doctors were commissioned to zap her brain with intense volts of electricity to erase her memories. Afterward, she felt like a wrung out dishrag, never able to measure up to society and their vicious score card. All her self-worth was validated by superficial beauty, a Scarlet O'Hara 24 inch waist and measured by her family's wealth. In the boarding schools, she often felt guided by an unloving hand. The nuns at the Catholic school never thought she'd amount to much. The words of the grim priests, their hell, fire and brimstone sermons and all their lifeless traditions, echoed in her mind during the coldest hours of the night. Looking around at the prison cell, the nuns must have been right.

That night Rhoda couldn't sleep. Down the cell block, she heard someone laughing like a lunatic. On the floor below, someone was tapping out a beat on the bunk's metal frame. Every sound was amplified as the cell block settled in for the night. Under her tough exterior, she was afraid. All her life she was surrounded by people who wanted to cut her throat. Tonight wasn't any different. It was easy to blow it a week before she was due to be released. With her mouth, she knew that she had made a few enemies. Some who'd like to see her rot in hell or this godforsaken place. After lights out, she was overcome with a feeling of dread. An impending doom chilled her to the bone. It wasn't the first time she'd felt this way.

Corrections Officer Clancy clocked in shortly before 8 pm. In his lunch box, he had a stash of his wife's favorite chocolate chip cookies. He hadn't worked this cell block since he got transferred. But he heard that Rhoda was getting out and wanted to give her something to remember him by. A wicked smile crossed his lips he punched the time clock. It was their dirty little secret. For this special occasion, he switched his shift with a buddy. A hour after lights out, he'd go make his rounds around the cell block.

The dim florescent light flickered overhead as Rhoda tossed and turned on that cold, hard bunk. At night, the sounds in the cell block seemed louder. Every sound reverberated through the cold concrete building. A chill crept up her spine as she heard his foot steps coming up the metal stairwell. Her body shivered. Tap. Tap. Tap. She heard him hitting the checkpoint on the door of each cell. But then it stopped. Suddenly, the lock on her door clicked and the door slid open. Looking up from her bunk, the first thing she saw in the faint light was his greasy smile.

"Well, hey there Rhoda," he started with a snicker. "I heard you was getting out and I brought you something to remember me by." Nothing pleased him more than a feisty mare that was well broke-in. And he had a hand in training this one for several years now. He'd hate to see her leave the stable without a farewell party.

A creepy feeling washed over her as she looked into his demon infested eyes. Without missing a beat, Rhoda put on her game face. She'd known rotten apples like CO Clancy before. "Oh," she said acting pleasantly surprised. "For little ol' me. You shouldn't have." CO Clancy slid the door mostly closed as he stepped into the cell.

When there is great pressure, one of two things will happen. Either the pipes will burst, causing a great flood and destroy everything. Or the pressure will build so much, that a chunk of black coal will transform into a diamond. This game of cat and mouse, predator and prey, was all too familiar.

In her first prison stint at Devil's Island, she was scared and vulnerable. This made her easy prey. It wasn't the first time someone in charge had taken advantage of her vulnerability. Growing up in an orphanage, it seemed to be a pattern of abuse she never got away from. But tonight, something inside her revolted. For the last few days, she could almost taste her freedom. The fear of losing that made her feel crazy inside, like a caged animal. A cornered animal is the most dangerous. A cornered woman, with a great need, can grow horns and hooves.

"I brought you some of my wife's famous chocolate chip cookies," his greasy smile turned into a smirk. "I remembered how much you liked those." He held the plastic baggy of cookies in his hand.

"Yeah well, you don't get a lot of chocolate around here," Rhoda deflected, feeling terrifically uneasy. She knew where this was going. But tonight she didn't want to go.

"Well, I'll let you have a cookie," he paused, dangling the baggie in his hand. "But first we got to take care of a little business," his voice grew firm, commanding. When she heard him start to unzip his pants, the voices inside Rhoda's head started screaming. Quickly, her heart turned to stone and she went numb. Trapped and cornered, her mind raced, trying to figure a way out of this wretched hell. But tonight, she couldn't afford to lose control. While he stood there grinning, her mind flashed back to the first time this happened. It wasn't long after she got transferred here from the county jail.

With an imbalance of power, it wasn't uncommon for correction officers to have sex with inmates. It's been estimated that there are 217,000 prison rapes a year committed by correction officers against prisoners. Even a priest was found guilty of having sex with inmates. Usually, there was an exchange: sex for cigarettes, drugs or cell phones. In a Baltimore prison, one male convict impregnated four female corrections officers. These female officers were charged with rape. Because with an imbalance of power, the inmate never truly consents. Just because something is common, doesn't mean it feels good. The poison is in the sugar.

In her mind's eye, Rhoda remembered the first time CO Clancy pulled down his zipper. While he clutched his puny, little manhood in his hand, she almost burst out laughing. But she knew better than to insult a man with a billy club and a gun.

In that instant, another episode flashed through her mind, back to a place long ago. As a troubled teenager, she got placed in a youth camp. It was a working horse ranch. For one of her chores, she spent time feeding and washing down the horses. Her favorite was a misty gray stallion. He was almost silver, with a long, flowing mane. Snorting and shaking his head, his fiery eyes dang near scared the life out of her. The first time she washed him down, she spied his male organ. His manhood was the biggest thing she'd ever seen. This feisty steed was the prize possession of the ranch, bringing the rancher lots of money for his stud services.

And then, of course, it happened. One afternoon, while Rhoda washed down the horses, a ranch-hand snuck out from behind the bales of hay. His boxer shorts were down around his ankles. Flashing a greasy smile her way, he gave her a wink. In his hand, he held his manhood. But having just washed down the stallion, Rhoda laughed uproariously when she caught sight of his puny swollen member. Next to the stallion's, the ranch hand had no bragging rights. Her cackling laughter found him humiliated. The ranch-hand lost his vigor and his manhood shrunk. Embarrassed, he sheepishly slipped away.

But she didn't think laughing at CO Clancy would get her out of this one. So without a choice, she played along. All the while, she hoped that she wouldn't blow it and end up in the hole. For the first couple years of her incarceration, he made a habit of coming by, offering up cookies in exchange for sex.

But something tonight was different. A disgust, a revulsion gripped her throat. She knew what she was being forced to do. Many times over the years of nightly visits, she wished she'd had the courage to bite it off. But she was afraid she'd be killed. Just like the other inmate girl who won a million dollar lawsuit against a prison guard who raped her. While he was incarcerated, her life became a living hell. After months of harassment from other correction officers, the poor girl was found dead in her cell.

"Only six more days. Don't blow it now," Rhoda thought to herself as she mustered up the grit to do this dirty deal. It's not that the business would take a long time. But she felt sick to her stomach, like she was going to throw up. Rubbing himself, he stood there staring at her with his greasy grin.

"Come to papa, little girl. Daddy's got a cookie for you," CO Clancy chimed. His obsession for an infernal Venus haunted him constantly. It drove him to work nights and drew him away from his marriage of too many years. "You remember what to do, don't you little girl. You'll make daddy feel good all over."

Standing there in the dim light, she wanted to scream. But there was no place to run to. Her mind struggled, trying to make this horror go away. But she had no choice. She had no choice. She had no choice.

The concrete floor was cold and hard as she knelt down in front of him. Stroking her red curls, he started to coo. "Oh, you are a good little girl."

"SICK! SICK! SICK!" her mind screamed. His flaccid manhood plopped in her mouth.

"Daddy's got a good lollipop for you," he said as he ran his hand through her thick red hair.

But this time something inside her snapped. A burning fury welled up inside her belly. Without even thinking, her teeth clamped down on his manhood like a pit bull.

"AHHHHHHHHH!" his screams echoed through the cell block, as her jaw locked down hard. Piercing his delicate skin with her sharp teeth, blood started spurting everywhere. With all his might, he slammed his fists against her head. Then he pulled her red curls to get her clamped jaw to release him. But the harder he pulled, the fiercer she clamped down. Inside her mouth, she felt her teeth tearing through his flesh. Her hands grabbed his balls, twisting them from side to side. Lightning bolts of pain shot through every cell of his body. The pain was excruciating. His knees began to buckle as he felt himself collapse. While his screams bounced of the cell block walls, his private obsession finally became his undoing. Everyone was awake, listening.

All over the cell block, alarms sounded and all the lights went on. Correction officers flooded into the cell block. Like troops on a mission, their heavy boots pounded up the metal stairs. Yelling commands, they stopped as one correction officer pushed open the heavy metal door. With blood splattered all over her face, Rhoda held the gnashed off manly member in her hands. CO Clancy lay there, collapsed in a pool of blood.

The next day it was all over the news: "INMATE BITES OF CO'S PENIS IN ATTEMPTED PRISON RAPE!" To save his reputation, CO Clancy spun the tale a different way. Rhoda was accused of assaulting an officer. She was placed in solitary confinement. Sitting in that dark hole, she felt trapped in an endless winter. This time, her whole world sank. Damned since birth, her unhappiness and bad luck seemed unending. Down in her gut, she knew she'd never see daylight again. CO Clancy was taken to the emergency room and his dismembered manhood was sewn back on.

Days later, at her arraignment, Rhoda sat shackled in the jury box. Over the loud speaker, played a tape recording of her Constitutional Rights. Wincing in pain, she could barely sit in the hard wooden chair. There were bruises on her back and legs where she was beaten with billy clubs. In self defense, she had broken the unwritten rules. Now she felt cursed. An overwhelming fear gripped the shreds of what was left of her twisted, tormented mind. She was afraid she'd never see her daughter again. Her unbridled spirit, now finally broken, was just a muddy puddle sadly clinging to the soles of her feet. Effectively, she felt like she lost her mind. Her inner soul was crushed. Feeling absolutely destroyed, her heart was so numb, there were no tears. Her head hung low in bone-crushing sorrow.

Outside the courthouse, the media frenzy was outrageous. Cameras flashed, reporters clamored, as Justice J. Booker got out of her black Mercedes that morning in the courthouse parking lot. This was just the kind of bad press the Department of Justice didn't need. When people lost faith in the justice system, all kinds of chaos followed. But that morning, she was determined to get down to the bottom of it.

In her chambers, Judith Booker found her black robe and went over some of the case briefs. Something about CO Clancy's assault charges against inmate di Cello, didn't add up. Nothing bothered her more than an abuse of power. She wouldn't tolerate it. But, all the facts had to be presented before she could make a ruling. Shortly before 9:00 am, she donned her black robe and left her chambers. Walking through the hallway into the courtroom, she said hello to the bailiff and the clerk. Then, she took her seat behind the bench. The morning docket was fairly full. She hoped to get through them all by noon.

Judge Booker called the bailiff over to the bench. "Now, I saw reporters out there this morning. I want you to instruct them, that I will not tolerate any cameras or disruption in my courtroom. Make that very clear, or I will clear the court. Is that understood?"

"Yes Judy," Bailiff Walker smiled. He'd seen other controversial cases come before court. If he didn't set the limits, it could quickly turn into a circus.

"Now is CO Clancy in the courtroom this morning? Or just his attorney?" she asked.

"So far, only his attorney checked in. I can't imagine the guy's walking already after what happened," the bailiff said, casting a knowing look.

"Yeah, I wouldn't think so either," Judy said. "Well, if you're ready, lets get started."

The bailiff went to open the courtroom doors and allow everyone in. Before he let in the reporters, he gave them a general warning about cameras and disrupting the court proceedings. Everyone filed in afterward in a respectful manner.

Among the people in the audience, was Merrie. She was a representative of a national human rights organization, "END PRISON RAPE." Their organization worked tirelessly to end the sexual abuse of men, women and young people behind bars. When word of Rhoda di Cello's case crossed the wire a few days prior, Merrie was on a plane to see what she could do.

Oftentimes dehumanized, the victims of sexual abuse in prisons are terrified of speaking out against their captors. Prison rape is a problem shrouded in shame and secrecy. Statistically speaking, one in 5 male inmates have experienced forced sex. While women inmates, who tend to be assaulted by male officers or staff, are raped or abused somewhere between 8 to 27 percent. Juveniles, who are tried and sentenced as adults, don't fair any better. Being so incarcerated, they are 5 times more likely to get sexually assaulted than if they had gone to a juvenile detention center.

With no windows in the courtroom, it was impossible to tell the passing of time. Dark stained wood paneling covered the walls. With the Wainscot molding, it gave the courtroom an austere ambiance, devoid of human compassion. What mattered here was what laws were broken, not how people felt about what happened. Like a shield, Rhoda's red curls hung around her face, as she stared down at her shoes. She picked furiously at a hang nail, ripping the skin and causing it to bleed. From her neck down, she felt nothing. Her heart and all her goodness was ripped out of her. She just wanted to die.

"ALL RISE," the bailiffs voice boomed over the courtroom. "Court is now in session. Honorable Judge J. Booker presiding."

From behind the bench, Judge Booker looked out at the courtroom. Behind her black leather chair hung the Great Seal of California, with the California flag and American Flag flanking the bench. It didn't seem too different from any other day. But something was brewing and she could feel it. "Good morning," she began. "Now, I know we all saw the news. Let me remind you that I will not tolerate any outbursts or photography in this courtroom. Am I clear?" There were a few murmurs in the audience.

In an emotional stupor, Rhoda just looked at her shoes the whole time, until she heard her name being called. "State of California vs. Rhoda di Cello." The shackles around her ankles cut into her skin as Rhoda stood up. For just a second, she met the judges gaze, then immediately looked down.

"Miss di Cello," the judge began. "It says here that you are accused of assaulting a corrections officer, David P. Clancy. Now, do you have an attorney?"

"No, your honor," Rhoda spoke in a muffled voice.

"Would you like one appointed for you by the court?"

"Yes, your honor," Rhoda dared to look up.

"Fine, you can meet on the side bar here, with your public defender. Then I will take your plea," the judge arranged. "Why don't you consult in the jury box and let me know what you decide."

While the harried public defender came over to talk to Rhoda, it didn't make her feel any better. Rhoda had already decided she was going to plead not guilty. Even though there was blood all over her face and she had the penis in her hand, she didn't consent to have sex with CO Clancy. She did it under duress.

After they consulted, the public defender approached the bench, ready to make the plea. Rhoda stood with her public defender behind the tables set up for the attorneys. Her heart beat furiously out of her chest. Not even 10 days ago, she was looking forward to spending the rest of her life with her daughter. But now, she might rot in this living grave and spend 25 years in prison. Since her mother died in childbirth, with no record of the father, Rhoda had been a ward of the court most of her life.

"Okay, Miss di Cello," the judge began matter-of-fact. "It says here that you assaulted correction officer Clancy by biting off his penis. That's when the other officers rushed into your cell. You had CO Clancy's penis in your hand and blood all over your face and clothes. How do you wish to plead?"

"Not guilty, your honor," Rhoda spoke out loud.

"Your plea of not guilty is accepted," the judge proceeded. Then she just shook her head. Something did not make sense. "Now, I realize this is the arraignment. You are not required to testify…" she paused before she asked the million dollar question. "But what I don't understand is HOW did you get his penis in your mouth?"

Waves of anxiety flooded over her. Every cell in her body was on fire. Rhoda couldn't hold back any longer. Streams of tears ran down her face. Quickly, she wiped them off with her sleeve. "He came into my cell at night," she said between sobs. "He told me that he'd give me chocolate chip cookies if I took care of his business."

"What was his business?" the judge coolly inquired.

"Whatever he wanted," Rhoda's voice got cold.

"You mean sex?"

Rhoda furiously nodded her head up and down. "YES!" she cried.

Thunderstruck, the judge leaned back in her chair. Glaring out into the audience, she spied CO Clancy's attorney. "Mr. Reinhold, were you aware of this?"

"No your honor. That is not what CO Clancy described to me at all," Attorney Reinhold stated.

"Who else knows about this?" the judge asked Rhoda.

"Everybody," Rhoda stammered, as she looked at the other women in the jury box. "All of us."

With an eagle eye, the judge looked over the women in the jury box and shook her head. "Is there anyone else here in this courtroom, you ladies in the jury box, that knows about CO Clancy's nighttime lewd behavior?"

In the jury box, scared glances shot from one shackled woman to another. Slowly, three hands went up. Then after a few moments, two more frightened hands went up.

Judith Booker's mind went racing through all the alleged cases of sexual abuse which were brought before her, regarding CO Clancy and the conduct of other correction officers. But as in any case of 'he said - she said', it was hard to prove beyond a shadow of a doubt. More difficult was destroying a man's career over such allegations. But this time, it was different. In the middle of the night, a woman inmate, close to leaving prison, bit off a man's penis in her own cell after lights out. He had no business being there to begin with. There was no prior emergency regarding Rhoda di Cello, recorded in the log book. The only emergency recorded on that fateful night, was CO Clancy's after his penis was bitten off.

"Mr. Reinhold, if your client wrongfully accused Miss di Cello, there will be consequences. From what I'm witnessing, CO Clancy is accused of forcible rape from several women inmates in my courtroom right now. There is nothing that troubles me more than an abuse of power," Judge Booker continued.

Merrie felt compelled to stand up, even though it might constitute a disruption of court. "Your honor."

"Yes and who are you?" Judge Booker asked.

"Your Honor, I am from the organization, END PRISON RAPE. I'd like to offer these women free counseling if you could so order it," said

Merrie.

"Oh," the judge sighed. A wave of exhaustion moved through her body, as she thought of the big impact this could make. As it stood right now, the import of this case and all its implications would surely tarnish the system of justice. "The court will take a brief recess to consider the matter. Let's say we reconvene in one hour." With force, she struck her gavel to add emphasis and stepped down off the bench.

Back in her chambers, Judy picked up the black phone on her desk. Keeping her emotions in check, she managed to control her growing anxiety as it washed over her. She needed to consult with someone who knew a bit more about these matters. Quickly her fingers dialed her ex-husband Jack, who worked for the FBI. It seemed as though an eternity passed as his cell phone rang and rang.

"Jack Booker," his cool voice came over the phone.

"Do you have a minute?" her terse voice quickly asked.

"Yeah, Judy... what's up?" It wasn't often that his self-contained, impenetrable ex-wife called him.

"I have a situation that could explode down here. I was wondering if you could make it over. We may have a CO in the prison, a sexual predator and 6 of the women inmates in the jury box know about it," her voice was strained. "There may be more."

"Ah Judy, prison rape is a common thing. For all we know, those women asked for it," he stopped short.

His flippant attitude broiled her insides. Years of witnessing the most heinous crimes on Earth had taken a toll on the man she'd met 30 years ago in a criminal justice class. Back then, looking through the hopeful eyes of youth, they still thought they could change the world. Instead the world had rotted out their passions, leaving them hollow and dead inside. Looking in disbelief at the phone receiver, she almost slammed the phone down, but decided against it. "SHE BIT OFF HIS PENIS, JACK!" Judy screamed.

"OKAY! OKAY! I'll be right over," he hung up the phone. Working for the Justice Department had its obvious downside. Their marriage was a casualty of the war they witnessed everyday. It was hard not to take their work home. But the constant hell they witnessed infected their relationship. Eventually, it destroyed their marriage. It was no one's fault really. But having their daily lives seeped in darkness, they just couldn't recover the love they once had.

Most of the courtroom had cleared out during the recess, except for Merrie and a reporter, Matt Carlson, from the Daily Reporter, who worked on his smart phone. Hoping to lend support, Merrie moved her seat closer to the defendant. Feeling utterly defeated, Rhoda hung her head. Without a sound, tears flowed freely from her eyes. They dripped off the edge of her nose, leaving wet marks on her orange jail suit. Sitting next to her, a wave of compassion came over the public defender. In kindness, she put her hand on Rhoda's back to console her. Rhoda winced in pain.

"What's the matter?" the public defender asked.

"It hurts there," Rhoda's small voice answered. On a whim, the public defender slowly inched Rhoda's sleeve towards her back. Looking underneath her shirt, made the public defender wince. The skin was scabbed with dried blood, colored in black and blue.

"Let me see your back," the public defender said. Like a helpless child, Rhoda allowed her to slowly lift up her shirt from behind. Black and blue marks covered her back. Some of them were fresh. In a few places, the skin was broken and fresh scabs had formed. Sitting behind Rhoda, Merrie gasped. The reporter looked up. For a moment, the bailiff was out of sight.

Watching this scene unfold, the reporter reached for his camera. Through his camera lens, Matt Carlson zoomed in for the shot. As Rhoda's shirt was lifted, he saw the bruises covering her back. His trigger finger started snapping photos. After he got the shot, he rushed out to the lobby and downloaded them to his computer. Within seconds, he sent them over the internet to his boss. This story would be breaking news.

"What happened?" the public defender asked, already knowing the answer.

"After they stuck me in the hole...," Rhoda stammered, her heart was beating as fast as a jack-hammer. "Those bastards ...." she sniffled, wiping the tears from her eyes. "Came by and beat me with whatever they had. If that wasn't enough, I got raped two or three times a day." Rhoda's shame rose to her throat. "They were paying me back for what I did to CO Clancy."

With gentle, humbled eyes, Merrie caught the eye of the over-worked, haggard public defender. The strain on her face said it all. There were no words.

CHAPTER TWO: GOING TO CALIFORNIA

STONE, WIND, FIRE AND RAIN

Stones will be hard, my love
As for the Wind, that is not so
The Wind can be cold, my love
From the North, it blows and blows

Rain will be wet, my love
Or it will turn into frozen snow
The Fire will burn, my love
Keeping us warm against the Winter's cold

Earthen Clay is soft, my love
Until through the Potter's fire it goes
The Sands of Time will shift, my love
As the Four Winds forever blow

Rivers continue to flow, my love
Home to the Sea, they go
The Sun will blaze, my love
No matter if you're young or old

When the body grows old, my love
The Spirit will long to go
To be with the Ancestors, my love
Into the Great Beyond, you know

White Lighting brightens the sky, my love
While the Holy Thunders roll and roll
When your heart-fire grows dim, my love
Soon, it will be time to go

You can't lasso the Wind, my love
Though your breath you might try to hold
Walk along the River of Life, my love
With the Star Marker and be forever whole.

Rambling down the interstate, a dry, dusty Santa Ana wind pushed Hal's old beater truck to the side. He clutched tightly to the steering wheel to keep from going into oncoming traffic. His mouth was parched and his legs were cramped after the long hours of driving.

"Spent my days with a woman unkind,
Smoked my stuff and drank all my wine..."

Crackling over the airwaves of Hal's old FM radio, sang the haunting voice of Robert Plant. The wandering minstrels of Led Zeppelin were playing one of Hal's favorite songs.

"Made up my mind to make a new start,
Going to California with an aching in my heart..."

Strumming guitars and mandolins floated through the air, as the wistful folk song, "Going to California," filled the cab of the truck. Decades ago, Hal ended up in California through the military.

"Someone told me there's a girl out there,
With love in her eyes and flowers in her hair..."

Down near San Diego is where he had his last drink. After a few months sober, he met Arlene, who later became his wife. It was hard to remember now, if she had flowers in her hair when he met her. But this classic tune brought back some good memories.

"You ever heard this band?" Hal broke the long silence as they barreled down the dusty highway, headed towards the West Coast.

"You mean Led Zeppelin?" Leroy shot back.

"Well, you were just a young pup, barely alive, when those balladeers wrote this song," Hal surmised with a chuckle. "Out West, they had a radio station, KMET, I believe it was, which played all the favorites. Every morning, Jeff Gonzer started out with Bruce JUICE. Bruce Springsteen, if you know who that is."

Throwing Hal one of his 'you gotta be kidding me' looks, Leroy shot back, "This song is from Led Zeppelin IV. The same album that "Stairway to Heaven" is on."

"Yup, you're right about that. It's a darn shame that the drummer, Bonham, drank himself to death. I think he was only about 30 years old or so. I'd say they were one of the best rock bands that ever lived," Hal went on. "Back then, we lost a lot of great musicians to the drink, Leroy. Alcohol is no respecter of fame or fortune."

Blasting hot, dry air came through the window as Leroy pressed a wet bandana to his forehead. The inescapable heat made him edgy. Falling back into his own thoughts, Leroy stared out the open window to the rugged terrain which made up the Mojave desert. Since they crossed the Great Divide, he'd been preoccupied. His own heartstrings were playing a distantly familiar tune of their own. One he'd tried for the last 400 miles to shove away, in the deep caverns of his heart. But it haunted him just the same. Out the window, for miles and miles, there was nothing but windblown rock formations, Joshua trees and cactus.

After they crossed the Arizona/California border, waves of sweltering heat radiated off the black top as the thermometer pushed 114 degrees. It was only 10:30 in the morning, when Hal pressed that old beater truck through Needles, California. When they started out that morning, Hal hoped to make Los Angeles before noon. But it looked like things were headed for trouble. From under the hood, steam started to billow. A few seconds later, the radiator blew. Green water gushed everywhere as Hal eased the truck over to the side of the road.

"Freaking oatmeal," Leroy mumbled under his breath as they got out of the cab. Whipping passed them on the interstate, semi-trucks blared their horns in warning. Blasts of hot, gusty Santa Ana winds pushed gritty grains of sand across the desert highway. The Mojave was dry and dehydrating. With his throat parched, Leroy found a water bottle in the ice chest and took a good swig. The wind gusts measured about 25 to 45 miles an hour. There was no break from the scorching, wind-blown heat.

"What'd you say?" Hal asked accusingly as he slammed the truck door and opened up the creaking hood.

"FREAKING OATMEAL!" Leroy bellowed as he threw his hands in the air. "I can't believe you put freaking oatmeal in the radiator! Now we're stuck out in the middle of bum-fuck nowhere."

"It ain't nowhere. We just passed Needles a few miles back," Hal surmised. "And it was either oatmeal or get stuck out in a small town, with a shady mechanic who said he'd have the radiator fixed in a week."

"Well," said Leroy as he took a fighting stance, squaring off in front of Hal. "You're the one who wanted to go off the main highway and take the scenic route!" Leroy raised his voice. "You know what I don't understand? Huh, you want to know what I don't understand? Why in the hell didn't we take Roy's air-conditioned, new truck to drive all the way to California? No, you got to take this old beat to shit truck, and get us stuck out here in the desert!"

"Aw hell, Leroy!" Hal backed off, not wanting to alligator wrestle in the heat. They'd been driving a long time. And sometimes, traveling brings out the worst in people. "Me and ol' Betsy here, we've been riding the range a long time. I know her like the back of my hand. I sure as shit don't want to be responsible for no fancy truck, if something were to happen," Hal said bent over the steaming engine, trying to find out where the leak was coming from.

"His truck is fully insured!" Leroy said exasperated. "It's a work truck!" This finally struck his last nerve. Grains of sand pelted his body, as hot gusts of wind dried out everything in sight. The sweat was already dripping from his temples. Except for the slim shadow of a Joshua tree, there was no shade to be found.

Under the front of the engine, streams of green water gushed out all over the highway. Steam spewed forth from the radiator. Doing his best to ignore Leroy, Hal went over to the passenger side door. The old door creaked as he opened it. Digging through the glove box, he found a small pouch of tobacco. Getting out of earshot of Leroy, Hal took a few steps off the highway. With a pinch of tobacco in his hand, Hal made a prayer. "Creator, looks like we need some help. Please send somebody quick to get this truck to a shop, before I lose my temper and twist Leroy's fool head off. He's been riding my ass since Colorado. I'm not sure what's gotten into him. But if it don't change, I'm gonna jerk that demon right out of his sorry ass! Before I kill him. Thank you Creator, I know You'll come through." Hal raised the tobacco over his head and gauged the wind. Opening his palm, the wind swept the tobacco from his hand. It went flying everywhere.

"Okay, that's taken care of," Hal said out loud as he dusted his hands off on his jeans. "Help will be here shortly." Finding an old bandana, Hal poured some water on it and tied it around his neck. It cooled him off for a short spell.

Getting blasted by the desert sand, Leroy just scoffed. Even though he'd witnessed many wonders, miracles of a sort, with this man, he never believed that you could just call on a band of Angels and they'd show up. In disbelief, Leroy watched as Hal pulled down the tail gate of the truck and started playing his harmonica. That old bluesy sound eased Hal's ruffled feathers. Laying in the back seat was Leroy's guitar. For a moment, he thought about joining Hal in some old show tune which Hal was always whistling. Just as Leroy decided to pull out the guitar, a Highway Patrol car pulled up behind them with its lights flashing. The officer took a moment to put on his hat before he got out of the car.

"How you doing today?" asked Officer Kent as he walked up to the truck.

"Blown radiator," Hal said as he slid down off the tail gate. "I'm right glad to see you."

"Yeah, it's not a good day to get stuck on the side of the road. In about an hour, the temperature's going to hit about 120 degrees," Officer Kent remarked. "I'll make a call and get you towed back to Needles. Stouts can repair the radiator." The officer went back in his air-conditioned car and radioed for a tow truck.

"Thank God he showed up," Leroy said, wiping the sweat from his brow.

"You know what Leroy? You know what I get about you? You got no sense of appreciation," Hal threw him a sideways glance.

"What's that supposed to mean?" Leroy said digging in his heels, his shoulders squared, thrown back in defiance.

"Well, the way I see it," Hal started. "We've traveled through some of the prettiest countryside and you got your blinders on! I don't know what that is, but you just don't see it. Somehow, your head is screwed on so tight that when Mother Nature shows you her finest wares, you got your eyes closed! And I'll tell you what Leroy! There are none so blind as those who refuse to see!" Hal paused a second while Leroy gave him a broiling look. "I'm just saying," Hal threw up his hands as he sat back down on the tailgate. Buzzing in his pocket, the cell phone rang. It was Roy. "Looks like Roy's calling. I better take that."

When Roy first asked Hal to go pick up a horse in California, he knew Hal loved the open road. The best way to keep a man like that employed was to give him a chance to see the countryside again. Horses were Hal's life and no one took better care of them. He had a knack of looking into a horse's eyes and seeing the condition of its soul.

"Hey Roy," Hal answered, wiping the sweat off his brow with his shirt sleeve as he turned away from the howling wind.

"How's the trip going?" Roy asked, leaning back in his office chair. His eyes wandered, staring out the window at the lone prairie.

"Well, we got a little waylaid here in Needles. The radiator blew and we're waiting to get towed," Hal admitted. "No big deal. It'll just put us back a couple hours."

"Look, I'll put extra cash on the debit card. You think $400 ought to cover it?" Roy sounded concerned. He was familiar with Needles and knew how hot it can get out there. "You know, I'll make it $600 and you and Leroy spend the night. Start fresh in the morning. I'm looking on the computer and it's going to get miserable on the road this afternoon."

"Yeah, that's probably a good idea. We'll be able to fry an egg on the tar top, in a minute. I'd say we're both pretty spent from the heat. It's already pushing 114 degrees out here and it's not even noon. I haven't spent time on the Colorado River in a while. That might be a good distraction," Hal felt relieved. Working for Roy was always a good thing. Even back in the day, when he was running lots of thoroughbreds through his ranch, Roy knew how to take care of his workers.

"Don't worry about a thing," Roy's voice came over the phone reassuringly. "Is a tow truck coming or do you need me to find someone from here?"

"Naw, we got the Highway Patrol making the call. They'll probably be here in a half hour or so," Hal replied as beads of sweat gathered on his brow. "This heat could turn a body into a prune in a half a day."

"Well, just stay hydrated. You got enough water?" Roy asked. Just then, Emma walked into Roy's office, overhearing her dad talking to Hal.

"Is that Hal on the phone?" Emma whispered, nudging her dad. Roy nodded his head yes. "Let me talk to Leroy," his little peanut girl demanded.

"Hal, Emma wants to talk to Leroy," Roy's voice was a little surprised as he handed her the phone.

"Sure thing," Hal answered as he handed the phone to Leroy. "The Little Miss wants to talk to you."

A shy smile crept across his face as Leroy answered the phone. "Hey."

"HI!!!" Emma squealed as she ran out of the office with the phone. Astounded, Roy turned around. Looking over his shoulder, he watched his daughter run back to her room and slam the door.

"How's your trip?" she quickly asked after she closed the door. "Are you having a good time?"

"It's alright," Leroy confessed as he moved out of earshot, towards the other end of the truck. "Hal decided to take the scenic route, and now we're stuck in the desert with a blown radiator!"

Suspecting that something funny was going on, Hal watched Leroy as he walk away. Just then, the CHP officer got out of his patrol car and walked over to him.

"Looks like a tow truck will be here in about ten to fifteen minutes," the officer said. "I called ahead to Stouts. They're expecting you."

"Thanks so much," Hal said as gusts of hot, dry wind pelted him with grains of sand. " I don't know if we'll make it back on the road today, given the heat."

"Well, there's some good places to stay along the river," said the officer. "Might even be a good day to get your feet wet." The local business owners were always hospitable to those traveling through. It was the only way they earned some money. Especially in the dry and dusty off-season.

"Got any recommendations?" asked Hal.

"Well, on Broadway, you could walk to Best Value from Stouts and up a little further is a Motel 6," replied the CHP officer. "The river is about a mile or so from there."

While he talked shop with the officer, Hal heard Leroy laughing it up, on the other side of the truck. "Well that's sounds good. We've been traveling for a few days. It might be good to take a load off and visit the river." As he finished his sentence, the tow truck pulled up in front of Hal's old truck.

"Hey look, I got to go," said Leroy as he spied the flashing lights from the tow truck. "The tow truck just got here. I'll talk to you later, okay."

"I miss you," her sweet voice pierced his heart as it echoed over the phone.

"Yeah, me too..." admitted Leroy as he hung up the phone. Smiling, he went back over to where Hal was standing and handed him the phone. "Emma says hi."

"Well, looks like that put you into a better mood," Hal commented as the tow truck back up in front of the truck. Leroy threw him a smile and said "Yeah. Hey, sorry about the grouchiness before."

"No problem," Hal replied, putting the phone back in his pocket. But something was up. There was no denying that Leroy's mood noticeably changed for the better, just because of a phone call. "Naw," Hal muttered to himself as he shook his head. *"Emma? Leroy? It can't be that,"* he tried to banish the thought from his mind. But from ear to ear, Leroy had a 'shit-eating' grin on his face. There was no denying it. A few minutes later, the tow truck driver had Hal's truck loaded up.

The town of Needles, nestled along the Colorado river, is in the midst of the Mojave desert. Speckled with Joshua trees, it has an arid, rugged beauty. The old, wind blown mountain peaks are poked through with holes. Though the city of Needles was founded in 1883 because of the Atchison, Topeka and Santa Fe Railway, the First Nations Peoples lived there thousands of years prior. From the 1920's to 1960's, the town of Needles was a major stop on the historic Route 66. During the 1930's, immigrants fled the Dust Bowl of the Midwest and landed in "Carty's Camp" which was depicted in the movie "The Grapes of Wrath." There was a lot of history in this small river town of a little over four thousand people.

Spanning this stretch of desert along the Colorado River is the Fort Mojave Indian Reservation. The Mojave are one of the traditional Native American Colorado River Indian Tribes. The Mojave Indians are called 'Pipa Aha Macav - The people by the river.' Their ancestry traces its earthly origins back to the people of Spirit Mountain, the highest peak in the Newberry Mountains, just northwest of Lake Mead.

When the Spaniards came in the 16th century, the Mojave were the largest population of First Nations people in the Southwest. But then gold-fever struck in the Golden State with the California gold rush in 1849. With a driving need to make it rich, more and more non-Indian people flooded through the desert from the East. In order to protect these American prospectors and immigrants while they panned for gold, the United States military established an outpost in 1859 on the east bank of the Colorado River. Originally the outpost was called Camp Colorado, but was later renamed Fort Mojave. The fort itself closed in 1891. Afterward, the buildings were turned into an Indian boarding school which operated until 1930. The ruins of this troubled time still remain on a bluff overlooking the Colorado River just south of Bullhead City.

"Ah," Leroy sighed as a blast of cold air hit his face, after he opened the door of the tow truck. Inside the air-conditioned cab, it was cool and comfortable. The driver was a quiet man. His dark skin was engraved with deep creases from years of living in the sun. With his wide jawline, Hal suspected that he came from one of the southern tribes. There were a few moments of uncomfortable silence as they settled into the cab. As the sun climbed high across the heavens, Hal and Leroy were grateful to get out of the overbearing heat. Finally, the driver broke the silence with some small talk.

"So where y'all headed?" the driver asked as he glanced in his rear view mirror and signaled his way into the flow of traffic.

"Los Angeles," Hal offered as he glanced at the dashboard. The inside thermometer read 115 degrees.

"Helluva day to get stuck out in the heat," the driver came back. "In a couple hours, you can fry an egg on the tar top."

"Yeah, I used to live out West. I can't say I miss the heat much," Hal conceded. While the tow truck bounced along the interstate, Hal looked out over the desert. In barely visible waves, the scorching heat was radiating off the asphalt.

"You get used to it after a while. But you got to plan your day around the sun. Get all your stuff done early morning, and stay inside in the afternoon," replied the driver. "It don't cool down until after 10 o'clock, though. That's when me and the misses go out for a walk, after being cooped up all day."

It wasn't long before they pulled into town and the tow truck driver released Hal's old truck to the repair shop. As promised, Roy put extra funds on the debit card. Hal felt better knowing the truck would get serviced. Before the truck went up on the rack, Leroy grabbed their bags. Hal found his fishing pole. They headed down to the hotel, which was about a half block down the road.

After they checked in at the hotel, Leroy opened the door to their room and turned on the air-conditioner. Hal set his bags down in the small closet and went into the bathroom to wash up. As the room cooled down, Leroy propped himself up on some pillows on the bed and turned on the TV.

"LATE BREAKING NEWS!" the news broadcast began. "We are here at the courthouse where Rhoda di Cello is being arraigned for allegedly assaulting a corrections officer in her jail cell. From all accounts, di Cello bit off the correction officers penis during the nightly bed checks. She claimed that the corrections officer offered her cookies in exchange for sex. A local reporter managed to get photographs of di Cello's bruised and beaten back, when the public defender lifted up the back of her shirt and revealed it to the judge." The television flashed pictures of Rhoda's bruised backside on the screen.

"Well, that's pure bullshit," Hal hollered from the bathroom. "The only way that girl got his pecker in her mouth is he put it there! Offering her cookies for sex, that man should rot in hell!"

"After having undergone reattachment surgery, the corrections officer is recovering tonight at University Medical Center. From our latest sources, we believe the FBI will be launching a full scale investigation. We will keep you updated as we get further developments," said the news caster as the TV station went to commercial.

Walking out of the bathroom, Hal pulled the floral blackout curtains shut, before he flopped down on his bed. It was high noon. The sun was bearing down on this small desert town. "I think I'll take a little nap," Hal muttered. "I'm plum tuckered out from this heat. I never did like it much."

"Yeah, me neither," Leroy agreed. "I'm hungry though. When do you want to get something to eat?"

"Aw, give me like a half hour to rest my eyes," Hal said as he sat on the edge of his bed, pulling his cowboy boots off. Then, he grabbed his pillow and lay down on his side.

After a rash of pharmaceutical commercials for every ailment known to man, the news caster came back on. "Now, in the news today, there's an intense investigation into the Veteran's Administration. This is concerning veterans, who are not getting the medical care they need. After returning from combat, as many as 40 veterans have died, just waiting for doctor's appointments. Apparently, the VA doesn't have the resources to handle the number of cases it's getting every day. Also, the number of veteran suicides are being investigated by the Department of Defense. It is estimated that 22 veterans a day are taking their own lives. More veterans are dying daily by their own hand, than they do in combat. The investigation by the Department of Defense revealed that, a high ranking doctor downgraded the PTSD diagnosis in order to save on government dollars. Once the veteran's diagnosis was downgraded, it effectively lowers their VA disability rating and their benefits. Nearly forty percent of veterans who received a PTSD diagnosis under this high ranking medical doctor had their diagnosis reversed," the news caster went on.

"What the hell is that idiot saying?" Hal felt really irritated as he turned over and looked at the television. "Some dumb ass doctor is reversing the PTSD diagnosis to save the government money!"

"Shh, I'm watching this," Leroy scolded, as he turned up the volume.

"Effectively, the PTSD diagnosis makes every veteran eligible for service connected disability, which averages about $1000 per month. With 3.5 million veterans diagnosed with these disabilities, the government pay out becomes HUGE over time. Most of our veterans are in their 20's and stand to live another sixty years," the news caster continued.

"NO SHIT SHERLOCK!" Hal yelled at the TV. He was clearly irritated by this news report. "I never got a dime of that money. I drank! And I drank hard to get rid of all those memories burned into my mind. It wasn't until Wyatt showed up and brought me to ceremony that things started to change."

"Now Pentagon officials also released reports encouraging doctors working with veterans to focus more on therapy and less on medication. One particular medication, benzodiazepines, such as the commonly prescribed sleep aid known as Klonopin, has more risks than benefits. One of the dangers associated with benzodiazepines is the loss of judgment. Regular users start practicing dangerous behaviors such as unprotected sex and criminal activity."

"YA THINK!" Hal yelled at the TV while the news caster went on.

"This might be one of the reasons why US prisons are now crowded with veterans returning from the Middle East. Other dangerous factors contributing to veteran suicide, are that benzodiazepines inhibit the 'natural fight for life' found in all living creatures. Veterans struggling with nightmares and terrible memories, are prescribed Klonopin for sleep disorders. But it reduces their defense against suicidal thoughts. Many families, who have lost loved ones to suicide, are screaming at the Veterans Administration, "Where's the help?" The news caster stopped short for a moment, as if the impact of his last story had gotten under his skin. "And that's our broadcast for this afternoon. Please join us tonight at 5 o'clock for updates on today's stories."

"That damn government don't give a lick about our troops," Hal festered. "We'd cost them less money if we're dead! You know what gets me Leroy? Most vets suffer this shit out alone. There ain't a talking doctor alive, who can look a veteran in the eye and truly understand what they've been through. Oh sure, those white coats will tell you that you have this or that disorder. But they don't really know, because they ain't ever been there."

Turning the volume down on the TV, Leroy listened to Hal's lament, fully understanding his frustration.

"After World War 2," Hal went on. "They didn't have any diagnosis for the guys coming home from the war. Those head-shrinks called a veteran's trauma 'shell shocked!' Those guys went through hell. It takes guts of steel to fight hand to hand combat. Where you look the enemy in the eye, kill them and watch the life go out of their bodies. Killing takes a toll on a man! And some vets never come back from it." Hal paused a minute. There's nothing worse than feeling expendable. Especially when a man risks his life for the love of his country. Hal's blood pressure was rising.

"And when those war heroes came home," Hal kept venting. "Their families didn't understand what they'd been through. Which makes the loneliness that much worse. Because they've got no one to talk to. Drinking was the only way to self-medicate, until they died. Some vets got real crazy after Viet Nam. Out in Los Angeles, you still find Viet Nam vets walking the streets, talking to themselves or to whatever spirits they got around them. You can't take a trained killing machine, whose gone on 14 deployments and expect him to come home, after fighting a bloody war, to play nice with others. He's got to have some help."

"Don't go getting yourself all worked up," Leroy shook his head as he turned off the TV. "I bet you're just hungry."

"Leroy, you know as well as anybody, if you killed someone, you're being haunted!" Hal sat up and stared at his buddy. "This whole situation is a tempest in a teapot. The government don't give a crap about the vets coming home. All their doing is feeding these guys pills, which sets them up to kill themselves."

"Don't you remember, I told you NO PILL PUSHERS!" Leroy thought back to his early days of sobriety. "I knew that's what they were doing." Leroy thumbed through some of the river brochures on the nightstand. One brochure from "Firewater Jet ski" caught his eye. "Hey, lets go down to the river and try out one of these wave runners."

"Naw, not me," Hal shook his head.

"Aw, come on! You only live once!" Leroy cajoled.

"Well shit, you know that ain't true," Hal laughed. "And though this is NONE OF YOUR BUSINESS, I don't swim."

"What?" Leroy laughed, mocking his good buddy. "How can you call yourself a warrior, if you don't swim?"

"Never liked cold water..." Hal mused. "It always gave me goose flesh and made my balls shrink up!"

Leroy howled. He never liked cold water either. "Shit, Hal! The water in the Colorado's not going to be cold. It's 120 degrees out there. Come on, I'll get you some floaties and you can splash on the water's edge." Leroy poked fun at his buddy.

"You know what Leroy," Hal shook his head. "You always were a smart alack! But you're right about one thing, I'm hungry. Let's go find something to eat. I can grab my fishing pole and you can wear yourself out on that sea pony. Then we'll get a good nights sleep."

Off Broadway, they found a U-haul store and rented a pickup truck. After Hal put his fishing gear in the truck bed, they made it to a restaurant that someone had recommended called "Wagon Wheel." Sitting down, in an air-conditioned booth, Hal started to relax. His trained sense of smell got a whiff of the chicken fried steak, gravy and eggs lingering in the air. The waitress brought over some menus and Leroy started reading.

"What are you going to get?" Leroy asked Hal after scanning the menu.

"Breakfast," Hal said with conviction. "You need to eat a good breakfast to start the day off right."

"You're about the most old fashion person I've ever met," Leroy shook his head.

"Just a diamond in the rough," Hal laughed. "What do you got against breakfast anyway?"

"Just never liked it," Leroy answered as he flipped through the menu.

The waitress came over, "Howdy boys! Can I get you two something to drink?"

"I'll take a coffee and a tall glass of orange juice," Hal ordered.

"Bring me a lemonade," Leroy started. "Oh, change that, mix the lemonade with ice tea."

"You mean an Arnold Palmer?" the waitress asked.

"I knew it had a name. I just didn't know what it was," Leroy said.

"Listen before you run off," Hal started. "Why don't you fix me up a chicken fried steak with my eggs fried over easy and you got those home fried potatoes?" The waitress nodded her head yes. "You ready, Leroy?"

"Yeah, I'll take the tacos," Leroy said.

"Do you want those with chicken or steak?"

"Chicken sounds good," Leroy said.

"Alright, I have a chicken fried steak, eggs over easy and hash browns, and chicken tacos. Do you want toast or pancakes with your breakfast?"

"Make it pancakes, but hold the butter. I'm watching my girlish figure," Hal laughed.

Anything else?" the waitress asked.

"You got the winning lottery numbers for the state of California?" Hal threw her a wry smile.

"I wish! I wouldn't be here if I did," the waitress laughed, putting her order book back in her large apron pockets.

"Well, that's good for now," said Hal as the waitress walked away. "Man, that story about the veteran suicides just frosts my balls. And you know what bothers me, it's the same thing with every war. Ever since World War 2, and Viet Nam, those dang white coats got fancy names for things, but don't know how to treat them."

"But we did treat it, Hal..." Leroy paused, remembering how Hal found him years ago. "You, me and Ben, we found an answer."

"Yeah, but how we gonna help the rest of these vets coming home?" Hal pondered. For him, there was nothing worse than the long suffering vets went through, after taking on the demons of the world.

"Beats the hell out of me," Leroy said as the waitress set down their drinks. "Look, we don't have to figure it all out today."

A few minutes later, the food came and Hal's blood sugar started to rise. After a couple refills of coffee and another orange juice, his mood got a bit lighter. "You know Leroy, it says in the Big Book that probably no human power could have relieved our alcoholism."

"Yeah, so what's your point?" asked Leroy biting into his crispy taco.

"Well, I got this knack of wanting to take on the problems of the world and I forget, that it's Creator's job. I just need to step out of the way and let Him do it. All I can do is be of service," Hal surmised.

"Listen, if it will make you feel any better, we'll go to the VA when we get to Los Angeles and talk to the guy about building a lodge," Leroy suggested.

"Hmm, I like that idea. I know a fella that runs lodges out there. Actually I know a few guys out there. Maybe we'll get something together and see if we can't make a dent in this problem," Hal smiled.

After a good meal, Hal felt a little less ornery. To escape the blistering heat, they moseyed down to rent Leroy a sea pony so he could get his Ya-Ya's out. It was a lazy, but hot afternoon. Hal looked forward to putting on his waders and getting out into the river.

Glints of sunlight reflected on the shallow waves near the water's edge. A warm breeze stirred through the tree-lined riverbank as Hal backed the truck down to the dock. Leroy was chomping at the bit to get this sea pony into the water. Sometimes Hal wished he still had Leroy's spunk. But he'd settle for the serenity of going fishing.

"Hey, don't forget to put on your life vest," Hal scolded as he watched Leroy put that sea pony in the water. Hal tossed it over to Leroy, who just threw him a scowl.

"I don't need that!" Leroy boasted. "I know how to swim."

"Just put the dang thing on, you ol' hard-head!" Hal insisted. "That way, at least you'll float, if I got to come fish your sorry ass out of the water!"

Knowing he'd never hear the end of it, Leroy gave in to Hal's demands. Out of willfulness, he refused to clip the vest closed, to avoid looking like some sissy. But he did put it on. Gunning the gas, it didn't take long before Leroy found some white water rapids. That became his afternoon challenge. Bouncing across the stormy waters, the sea pony bucked and bolted. Leroy rode that sea pony like a bucking bronco. Hal could hear him hooting and hollering all the way down river. He watched from afar, with his fishing pole in the water.

"Crazy kid," Hal mutter out loud. It wasn't that many years ago, when he'd done the same kind of stunts at the rodeo. Bull riding wasn't for sissies. Neither was being a rodeo clown. But those days were long past. A gentle breeze pushed his iron-colored ponytail across his chest and he felt a nibble on the end of the fishing line. Just then, Leroy roared by, waving in Hal's direction. Showing off, Leroy whipped around, doing a few donuts and roared past Hal again. "Come on Hal," he hollered. "You got to try this thing!"

"GO ON! Get out of here! You're scaring the fish!" Hal hollered back as he waved him off.

A moment later, a flashy speed boat came flying by, creating a mighty wake behind it. Spurred on by the challenge, Leroy gunned the gas and gave chase. He pushed that sea pony with everything it had. Jumping the wake, Leroy caught some air and flew across the water. "YEE HAW!!!"

Watching from the sidelines, Hal just shook his head. It was good to see Leroy having a good time. The searing desert heat bore down on his back, so he dunked himself under the water. But something gave him a feeling of foreboding. After dipping his head under the water to cool off, Hal looked up just in time to see Leroy flying off another wake. Only this time it didn't go so well. Hitting a wall of water, Leroy lost his grip from the handle bars and flipped off the back of the sea pony. Crashing down, his head struck the back of the wave runner with a bang. All Hal could see was Leroy falling off the sea pony with a big splash.

"Aw shit Leroy," Hal muttered as he watched the sea pony go around in circles. Fearing the worst, Hal pushed through the water. On the shore, he ran up river to where the sea pony circled round. From the riverbank, he didn't see anything moving. And then Leroy's life jacket floated past him going down river. Hal's heart sunk. "SHIT! SHIT! SHIT!"

Up river, seeing Leroy flip off the sea pony, the speed boat turned around and came flying back. The passengers watched while Leroy performed his crazy stunts behind them. Kenny, the driver of the boat, saw Leroy's body floating face down, slightly under the water. Without a lifeguard on the river, Kenny dove into the water and pulled Leroy's body onto the boat. He was unconscious.

Wading up to his chest, Hal called out from the river's edge. "HOW IS HE?!"

"He doesn't have a pulse!" Kenny hollered back as he headed for the dock. There was a huge bloody gash on Leroy's head. In a panic, Hal got out of the water and ran over towards the dock.

It all happened in slow motion. Bound and determined to jump the wake, Leroy pushed the sea pony full throttle. But the curl of the wake had a trough. The sea pony hit the trough like a wall. Which forced it to go straight up, rather than over. Jolted by the upward force, Leroy lost his footing. As he slipped backwards, he cracked his head on the back of the sea pony before he fell into the water. The conk on the head knocked him unconscious. When he fell backwards, he swallowed a big gulp of water. That's when he started to drown.

Like a snap, his Spirit was yanked out of his body and hovered over the river. With Spirit eyes, Leroy watched Kenny turn the speed boat around and race back to where his lifeless body floated beneath the water. Sputtering away, the sea pony paced round and round. The sound waves of Hal's booming voice echoed across the ethers. Suddenly, Leroy spied a pinpoint of glorious Light. Turning towards the pinpoint of Light, he saw all around him was black. The Light was the most brilliant thing he'd ever seen. It didn't hurt his eyes to look at it. Then he felt himself rushing through a tunnel, towards the Light.

Beyond the outer walls of the tunnel, Leroy saw dim lights coming and going like fireflies in springtime. Uncounted millions leaped before him, glowing faintly from the edge of the darkest night. These lights were the souls of men who drank from the cup of death. Having drifted down into the darkness, some spirits clung to the outer tunnel walls. Leroy heard their cries for help. They were stuck in the In-between. But somehow Leroy knew he couldn't stop, otherwise he might not get back.

Racing back to the dock, Kenny, a retired battlefield corpsman, knew he only had a few minutes to bring Leroy back. Otherwise, he might end up brain dead. As soon as they hit the dock, Kenny rolled Leroy's lifeless body on his side to allow any water to drain from his lungs. Then, he started performing CPR to get his breathing started again. There was a major cut near Leroy's hairline where he hit the edge of the sea pony. It would probably need a few stitches.

Embraced in overwhelming Love, every tree and blade of green grass shimmered as Leroy walked from the tunnel into a large, flower-covered meadow along a sparkling river. A young boy with eyes the color of soft earth, came running over to greet him. It all seemed so familiar, as Leroy walked across this sunny meadow.

"Grandpa's waiting for you," the little boy said as he took Leroy by the hand and led him to a large teepee. Opening the door flap, Leroy recognized his great grandfather. Sitting beside him was a great Being of Light. The power of Love which flowed from the great Being was overwhelming. For a moment, Leroy felt struck with awe.

"Call 911 and get my medical bag!" Kenny commanded his friend. "It's under the front seat in the truck." After wading through chest high water, and racing back to the dock, Hal ran up completely out of breath.

"How's he doing?" Hal asked tentatively as scorching rays of sunshine beat down upon the blacktop.

"Is this your friend?" Kenny asked, as he lunged over Leroy's body, doing chest compressions.

"Yeah," Hal huffed and puffed. "How's he doing?" Hal asked again, not liking how this was looking.

"He's not breathing," Kenny said.

"How long you think he's been out?" Hal asked, knowing it was a race with time in matters like these.

"A few minutes. By the time I saw him go down and turned around, it's hard to say," Kenny kept working on Leroy. "What's his name?"

"Leroy," Hal whispered watching Kenny work on him.

Bathed in a beautiful, bright, loving light, Leroy recognized the Being of Light from pictures he'd seen as a little boy. No words were needed on this side of the Veil, because everyone talked through their thoughts. "When you were a small boy, Leroy, you used to pray to me. I was never far away," began the Being of Light. "Sometimes I couldn't answer your prayers right away, because they interfered with another person's free will. I know you felt disappointed in me and thought I was part of a fairytale or a myth, which people tell themselves at Christmas time."

"That was because of my dad's drinking," Leroy replied. "It destroyed our family."

"It was your father's free will that lead him down that dark path. But now, he's made another choice. The lesson was learned," the Great Being said with compassion. "Humans are great spiritual beings, Leroy. They're meant to come to Earth to create good, by doing small acts of kindness, rather than great demonstrations. It is the little things that count because they show your true nature. Sometimes humans are tested, and venture off into much harder lessons. Through their experience they gain knowledge. Either way, the lesson is learned. Then they can drink from the cup of wisdom. Love of others and learning inner truths are the most important aspects of this journey." Leroy pondered these thoughts a moment before the Great Being went on.

"Are you ready to die?" the Great Being asked, as His all knowing eyes gentled Leroy's soul. "Show me what you've done with your life so far."

There was no judgment in His Voice, only compassion for all that Leroy had experienced. No sooner did those thoughts transmit, when Leroy's mind began to fill with moving pictures from his early childhood. Like a slide show, every memory zipped through his mind at record speed. Watching his life story unfold, he became immersed and relived each moment. He felt all his feelings and the feelings of everyone in his life whom he had touched. There were moments when he was purely selfish and saw how his actions badly affected others. He wished then he could change that. Other moments were compelled by great love, a feeling of Oneness with all life. Every victory and every disappointment was revisited. The mystery behind them was still to be revealed.

Looking at his life, Leroy knew he wasn't finished. There were so many things he still wanted to do. But nothing inside him wanted to leave this beautiful Being of Light, or his Home. Flowing through his heart was this great indigenous wisdom, a limitless consciousness of divine Love. Behind all created Beings was a Great Being; the Star Maker, the Great Self, the I AM THAT I AM. This insight fell on him like a gentle, spring rain. It melted away the harshness of his inner winter landscape, where his heart had lain frozen beneath the fields of fear. Now he drank from the living waters of pure Knowing.

In the sparkling eyes of the Great Being, came only true compassion. Leroy was given two choices, to stay in the Upper Realms or to finish his Soul Contract back on Earth. In moving pictures, he was shown what would happen to his family and others if he stayed and didn't complete his mission. If he went back to Earth, he'd have the opportunity to fulfill his Soul contract and finish his learning. Everything that happened to him was either something he chosen to learn or a debt of his, which had to be repaid. In these few moments Leroy saw the purpose of his life. Reading Leroy's thoughts, the Great Being told him it wasn't his time, but it was his choice to go back or not.

Powerless to do anything, Hal paced back and forth across the dock. He felt more and more anxious as Leroy's spiritless body lay on the black top in the baking sun. Kenny worked ceaselessly to resuscitate Leroy, but time was running out. In the distance, Hal heard the sirens coming down the highway. The hospital was another ways off. Finally Hal was at his wit's end. In a fit of fury, he just started yelling.

"DAMN IT LEROY! GET BACK IN YOUR BODY RIGHT NOW! YOU HEAR ME LEROY! I SAID GET BACK IN YOUR BODY RIGHT NOW! BEFORE I COME OVER THERE AND GET YOUR SORRY ASS! IF YOU THINK, FOR ONE MINUTE, I'M GOING TO BE THE ONE TO TELL YOUR MOTHER ABOUT YOUR STUPID SHINNANIGANS, YOU ARE SORELY MISTAKEN BUDDY! DAMN IT LEROY! GET BACK IN YOUR BODY RIGHT NOW!"

"I got a pulse," Kenny said looking relieved.

"YEAH!" Hal hollered out to the Universe. He felt so good, he could dance for days!

Falling back to Earth, Leroy felt the cold blackness and fear which veiled the planet. With the icy rigidity thawed from his soul, he felt to the core of his bones the changing of these times. He knew it was good. Like a bullet, his Spirit shot back into his body. Choking, gasping for air, water gushed from his lungs as he took his first raspy deep breath. His body was racked with pain.

A wave of relief swept over Hal as he saw Leroy coughing, choking up the water he'd swallowed. In the nick of time, Leroy came back to life. Hal had seen death up close and personal. It wasn't his favorite experience. Just then, the ambulance pulled up with the county sheriff. In the river, the sputtering sea pony was still circling, where Leroy left it. While the paramedics checked out Leroy, Hal grabbed the life vest. He put it on and went out in the water to retrieve the sea pony. It had been a helluva day.

Of course, Leroy didn't want to go to the hospital. He told the paramedics he'd take his chances with catching pneumonia, when they started to warn him about the risks of drowning and the things that he can get afterward.

The sheriff took down an incident report. Afterward, Leroy thanked Kenny for all his life saving work. Plum wore out, Hal finished loading up the sea pony and they got in the truck and left. Neither one of them said a word for the half hour drive back to town.

Back at the hotel, Hal pulled into the parking lot. Leroy was slumped in the passenger seat. He was exhausted from a day of hot sun, heavy riding and a near-death experience which would forever change his life. As he walked over to the room, Hal pulled out the key. After he unlocked the door, Hal turned to look at his buddy. "You know, Leroy. Today you really scared the shit out of me. Watching Kenny working on your body, and you just laying there, like a wet towel. I got so dang mad! I was ready to shake you like a gorilla and smack the life right back into you."

Leroy started to laugh. "I could hear you yelling all across the heavens. But I was right in the middle of a conversation, and couldn't break away."

"Something happened over there, didn't it. You saw something! I knew it! I knew it all along!" Hal pushed open the door. The cool air-conditioned room felt welcoming as Leroy flopped down on his bed. "WELL!" Hal said standing at the end of Leroy's bed. "You gonna spill or what?"

"Lets just say I understand Ben a whole lot better now," Leroy admitted. Longing for sleep, he just wanted to close his eyes. The whole experience wore him out. Within moments of hitting the pillow, Leroy was fast asleep. For the longest time, Hal just sat on the edge of his bed and stared at Leroy. Watching Kenny work on Leroy, not knowing if this was going to be it, changed something in Hal too. He realized that nothing was more important than caring about the people who mattered to him. For all he knew, this could have been Leroy's last day. Down at the bottom of his suitcase, was his pipe bag, where he kept his Cannupa. It was a sacred pipe, one he'd carried long before he ever sun danced. It seemed appropriate to load it up and give thanks.

Like a father, Hal found a blanket and threw it over Leroy. Then he slipped out of the room and drove a few miles to find a quiet place to load his pipe and give thanks. Out in the middle of the Joshua trees, cactus clusters and gritty desert sand, Hal found a sweet little spot at the foot of a rugged, rocky mountain. The air was dry as could be. A slight breeze was blowing, coming up from the south.

In the long of the afternoon, the sinking sun cast tall shadows of spindly Joshua trees. After he lay down a blanket on the hard, gritty earth, Hal unpacked his Cannupa from the pipe bag. In an abalone shell, he lit some sage and smudged off the pipe stone bowl and pipe stem. Tears welled up in his eyes as images of Leroy's lifeless body flooded through his memory. In those long helpless moments on the dock, he felt so powerless to do anything. But at the same time, there was an immense gratitude, knowing Leroy pulled through. As mentor and student, they'd walked together so long now. Hal couldn't really imagine his life without his buddy.

"WEY HI YA HEY HI YA, WEY HI YA OH WEY OH HEY…" Hal began to sing. Watching the sage smoke drift into the wind, Hal's heart filled with deep appreciation to Great Spirit, the Red Road and the circle of Life. Taking the first pinch of Chan-shasha, Hal held it over his head. "Great Spirit, Grandfather, I almost lost my good buddy today. I guess Leroy went home and paid y'all a little visit. All he said to me was, he was having a conversation. Thank you for bringing him back, or sending him back, since it wasn't his time. I pray that there's nothing wrong with that hard-headed, you know what! And that he makes a full recovery from his near drowning accident. One good thing came out of it, he said he understands Ben a lot better. Please take good care of us as we keep traveling along. Aho."

Hal packed the pinch of pipe smoke in the Cannupa, and reached in his pouch for another. This time he said a prayer to the Spirit Helpers of the East. While he held the Chan-shasha in his hand, he thought of Ben and all the good people he'd met since he moved out there. It was never his intention to stay so long. Usually, his feet got itchy and he'd ramble on to the next rodeo. But Spirit had other plans. Like finding Roy at WalMart, with little Emma, full grown, in tow. Well, it's all gone that way since. "Great Spirit, Grandfather, thank you for taking such good care of me… I don't know that I rightly deserve it after being such a screw up for so long. But now, I got me a place to live and people I care about. I found friends and people I consider my family. I thank you for bringing Ben and all those back "home" into my life. Bless them all up, Grandpa! They make my heart smile, just knowing they're there."

After packing that pinch of pipe smoke into the sacred pipe, Hal reached for another and prayed to the Ancestors of the South. It wasn't but a couple hundred miles from here, as the crow flies, that Hal crawled out of a chicken coop years ago. Dirty and hungover, he was lucky enough to find some spare change at the bottom of his pocket to call Alcoholics Anonymous. So as he looked towards the South, he was filled with gratitude for his sobriety. "Great Spirit, Grandfather, thank you for my sobriety. I was pretty useless as a drunk. Thanks for Leroy's and Ben's sobriety too. I don't think we'd be much use to each other or to You, if we were in a drunken state of mind. Bless up all them alcoholics, drunk or sober. Give them the same chance that you gave me. Aho Mitakuye Oyasin!"

Placing this pinch in the sacred pipe stone bowl, he took one more out of his pouch. As he prayed to the Spirits of the West, he thought of the Thunder Beings. From the look of it, they could sure use some rain out West. A great drought had spread all over the western states. Ranchers had to sell off their cattle, because they had no water and couldn't grow feed. In the Central Coast, the old Oak trees were dying from years without good rain. Farmland in California was cracked and bone dry. Everyone was fighting over the water. Then the hot, merciless Santa Ana winds turned most of the western states into a tinderbox, igniting one fire after the next. Nowadays, fire season lasted the whole year, rather than a few short months.

"Great Spirit, Grandfather, thank you for my life. I call to my Brothers the Thunder Beings and ask that You bring some rain out West. It's pretty dusty out here and California grows a lot of food. Thanks for blessing up all the crops with Your gentle, loving rain. Also, help me let go of whatever doesn't serve me anymore. I realize I still got a couple of character defects. After the day I had with Leroy, I was just plum pissed off that he put himself in harm's way. He's such a dang show off. But then, he went to have a talk with You. So I can see it was a good thing. Remove my fear from me and whatever else stands in the way of my usefulness to You and my fellows. Help me to see people the way You see them. Grant me whatever I need to go out from here and to do your bidding. Aho."

Putting the pinch of pipe smoke in the Cannupa, Hal started to feel pretty peaceful. Taking another pinch of pipe smoke out of his pouch, he held it over his head, calling to the Ancestors of the North. "Great Spirit, Grandfather, we've got a problem with all the soldier boys coming home from that blasted war. From the looks of it, 22 veterans a day are taking their own life. Maybe they got too much blood on their hands. Maybe they're getting haunted. I ask that You show me a solution and how to make it happen. Grant me the resources that I need and the right people to get these soldier boys cleaned up, so they don't destroy themselves and their families. You did that for me so many years ago, and I got to help out Leroy the same way. Help me to be useful to these young men and women, who are tormented by what they saw, so much so that they are killing themselves. Thank you for helping me all those years ago. I'm a much better man. Aho."

Placing the Chan-shasha in the bowl, his next prayer was for Mother Earth, who provided for All Life. He took a pinch out for this blessed Mother of all Life and placed his hand on the Earth. "Great Spirit, Grandfather and blessed Mother Earth, thank you for my life. For all the years I've lived on You, you've given me everything I needed. I thank you from the bottom of my heart. Thank You for this fresh air, clean water and good food. For giving me a place to lay my hat and people to love. Thank You for all these blessings. Please bless up this great Mother with all good things. Help Her thrive in times of adversity and clean up whatever is wrong, forever more. Bless Her in all ways. Aho."

This last pinch of pipe smoke was for the Sacred Place Within. With mindfulness, Hal took out the last pinch from his pouch. Looking all around him, he was filled with a sense of deep inner gratitude. It welled up in his heart. For many years now, the Earth was his home and doing good was his religion.

Along the way, he'd learned a great many lessons from everything that was put in front of him, including almost losing Leroy. He realized he was given a second chance. "Great Spirit, Grandfather, it was almost Leroy's last day here. Thanks for all the days You've given me and all the days I have left. I pray to make the most of them. That whatever or whoever You put in front of me, I treat them with the same love, honor and respect that You have given me. Help me to love all life, regardless of whether I like it or not. Help me to learn all there is to know, so I can be useful. Thank you for all the good You've given me and the not so good, You've taken away. Thanks for all my blessings. Aho Mitakuye Oyasin!"

Standing on his knees, Hal offered his Cannupa to the seven directions. Then, he struck a match and had a good smoke. With the sacred smoke, he blessed off the pipe stone bowl, then the stem. He also blessed off his own body and blew some smoke in Leroy's direction, back at the hotel. With heartfelt intentions, he sent a puff to Ben, Roy and his family back home. He pulled hard and blew some smoke at the Earth. Then towards the heavens. Thanking the Creator of all Life for his time here.

A slow moving peacefulness filled his Being after he was done. It had been a long, full day. In the West, the sun was just starting to dip behind the rugged mountain range, casting long shadows across the land. A cooler wind started to whip up and blow the gritty desert sand around. All in all, packed with tough lessons, it'd been a good day. Hal packed up his sacred pipe, grabbed his blanket and headed back to the truck.

When Hal got back to the hotel, Leroy was sitting up, watching Andy Griffith on old antenna TV. Thankfully, the color was back in his face. Though he was quite tired, he felt alright.

"Where'd you go?" Leroy asked as Hal opened the door.

"I went to take care of my pipe. I hadn't done that in a while and I figured it was time," Hal explained, setting his truck keys on the dresser.

"Yeah, that's a good idea, I think I'll do that in the morning. Right now, I just feel drained," Leroy yawned, stretching his arms over his head.

"Well, you had a helluva day, little buddy," Hal said concerned, as he put his pipe bag back in his suitcase. "Do you want to talk about it?"

"It's hard to explain, really," said Leroy as he sat up straight. "All I know is, I got jerked out of my body. I can see all the details. Kenny turning his speed boat around and pulling me out of the water. I saw you in your waders, heading for the shore. But then, it all changed. I remember seeing this Light. At first it was small. But then, I was rushing through this tunnel. No, that's not the right word. It was more like a tube. I saw these spirits on the other side of the tube."

"Spirits?" Hal interrupted. "Like they were stuck, caught in the In-between?"

"Yeah, something like that," Leroy admitted. "They were clinging on to the outside of the tube, wanting me to help them. But I knew I couldn't stop, or maybe I'd get stuck too."

"Oh," Hal toned, understanding this more and more from all Ben's talks. "You think they missed their bus? And now they wanted to hitch a ride with you?"

"Maybe," Leroy hugged his pillow, as he was talking. This was never his area. All this spiritual stuff made him feel uncomfortable. He left it to men like Ben, who'd been talking to Spirits their whole life. "I could feel how desperate they were. Like they were trapped and couldn't get out."

"Hmm," Hal toned. "Sounds like you had an adventure on the Other-side."

"Yeah, no doubt. That's not even all of it. Do you remember that dream I had, the first time I went to Sun Dance?" Leroy looked over at Hal, seeing if it registered in his memory.

"The one where your grandfather gave you a Cannupa?"

"Yeah, well I went back there. But this time, inside the teepee was this Great Being," Leroy began. "He was of the Light, like he glowed."

Hal stood there, thunderstruck. He'd read about this so many times, but never knew anyone who went through it. "Hmm," Hal pondered as he sat down on his bed. "So then what happened?"

"Well, we had this conversation," Leroy sat up. "It was mostly about what I'm supposed to do down here. And that if I left early, it wouldn't get done. Also that the most important thing on Earth is Love and learning."

"Hmm," Hal nodded his head. "I'd agree with that."

"I was surrounded by the most powerful love I'd ever felt," Leroy recalled. "I didn't really want to come back. This world is filled with mostly pain and suffering."

"Ya think," Hal laughed. "Today turned my head around in a way, I wasn't ready for. It gave me pause to really see what's important to me and what I'm doing about it."

"Yeah, me too. But now I know that there is more to this life than what we're living down here. We come from a powerful love..." Leroy paused, remembering how it felt to be loved so completely.

"You hungry yet?" Hal asked as his stomach growled.

"Yeah, I could eat," Leroy replied. "What are you in the mood for?"

Road food, restaurant eating, made Hal miss his little camp stove and home cooking. Nothing was better than fresh food, whether it came out of a garden or a fresh water lake. "Aw Leroy, I'm just tired of road food. If I'd a caught some fish today, we'd be frying them up. Let's go take a walk and see what they got on the main drag out here. Maybe I'll see something I like."

"That's all right with me," Leroy said getting off his bed and washing up. Looking in the mirror, Leroy surveyed the damage he did to himself that day. The cut on his forehead hurt pretty good. Thankfully, inside his medical bag, Kenny had sutures to stitch up Leroy's cut and cover it with a white bandage. Leroy would have to keep the stitches dry until they healed.

The last rays of sunlight glowed in the West, painting the southwestern sky with neon pinks, oranges and deep shades of blue. As they walked out of the hotel room, the temperature was still over 85 degrees. It didn't seem like it'd get much cooler. "I think I want a salad," Leroy said after a while.

"You want a what?" Hal asked amused, knowing his meat-eating buddy pretty well.

"Yeah, I don't feel like having anything heavy, no meat," Leroy paused. "It's too hot."

"All righty then, let's go find some rabbit food," Hal jested. "I could stand to lose a pound or two, myself. Though I might still have some pie."

Leroy laughed. "Yeah, that will take the weight off ya!"

After indulging in a couple of Cobb salads and a slice of fresh berry pie, Hal's mood seemed perceptively better. But what really held his attention, as they walked out of the restaurant, was the sapphire dome of the night's desert sky. For as far as the eye could see, it was afire with all the twinkling stars of the Universe. No matter where he traveled, the Big Dipper always followed the North Star. The Milky Way was thick and bright, while shooting stars streaked across the deep blue backdrop. Grandma Moon rose slowly in the East, as puffy thunderheads formed over the silhouette of the craggy mountains. A warm breeze swept across the star-studded heavens. The walk back to the hotel felt good. There was no need to rush. It'd been a big day.

As night fell, Hal could barely keep his eyes open. With a big yawn, he pulled the black out curtains shut and shuffled off to bed. After his head hit the pillow, he drifted into a deep sleep. In his dream time, he found himself sitting on top of a great mountain, overlooking the land near and far. Suspended far above him, in a Sea of Love, clusters of stars were twinkling. As he sat there, he heard a distant singing. He glanced around and saw an Elder of the Stars singing his soul song to Mother Earth. This seasoned Traveler of the Milky Way came walking up the path and quietly took his place beside Hal. In silence they sat there a while, until the Elder finally spoke.

"Do you remember the Time before Time? Before the Star Maker's songs called forth the flowers and clouds, the trees, the waters and the stone?" asked the Star Traveler, who had come from the farthest fields of the Milky Way. His kind, soothing voice was deep and rich. As his gentle loving eyes rested on Hal, he peered through the window of Hal's soul. "Before the first morning of the world," his hand swept across the fertile fields of Earth, "you were One with us. Even in the days when the world was young, and the waters were pure like a mountain stream, we walked beside you."

As Hal took in the stillness, he felt the Elder to be a familiar. "It just seems like we've gotten a little off track down here."

"Yes," agreed the Star Traveler. "Man, with his spirit sleeping, has become lost in the wonders of Time. In their dreams of chaos and separation, they have produced this baneful Harvest."

"You mean nightmares," Hal chuckled. "It'd be a good time to wake 'em all up, before they destroy the place."

"For twenty centuries," the Elder began. "The Star Maker has sent Many who carried an ancient wisdom from the Angelic Tribes. Riding on the clouds, they came to gently awaken humanity. Mankind had fallen under the 'spell of matter' and had become spiritually blind. Before the Fall, when the cloud of darkness passed over the Eternal Sun and temporarily blocked Its Light, we shared the ancient Wisdom which came from the Stars. The life force of the Stars flows through each of your veins."

Like silken rain drops on dry soil, these gentle words of wisdom worked their way into Hal's heart. He'd seen the damage done by those stumbling sleepwalkers of society. They were always looking for something or someone outside themselves to fix it, to ease their soul hunger. Since they lost touch with the Inner Voice of Great Spirit, they had no faith in a Higher Power. From then on, they depended on human beings, things or solely on themselves, to ease the ache in their soul.

"Don't blame them," the Star Traveler said, hearing Hal's thoughts. "Under the 'spell of matter,' they were lost in the dust of Creation. They forgot the true fire burning at their core. They felt cut off from the Love which quells all desire. But soon the long winter nights of man's history will grow shorter. As the ice melts, those human hearts, long frozen in dis-ease or disappointment, long frozen in time, will soften."

"It just seems to me that the needle in the compass of their heart must be broken," Hal confessed. "It don't point true North anymore."

"When you serve the god of fear, you're afraid to make mistakes," the Star Traveler offered. "But this Fall is not lasting. It's a passing cloud, that the Winds of Change will move across the Heavens and disperse after the long rain. History is not destiny."

"I pray you're right," Hal shook his head after all the trouble he'd seen this life time. "Now don't get me wrong, I mean no disrespect," Hal started, needing to say his peace. "But there only seems to be a 'Stairway to Heaven' and a 'Highway to Hell,' and from what I've seen, the traffic is all going in the wrong direction."

The Elder chuckled looking at Hal's serious expression. "Well, there are a few explanations for that," he began. "Ages ago, the Tempter swayed humanity by enticing them with things. That's when the Fall began."

"You talking about that fella Adam, a serpent and an apple?" Hal laughed. "I read that story. The way I see it, Adam didn't have much luck with women. His first wife wanted nothing to do with him. And then the second wife gives him forbidden fruit and they get thrown out of Paradise. After that, his first born son kills his second born. Not much since then has changed."

"Oh, there were some rough beginnings after the Fall of Man," the Elder chuckled. "But Earth wasn't the only planet to have its struggles."

"Oh, do tell," Hal said, as this story of life unraveled.

"As it happened, the children of Mars destroyed their planet, leaving it lifeless and barren," The Star Traveler began. "The star-seed of those wayward children were stuck in the Ethers, unable to return to Mars. It was the generous Spirit of Gaia, along with the Star Counsel, which allowed their souls to be rescued. While the physical planet of Mars healed itself, these souls were allowed to come to Earth, only if they agreed to amend their ways. If you noticed, there is great desire for these star-seed to return to their planet, but their destructive ways have not changed."

"Well, Mars is the god of war," Hal surmised, seeing how these wayward souls affected the life around them. "It makes sense that his kids would tear the shit out of things."

"In their spiritual slumber, it was their infatuation with the plains of matter which caused these chattering monkeys to forget the Spirit who lives in the forests and the stars," the Elder surmised.

"Are you telling me that some kind of puppy love with things turned all these people into idiots?" Hal couldn't believe his ears.

"Not right away," the Elder started. "But as they turned away from their true Heritage, it wasn't long before they lost touch with Spirit. Such people don't value rainbows and butterflies. Even the inner nature of their countries have become ill. When the Mind of the nation sorely declines from greed and deceit, it leaves the happiness of the people to whims and passing fancies, rather than caring for their genuine needs. Secrets equal distrust, just as lies create dis-ease. To be truly human, was a partnership between Spirit and matter. Once mankind was blinded to its deeper reality, it could no longer hear the Wisdom which came to them through the Spirits of the Forest."

"Man, this is deep," Hal rested his head in his hands, feeling the immensity of it all. "So what's the answer?"

The Elder laughed. "Love. It may not be the fastest way to solve a conflict. But in the end, where Love enters, the problem is resolved."

"That sounds pretty simple," Hal replied. "But if you looked around Earth lately, there ain't much of that song being played. Everyone's beating the drums of war."

"Yes, warfare is an expensive way to communicate," the Elder agreed. "Being quite harmful to both parties. You see, every exchange of violence is even and balanced. Whatever pain is inflicted, it comes back with an equal and opposite pain. This high price is paid by both winner and loser alike."

"What you're saying is," Hal began. "Whatever we do to someone else, we do to ourselves."

"You can't harm another without doing great damage to yourself," the Elder agreed.

"That's why 22 vets are killing themselves every day," Hal put together. "They can't handle the pain of what they were a part of. Those memories eat at their mind."

"It takes many decades for people and a nation to recover from war," the Star Traveler stated. "It's much better to talk than it is to kill."

"Yeah, I see your point. It just seems that some people ain't got much use for talking," Hal replied.

"All life is learning," the Elder began. "But understand this. To break the yokes of tyranny, hearts must be awakened to the seeds of perfection which reside within them and be transformed by the power of truth. The Father of the Stars has never left His Creation or His Children. He is closer to us than the Ocean is to the Shore, no farther away than your in-breath. The River of Life is rising. It will touch all Life. Either the children will dive in by choice or the living waters will come to them. Creator's divine love will bridge the deep canyons carved out by hate, anger and disappointment. Ever so gently, the Star Maker will awaken within the hearts of all Creation."

Under the canopy of stars, both were enveloped in a quiet moment, as Hal took all this information in. Then the seasoned Traveler of the Stars looked deeply into the eyes of Hal's soul and recalled the reason for his visit.

"You made some big prayers earlier," the Elder said gazing across the wide panorama of snow capped mountains and fertile valleys.

"I suppose so. There seems to be a lot of needless suffering going on right now," Hal responded.

"Our suffering is created out of our actions," the Elder offered. "What we create returns to us, sometimes many fold."

"You can say that again," Hal agreed.

"What did you have in mind, for those young men and women coming home from the war?" the Elder asked finally after a long silence.

"I'm not rightly sure," Hal pondered. "I know ceremony worked for me and Leroy. I can't see why it wouldn't work for others."

Then the Star Traveler swept his hand from East to West. As he did, Sacred Fireplaces were set ablaze, emerging out of the darkness from coast to coast. "Is this what you had in mind?"

"Yeah, I can see that. But how do I get something like that going? Starting a fire with green wood or wet kindling just makes for a lot of smoke." Hal replied, seeing the enormity of the mission being presented.

"To rekindle the fire of awareness just takes a spark," laughed the seasoned Star Traveler, knowing all you needed to strike a fire was a piece of flint and steel.

"Awareness of what exactly?" Hal wanted detailed instructions.

"Of the Star Maker who resides in the hearts of All," said the Elder. "For this fire to be lit in others, all you need to do is seed the prayer and allow it to work through the soil of their souls. Much like the work you did with your good friend. Spirit will manifest the rest," the Elder responded.

"You mean Leroy?" Hal shot back. "That hard-headed you know what, almost got himself killed today."

"It was a small detour on his Spirit's journey," the Elder laughed. "Don't forget, we are eternal. Your Spirit is older than stardust."

"After the day I had, my bones feel older than stardust," Hal responded. Looking out at the sea of Sacred Fireplaces, Hal's vision came back to the matter at hand. "You think this is gonna work?"

"Ah," sighed the Elder, his gentle eyes full of untold knowing. "With each tide, there is an ebb and flow. Some will awaken more slowly than others. Yet the awareness of Spirit will wash over them like a gentle rain. Everything you need will come to you. Spirit has no boundaries or limitations like that of the human mind. The prayer was made and Spirit responded. Now it's up to you to carry forth the dream as it is presented. Many are called to help right now. And you will see, this work will go far."

"Oh," Hal pondered as he looked out over the land speckled with Sacred Fireplaces. "Just seed the dream..."

"Yes, seed the dream. These festering wounds must be well cleaned before they can heal. What you do not see, is the opposition to this work," the Elder added. "The dark forces do not want healing for those afflicted with a dis-eased mind. Especially those who take their own lives. Out there, in the midst of it all," his hands swept across the land. "Is an angry army of earthbound spirits. They thrive by tormenting the living because of the war. They don't want humans to go free. With their cunning sway, they draw the living down into their world by anger, hate, fear, and dis-ease. But, Creator's Love can counter the dark. All you need do is call on the Higher Powers. They will answer you. What you must never forget, is that Creator's Light, which moves through the darkness, makes the shadows disappear. Stay within that Light and you need not worry."

As this ancient wisdom echoed down through his insides, Hal knew it to be true. It didn't matter to the Higher Powers what tribe or nation a person came from. It only mattered that a call was made and help could be rendered. "Whenever you're doing anything great," Hal began. "You gotta expect some devil monkey to throw a wrench in it. The stronger the enemy, the greater the battle, the sweeter the victory."

"Quite true," the Star Traveler agreed. "Those snared by the demon of despair, struggle the hardest. When their souls finally laugh, that laughter breaks that dark spell which has colored their world black. Their victory is great. You see, those who take their own lives are held captive by darkness, which they themselves created," the Elder put forth. "Their deep sadness cocoons them like a thick turtle shell."

"What's the solution?" Hal asked, knowing this was no easy task.

"Love," the Elder answered simply. "A Love so deep and true that

It knows no bounds. Unless prayers are made to rescue the lost ones from their self-imposed prison, they will remain stuck in the Shadows, until they themselves ask for help," the Elder continued. "Most people who make that wrong choice, don't want to die. They never saw themselves through the eyes of the Great Spirit who created them. They viewed their painful lives solely through eyes of flesh, never knowing their true value."

"I can see that," Hal replied, watching the Light of the Sacred Fireplaces expand, growing bigger until the land had a holy glow. "The heartache was just to great to handle."

"It is well that you made those prayers. For only those who have suffered the same way, can fully understand and help another to get free. You'll see, these gatherings will welcome in a season of change." With that, the Elder rose from his seat. Out of respect, Hal stood and thanked the Elder for his teaching and watched him walk down the misty mountain trail.

CRACKLE! CRASH! BOOM! BANG! Almost breaking the sky in two, a great crack of Holy Thunder jolted Hal out of his sleep. Rain fell in torrents as a streak of white lighting flashed through the deep gray underbelly of the clouds. The silver-skirted Thunder Beings, the great lords of the upper sky, danced in time to the steps they knew all too well. Creating a Wind of Change, the powerful Thunderbird's wings spanned the Heavens, reaching out in opposite directions. With great power, these wings beat against the sky, sounding a vibrant song of wind and rolling holy thunder. This victorious Rain-bird, with its supernatural powers and strength, caught the Spirit of Nature in its wings and together they soared across in her heavens.

Over the thirsty Earth, the Spirit of the Rain danced across the cloud covered sky. From the Most High, it sprinkled its holy waters to nourish the fertile soils of the Mother. Gathering in small pools and puddles, the water formed a union with all the waters of the Earth. Running creeks became streams, which forged into mighty rivers, all running back to the ocean, where the heat of the Sun would compel the waters once again to return to the heavens.

Hal sprung out of bed like he heard a gun go off. Sitting in the dark by the open window, Leroy was already awake, gazing at the pouring rain.

"Huh, what happened?" Hal yawned, seeing the dim light from the street lamp flood into the room.

"Thunderstorm," Leroy answered as the sweet smell of pouring rain came in through the open window. "You were talking in your sleep. Something about a dream."

"Did you take notes?" Hal said as he pushed himself out of bed. In the dim light, he rummaged through his things to find his tobacco pouch.

"All I heard you say was something about seeding the dream," Leroy recalled. "I was asleep until the Thunders showed up a half hour ago."

"Yeah, I was out," Hal opened the door and stood under the awning. Torrents of pelting rain gush down from the heavens. The cool water splashed his bare feet. Streams of water gathered into large puddles throughout the parking lot. From his pouch, he took a pinch of tobacco and raised it above his head. "Thank you, Tunkashila for answering this prayer and for guiding me on my next step." Within an instant, holy thunder clasped over his head. Flashes of white lightning crackled right behind it. Hal tossed the tobacco out into the rain with a feeling of gratitude.

"So what's the dream?" Leroy probed Hal for answers.

"Sacred Fireplaces," Hal answered as he turned around and looked at Leroy. "Far and wide, Sacred Fireplaces." Walking outside, he stood under the awning, breathing in the cool rain. Drops of water dripped down into the crevices of his copper-toned face as he looked across the wide open spaces.

Crackles of white lightning lit up the night sky drawing Hal's attention toward the street. Strong currents of water were already lapping over the curb, rushing down the street. Out of the corner of his eye, he spied someone stumbling in the middle of the main highway. In the midst of a cloudburst, the street lights cast an eerie glow over the shadows as the man hobbled across the road. Just then, Hal heard the blaring horn of an eighteen wheeler. It whizzed passed the man who was caught in a drunken stew, sending a wall of water flying at him. Sluggish to react and walking with a limp, the force of the wave threw him off balance. The man stumbled and fell back into the puddle.

"AW HELL!" Hal swore as he bolted in the room. Quickly, he pulled on his jeans and found his boots. "Come on Leroy, looks like we got trouble." The blaring horn of another eighteen wheeler echoed through the room.

Running across the highway, they found a man slumped in a puddle. His wet, bedraggled clothes were worn and full of holes. Under the dim glow of street lamp, Leroy saw "USMC" tattooed on the man's forearm. With Hal on one side and Leroy on the other, they hoisted him up, over their shoulders. The smell of booze wreaked from the stranger's mouth, as they dragged his limp body across the highway. Halfway across, the man started to wretch. Streams of puke and bile flew from his mouth. Standing down stream of this unwanted mess, Hal's boots got baptized by this yuck.

"Dang it!" Hal lamented. "I haven't had puke on my boots since I got sober!"

"It'll wash off," Leroy scolded as the rain gushed down his worried face. "Hurry up! Before the next semi comes!" Within seconds, they'd made it safely back to their room.

"Let's put him in the chair. In case he throws up again. At least, he won't choke on it," Hal directed as they maneuvered the stranger across the room.

"What do you want to do with him?" Leroy asked after they got him settled in.

"Beats the hell out of me. That's about the way you looked, minus the rain of course, when I dragged your sorry ass out of the gutter," Hal reflected, grabbing a towel to wipe the puke off his boots.

"You think we ought to get him in the shower?" Leroy asked, knowing it would take the both of them to do this.

"Well, he'll sure as shit smell better," Hal mused. "Go grab one of them beach chairs by the pool. It'll make the job easier."

Making a run for it, Leroy spied across the street. The rain wasn't letting up. Across the highway, a bright red neon sign flashed over the door of a saloon. "Huh, that's probably where he came out of," Leroy said to himself as he grabbed a plastic pool chair and dragged it back to the room.

"Go ahead and set it in the shower," Hal directed. "Then we got to get him down to his skivvies and clean him up. Did you see his tattoo?"

"Yeah," Leroy shook his head. "He's a Marine."

"We got ourselves another one," Hal said sadly. "Our boys are dropping like flies, coming home from this dang war."

"There doesn't seem like an end to it," Leroy said as he put the chair in the shower.

After about an hour, the Marine was finally cleaned up. Partway through the shower, he started coming round. Drunkenly, the man surveyed his surroundings as the warm water pelted his skin. His tired eyes were bloodshot and bleary. As Leroy rubbed a soapy wash cloth over the stranger's back, distant memories flooded into his mind. He recalled that fateful day, years ago, when Hal and Kyle had him in the shower at the truck stop. Now it was his turn to give back.

Only those who've been burned by the alcohol fire can fully understand its madness. Many less fortunate souls had sung its death song. Like an ancient breed of hard-bitten sea rovers, these restless travelers, from lands near and far, possessed a harder, more tragic wisdom. As wayfaring shipmates, they bonded together over hard stories and a frothy drink, yet few survived the assaults of alcohol's raging storms. Truth be told, only the gypsies of the firewater tribe understood its language. With wizened, tattered hearts, they alone could preach about its tempest. For after sailing through many lonesome waters, weathering every chilling storm, only they could fully appreciate the peaceful shores of sobriety.

By the time Leroy finished, Hal dumped the soiled clothes in the washer down by the stairwell. "Hold on, soldier," Leroy said gently as he eased the man out of the shower.

"Sarge..." the stranger slurred, his brain swimming from the strong soul poison which crucified his pride. "Sorry Sarge," he wept bitterly. "I won't let it happen again."

Something sounded familiar in the man's voice. But this guy was practically skin and bones. *"Naw, it couldn't be,"* Leroy thought to himself. "Daniels? Is that you Daniels?"

"Yes sir, Sarge," the man muttered under the unforgiving florescent light of the bathroom.

Leroy grabbed the man's chin and looked dead into his bloodshot eyes. "Mike Daniels, is that you?"

"Yesssss sir, Sarge," his words slurred.

"You're alive," Leroy stood there in shock. He hadn't seen Daniels since the morning they got ambushed, all those years ago.

"Well, just barely Sir," Daniels muttered. The alcohol fog started to lift a little. "My wife kicked me out about 3 years ago. I woke up choking her in my sleep. I didn't even realize I was doing it. Until she started fighting back with all she had and I woke up."

"Man," Leroy shook his head. "I've heard stories like that."

"Yeah, well they're true," Daniels uttered. "I guess I scared her pretty good."

Just then, Hal walked back into the room. "The clothes will be dry in about an hour."

"Hal, this is Mike Daniels. We were in the same Unit together," Leroy said still a little stunned. "I thought he was dead."

"Well, he damn near could have been!" Hal scolded, clearly upset. It pained him to see a veteran in such sad shape. "Had he gotten tangled up with that eighteen wheeler! BOY HOWDY! You came damn close to getting squashed like a bug!" Hal sat down on the bed. The clock read 4:32 am. His sleepy eyes felt like gritty sand paper. "You know what gets me? If it weren't for that thunderstorm, I'd have slept straight through. And we'd be reading about you in the morning paper."

"Don't mind him! He's grouchy like a bear, when he don't get much sleep," said Leroy as he tossed Daniels a pair of sweat pants and a tee shirt.

"Look, I don't want to be any trouble," Daniels stumbled around as he got dressed. "I'll just get my things and be on my way. Thanks for getting me out of the rain."

"Aw hell, you ain't going no wheres," Hal started to calm down. "I think we got some orange juice and bread left over in that mini-fridge. Leroy can get you a glass, to get your blood sugar up. The bread will soak up the poison in your stomach. Then, we'll get some shut eye. Come sun-up, we'll eat some breakfast. We can figure it all out in the morning. Right now, I figure I got about 3 good hours of sleep left. Sound alright to you?"

"Sure," they both shot back as Hal put his exhausted body back in bed. Within seconds of closing his eyes, he was snoring like a big bear. After fixing Daniels a glass of orange juice, Leroy tossed him a hunk of French bread. With a pillow and a blanket, Daniels gratefully settled down on the carpeted floor. It was a much better than trying to catch 40 winks in the pouring rain. Stunned at the whole last hour, Leroy turned out the light. As the storm raged on, Leroy listened to Hal snore, while the rain beat out a pounding, steady rhythm on the roof.

In the quiet hush before the dawn's early light, twittering songbirds called in the morning. Gathered in the sacred arbors of yesteryear, the Spirits of their Ancestors danced to the love songs of the wind and rain. Their all knowing love was carried across the heavens by the Four Winds. Nature's minstrels were joined by the piping shrill whistle from their

Eagle bone whistles. With their voices raised in chorus, the Ancestors called to the Higher Powers.

Throughout the centuries, battles fought on the blood-stained killing fields, brought together warriors from every war, all longing for peace. As Grandma Moon slowly descended below the Western skyline, their Spirits made prayers for health and healing. To give life to their prayers, they danced in sacred arbors just before the crack of dawn. Soon the rosy glow of the bright shining sun would illuminate the Heavens and Earth alike.

Something was shifting. A call to a greater purpose. A healing for all mankind. By the heavenly farmers, this spiritual seed of peace was strewn out through the fertile fields of the Cosmos. For those who were awake enough to sense it, this spiritual seed settled itself into their hearts and minds. Seeding the dream, the Spirits of the Higher Realms sprinkled visions of peace, harmony and healing throughout the land, for those with eyes to see.

CHAPTER THREE: FREE AT LAST

CROSSROADS

Where to go tomorrow?
Seemed the question on her mind
These granite walls brought sorrow
A dead end for all time

Standing at the crossroads
Between Hope and hell
That fateful day she took her fall
She remembered very well

She could see it from the distance
It loomed so tall and gray
The immensity of those granite walls
Took her breath away

The sun, it now was setting
With a half moon on the rise
The clouds they were amazing
With deep crimson colors painted across the sky

The stars began to twinkle
Across the Heavens from afar
She glanced up at that moment
Suddenly wished on a shooting star

For Love, it is so Infinite
It knows no stops or bounds
Those who place their faith in It
Somehow always will be found

    High on the wire, a black crow cawed, sounding its alarm. Flying over the fields of grain, two red-tail hawks circled the blue, cloudless sky in their hunt for field mice. The smell of freshly tilled earth and newly cut grass lingered in the soft blowing, gentle breeze. Dressed in their black and gray attire, the undertakers of the animal kingdom sat high in the branches of a towering row of eucalyptus trees which lined the fields. Being the clean-up crew, these buzzards waited patiently for their next meal. Off in the distance groaned the hum of a diesel tractor as it churned up the deep, rich earth. Sparrows, Finches and Mocking birds chirped and chattered away in the shrubs planted along the walkway near the storefronts. Otherwise, it was a relatively quiet day on the outskirts of town. Nestled in farm country, the woman's prison was surrounded by a checker board of fertile farmland in the midst of big valley.

    Off in the West, a great rack of billowy thunderheads were building with amazing speed. The buzzing hum of honey bees came from the lavender flowers planted in a windowsill. This morning, nothing felt as good as freedom, when she finally walked out through those prison gates. A new door was opening. A new road beckoned. Not wanting to repeat the mistakes of her past, a inner longing filled her heart. More than anything, she searched for a meaningful way to spend the rest of her days. Something told her she couldn't become successful on her own.

    Miles away, Rhoda occasionally heard the train blowing its horn. Waiting for the afternoon bus, beads of sweat poured down her neck while Rhoda sat on the bench in the sweltering sun. It wouldn't be there for over an hour. Much like a gypsy wandering through the landscape, her meager belongings were stashed in a trash bag which sat by her side. In a storefront window behind her, buzzed a pink neon sign, which read: "PSYCHIC." Beneath it, was a small handwritten sign which read: "SPECIAL: Readings $5.00."

    "Hmm," Rhoda sighed as she fanned herself with an old newspaper. With the summer monsoon thunderstorms over in the desert, it was a sticky, miserable heat. One that made her sweat. Her mouth was parched. Her lips were dry and cracking. She'd give anything for a cool drink of water. Especially, one that didn't taste like soap. The buzz from the neon pink sign sent Rhoda's mind wandering back, into a daydream, long ago, when she was just a kid.

That particular day, it'd been a rough afternoon. The boys in the neighborhood liked to pull her red pigtails. Over and over they chanted, "Fatty, fatty, 2 x 4! Can't get through the kitchen door!" One boy, Dante, was the worst. His brutality knew no end. With an evil look in his eye, he found a rock and threw it at her head. It hit her skull with a powerful force. Though it wasn't her fault, she lived in a group home full of other throw-away kids. Feeling the blood trickle down into her eye, Rhoda raced screaming down the block, looking for a place to hide. Under the wooden porch steps of a house around the corner, she finally found some shelter. It was a small, shady spot where Rhoda cried softly to herself. No one loved her. No one.

That's when she heard the screen door creak open and slippered feet shuffled across the porch. "Who's there? Who's there?" the old woman's voice called out. Rhoda was as still as a mouse in a falcon's sight. She barely breathed, hoping the old woman would go back in the house.

"I know you're here," the old woman softly said. "I can hear you breathing."

Still Rhoda said nothing. The last thing she wanted was trouble. All day long, her foster mother screamed at the kids. In that house, there was a constant revolving door of kids coming and going. Rhoda had been there less than a year, but already she'd seen kids getting shuffled from one place to another.

"You're a little girl," the old woman's voice cooed. "Oh such sadness, you've had in your young life," she went on. A sweet smell of cinnamon and sugar wafted through the air.

Terrified, Rhoda listened intently. *"How could she know I was a little girl?"* she wondered.

"Now if you come out, I have a cookie for you," the old woman offered. "But there is something you must know about your mother..." her voice trailed off.

"How do you know about my mother?" Rhoda's young voice demanded, as she crawled out from under the porch steps. The lady from the orphanage told her foster mother that Rhoda's birth-mom had died after delivering the baby.

"Ah, there you are," the old woman cooed. "Come up here, and I'll tell you."

Sheepishly, Rhoda crawled out from under the steps. The bump on her forehead was growing from the rock that Dante threw. Her chubby, white freckled legs were skinned at the knees. Red scabs of dried blood covered her kneecaps. Her round freckled puffy cheeks pouted. Her light blue eyes stared straight forward. To protect herself, she crossed her arms in front of her chest. Rhoda looked at the old woman, dressed in a yellow and white checkered house dress. The smell of garlic was coming through the front door. But there was another smell, something smoky.

"My," the old woman sighed, looking at Rhoda through her dark horn rimmed glasses. The lenses were thick, making her eyes look big like an horned owl. "Well, I can tell just by looking at you, you haven't had an easy life. How old are you?"

"Seven," Rhoda offered. "How do you know about my mom?"

"Well, because she whispered to me that you were under the porch. That's why I came out," the old woman smiled. "I was busy baking cookies, when I felt a tap on my shoulder. That's when your mamma told me to look outside."

"My mom is here?" Rhoda looked surprised.

"Oh yes child…" she began. "Come inside, before my cookies burn. I can't hear the timer from out here." Rhoda bounded up the porch steps and moved quickly through the screen door before it slammed shut. The house smelled of sweet maple and brown sugar mixed with garlic and another smoky smell. Sitting on a small table, covered with a golden, crocheted doily were three white candles, their burning wicks gave the front room a warm glow. Old Persian rugs covered the worn wooden floor boards. Ornate hand paintings in golden wood frames speckled the fancy papered walls. A red velvet lamp with gold trim sat on top of a wooden table in the corner by a soft, blue velvet couch.

Quick as a whip, the old woman pulled the pans from the oven. The smell of fresh cookies lingered in the air. Rhoda plopped down on a wooden stool on the corner of a maple butcher block table, looking over at this curious old woman. "How come I never met you before?" Rhoda finally asked.

"Well, sometimes special meetings have to wait for the right time," the old woman offered, as she took the cookies from the baking sheet and put them on a plate. "I suppose that this was the right time for us to meet."

"Did you know my mom?" Rhoda's young blue eyes waited with anticipation.

"No, I just met her today," the old woman said.

"But how?" Rhoda looked confused. "My mom died when I was born."

"Her vessel died, but her Spirit lives on forever," the old woman offered. This chubby, freckle-faced, little girl's face looked quite confused. No one had ever talked about her mom before. No one ever told her the story about what happened.

"Hmm," the old woman sighed. Then she had an idea. She pulled out a glass from the cupboard and got the bottle of milk from the frig. "You see this glass," she started to explain. "Let's say this glass is your mom's body. And the milk in this bottle, is her Spirit." The old woman poured some milk from the bottle into the glass. "Now, when her spirit is in the glass, her body is alive. But when her Spirit leaves the glass, the body isn't needed anymore. But her Spirit still lives." The old woman put the glass of milk in front of Rhoda. Then she poured herself a glass of milk and put the plate of cookies on the table.

"Your mom wasn't for this world, not really," the old woman began, glancing at the ceiling. "She was more like an Angel, who came here for a short visit. But there is something you should know."

"What's that?" Rhoda asked, afraid to drink the milk because her mom's Spirit was in the glass. The old woman dunked a cookie in her milk and put it in her mouth.

"Your mom is around you all the time. She watches over you. And she sings to you when you're asleep," the old woman's eyes twinkled. They were soft gray-blue wizened eyes. Her cheeks were creased and wrinkled. But there was a gentleness about her, which made Rhoda feel safe.

"But what about my dad?" Rhoda soft voice asked anxiously. "Do I have a dad?"

The old woman looked up at the ceiling and got a faraway look in her eyes. It was as if she was listening to something, something Rhoda couldn't hear. "Hmm... your dad never knew about you," the old woman started. "He lives faraway... way over the ocean," her hands were waving to the east. "He lives in the country where your mother was from."

"I think she came from Ireland," Rhoda said. "That was on my birth certificate. I got to see that once."

The old woman's eyes narrowed on the cut above Rhoda's left eye. There was a small bruise forming. "What happened to your eye?" she asked.

"Dante...," Rhoda looked down at the lime green linoleum covered floor. "Dante threw a rock at my head. He hates me."

Quick as a whip, the old woman grabbed a large butcher knife off the counter and pressed it to Rhoda's head wound. The cold steel pushed hard against the bruise, pressing down the swelling. "Ouch!" Rhoda whimpered as the old woman kept pressing the cold steel against her swollen head.

"Sit tight child. Don't squirm. Otherwise you'll have a nice knot on your head," the old woman said. In the silence, she started humming a old lullaby. The old woman's humming soothed Rhoda's hurt soul while the force of the cold steel pressed against her bruised head.

"Your mamma loves you very much," the old woman finally confessed. "She never meant for you to go through so much pain on your own. But her body wasn't strong enough to birth a child. That's why she ran away from home and came to have you over here. She hoped to start a new life."

Her young mind whirled, as the old woman talked about her mamma. All her life, Rhoda had felt so alone, so unloved and unwanted. But now, she knew that wasn't true. Finally after a long while, the old woman released the blade from her forehead.

"It looks like we got that swelling right in the nick of time," the old woman said. "If you didn't come out from under that porch, that would have been a mighty big bruise." She laid the big butcher knife on the counter.

"So my daddy, he doesn't know I'm alive?" Rhoda asked as she munched on the maple cookies, dunked in milk.

"Afraid not," the old woman said. "Seems to me, your mamma was afraid of him, somewhat," the old woman waved her hand sideways. "I have a feeling she didn't trust him."

"Do you think I'll ever meet him?" Rhoda asked quietly. She wanted so much to belong to somebody. Her whole young life was orphanages and foster homes.

"Hmm, I'm not sure. I don't think your mamma wanted that. It seemed to me, that she was trying to escape from that life over there. I can see her running for the train, running to get on the plane and finally when it took off, she felt she was safe. I'm not sure you'd want to meet him." The old woman shook her head. "Seems to me, you're safer without him."

In the sweltering heat, the bus blasted by Rhoda without stopping. Jolted out of her day dream, she could still see the old woman's smile and kind eyes as the memory faded away. "HEY!" Rhoda jumped up and screamed after the bus. It would be the last one of the day. Buses didn't travel much out here on Saturday. "Aw, damn," she sighed as she sunk back down onto the bench. The pink neon sign still buzzed in the storefront window behind her. "What the hell..." she said and dragged her garbage bag with her belonging through the front door of the shop.

A small bell tinkled as Rhoda shut the door behind her. There was a familiar smoky smell. She recognized it from the old woman's house in the old neighborhood, where she grew up. The front parlor was cool, with a few candles burning on a table. There was a counter, with a small cash register along with some brochures. Along the wall was a large glass case. Inside were different colored crystals, trinkets and bracelets. A half split open amethyst geode sat on a small table near the door. Hanging from a wall cabinet, were several kinds of incense packages, filled with long sticks covered with different resins. On the side of the counter was a small box filled with tin-foiled cylindrical packages. "KING'S CHARCOAL" it said on the side of the box. Next to that, was a small rack that had different incense in small plastic bags. "COPAL, FRANKINCENSE, MYHRR," were some of the labels.

Through a curtained doorway, came a middle-aged woman. Her long dark hair flowed over her shoulders. She looked directly at Rhoda with her piercing gray blue eyes and spied the trash-bag full of her belongings. "Can I help you?" she asked.

"Oh, yeah, I was interested in the $5 reading special," Rhoda said nervously, as her flaming red curls covered her face. Her freckled, white cheeks blushed, as she realized how disheveled she must look. The scent of prison life hadn't washed off yet. Sheepishly, she tried to shove the trash-bag with all her belongings behind her.

Suddenly a look of recognition crossed the woman's face. She'd seen Rhoda's face on the news. But she wouldn't let on. If she felt comfortable, Rhoda would need to bring that ugliness up herself. "Of course, dear. Let me show you back into my parlor. You may bring your things with you," she said as she acknowledged the trash-bag.

Self-consciously dragging the bag behind her, Rhoda followed the woman through a doorway, covered with deep maroon velvet curtains. There was a long hallway which went towards the back. As they walked, Rhoda realized that the storefront was part of a house where the woman and her family lived. It just happened to be on the corner in front of the bus stop.

The woman lead her back into a small room. Inside, there was a small wooden table with two chairs. Along the wall was a tall statue of the Blessed Virgin of Guadalupe. White candles burned on either side, along with small offerings of water, fruit and the stump of a cigar. Rhoda plopped the trash-bag down next to the chair and sat down. It was much cooler in this small room and she was grateful to be out of the heat.

"Do you have a glass of water?" Rhoda asked, feeling how parched her throat was. "It's really hot out there today."

"Of course, just go outside the door. There is a water cooler with cups. Please go help yourself," said the woman as she found her deck of Tarot cards. With an old wash clothe, the woman dusted off the table and took the Tarot cards out of their wooden box. She placed a royal blue silk cloth over the table, on which she would lay down the cards.

Rhoda walked outside the door and spied down the hallway. The giggling voices of children playing sounded from outside. From the kitchen, came the lingering smells of someone cooking. The aroma of spices, sauteed butter and garlic filled the house. By the wall was a water tank with a cup dispenser on the side. Rhoda took a cup and filled it with water. The first cup she gulped down, realizing how thirsty she was. The second cup also went down in a hurry. Then she filled it one more time and brought it with her into the small reading room.

"Somebody's cooking sure smells good," Rhoda said as she sat back down.

"Yes, that is my mother's recipe," the woman smiled. "My name is Esmeralda. And what is yours?"

"Rhoda," she replied. "When I was a kid, I used to live down the street from an old gypsy woman from Romania. It's funny, when I walked in I smelled the same smoky smell that she used to have in her house. But I never asked her what it was."

"Ah, you must smell the Frankincense. It is an incense given to Jesus by the Three Kings. I burn it often," Esmeralda offered.

"That must be it," Rhoda replied. "I remember her saying something about Frankincense. But I was just a kid, so I didn't really pay attention. She told me about my mom..." Rhoda's voice trailed off.

"Yes, I sense there is something about your mom, something that is unhealed. Something that disturbs your peace." Esmeralda's dark eyes were intense and penetrating when she looked at Rhoda. It was almost a little unnerving.

"Yeah, she died when I was born," Rhoda offered. "The gypsy woman told me she was around me all the time."

"I can only imagine what it must be like to mother your child from the Spirit World," Esmeralda said. "I have children of my own and I cannot imagine my life without them."

"I have a daughter," Rhoda said. "I haven't seen her in four years."

After lighting a white candle on her table, Esmeralda shuffled the cards. Sensing the density around Rhoda, she decided to light a stick of Frankincense and allow the smoke to clear away any negativity which may have come into her reading room. She was familiar with the need for the client to purge their worst sorrows when the cards came out. After they'd been shuffled sufficiently, Esmeralda passed the cards through the smoke from the incense, clearing the energy on the cards.

"Now, hold the cards in your hand," Esmeralda said as she passed Rhoda the cards. "I want you to ask the questions you want to know. Just a simple prayer."

But Rhoda was never taught how to pray. Being shuffled from the orphanage to foster homes, no one ever took the time to teach her how to pray. Honestly, she didn't even know if she believed in God, especially after the life she had. Holding the deck of cards in her hands, her thoughts whirled. She closed her eyes. Somehow the only question she had was "What happened? How did everything become such a mess?"

After Rhoda opened her eyes, she handed the deck back to Esmeralda. There was this anticipation in the air. Something felt hopeful. Esmeralda held the deck in her hand and shuffled them through once more. "Okay, now cut the deck three times, toward the left, and re-stack them again," said Esmeralda as she put the cards on the table.

Rhoda did as ask, cutting the cards and re-stacking them. Afterward, Esmeralda picked up the deck and laid down the first three cards. "The first card represents your past," she sighed as she placed down the "DEVIL" card. "The second card is your present," she said as she laid down the "TOWER" in reverse, upside down. "And the third card represents your future," as she laid down the card "SIX OF WANDS."

Looking over the cards, Esmeralda saw movement, but also a life filled with chaos. A life lived in the dark. "In all the years I've been doing these readings," she began, "I rarely get this card, 'The Devil.' It says, up to now, you lived your life in fear. There was chaos and lies. Bad decisions were made out of ignorance. Too much materialism and bad influences. You lived in the dark."

Esmeralda looked up to meet Rhoda's eyes. Her head hung in shame. It was even obvious to the cards that her life was cursed. "Basically, this card is a dead end street. That your life was off course. There was a lot of pain. The only way out is to make amends," Esmeralda sighed.

Tears streamed down Rhoda's face. "I just got out of prison," she sobbed. "My life's been a holy hell up to now. My mom died when I was born and they shipped me off to an orphanage. Then I got bounced in and out of foster homes for years. I never stayed in one place for long..." It all poured out.

Esmeralda reached behind her and found the box of tissue. How many people poured their life stories out in this small room? How many took this knowledge and turned their lives around? It was a simple living, selling trinkets and charms, helping people find love. But the love rarely lasted because the people themselves were broken.

Rhoda took the tissue and blew her nose. In a storm of emotion, she felt like someone ripped the band-aid off a festering wound and exposed it to everybody. Gawd, she was such a loser. Maybe she should have offed herself when she had the chance. Esmeralda reached her hand across the table and placed it over Rhoda's hand. Her pain was tremendous. Like a tremor, it vibrated throughout her body.

After a few moments, the tears subsided and Esmeralda refilled Rhoda's water cup from the water cooler. "Here, take a drink of this water and let it wash the pain away," she said.

Gulping the water down, it tasted so good. Rhoda quickly got up and filled the cup again. It'd been years since she cried or let her guard down. It was like a huge weight was lifted off her shoulders. "Does it say anything good in those cards?" Rhoda sat back down with a thud. "Because I don't think I can take anymore bad."

"Well, that always depends on how you look at things," Esmeralda began. "This upside down card is the Tower. It means change, no matter which way it's facing. But if it was right side up, the change would be like a bomb exploding. BOOM!" Esmeralda's hands shot up like they were making an explosion. "The way it's laid out now, means that the change is still coming but in a gentler way. Of course, change is always up to you. No one can make you change against your will. It takes courage to start over and do things differently. To let go of the old way of doing things, you must find your faith. Otherwise the devil will rule your world again."

Rhoda never thought of the devil ruling her life. But she couldn't escape the fact that she'd made really bad choices. Oftentimes she was tempted to get things the easy way, rather than work for them. "It killed me when I went to prison. My attorney kept telling me he could get me off. And I believed him. Then the judge banged that stupid gavel and convicted me of shoplifting and writing bad checks. I got sentenced to four years. Can you imagine four years for writing bad checks, when a rapist only gets 8?"

Esmeralda shook her head. "But you see, that is where you were tempted. You didn't trust that the Holy Father in Heaven would take care of you. You went against the Law of Love."

"What Holy Father in Heaven?" Rhoda scoffed, tossing her head back. "How could there be a holy anything on this Earth?

"I agree, it seems this world is run by the beast," Esmeralda said, staring off. "When my mother was but a girl, 1000 bomber jets flew over her house. The whole sky was full of silver!" Esmeralda's hands flew apart, encompassing the whole room.

"That must have been scary!" Rhoda chimed in.

"It was!" Esmeralda exclaimed. "During the war, all the churches were closed and God was dead. Many times, she hid with her family in the dark cellar. But that day, she ran outside, to see this sky filled with silver. Her uncle warned her that the soldiers would hurt her. Do you know what she said?" Leaning across the table, Esmeralda's deeply passionate eyes bored into Rhoda's soul.

Rhoda shook her head.

"Why would they hurt me? I never did anything to them." Esmeralda sighed. "She didn't understand this evil called war."

"Yeah, me neither," Rhoda shook her head. "Why do all these bad things happen?"

"Because of temptation," Esmeralda explained. "Man is a weak creature, who is easily lured astray through his lower nature. This is a world of duality. Both sides, Angels and demons were invited to this game of life. You see," Esmeralda paused as she heard her father's words coming out of her mouth. "It takes a great adversary to make a Master."

"Master," Rhoda scoffed. "Yeah, the only master's in my life were drunks and losers. They treated us kids like slaves."

"But that is what the devil try to do," Esmeralda shook her head. "Either you will master life, or the devil will master you!" For a moment, she wondered if any of this would even make sense to Rhoda. But she'd give it a try anyway. "You see, there are only two ways that this dark prince can overtake us. Either the adversary destroys us through our weaknesses or he will use our love against us. He'll try to make your heart dead, so that he can tempt you with things. He is the god of the material world. And many times those with the biggest hearts are given the greatest challenges."

"Yeah, you can say that again," Rhoda shook her head.

"Many people are haunted by the mistakes they made in the past," Esmeralda tried to console Rhoda with her words. "They live under staggering guilt which slowly deadens their heart. Until we make right our transgressions, the harm we have caused others, we cannot be free. The Adversary knows this. He keeps people locked in fear, so they die heartsick and broken. To be free, we must face our fears and correct the wrongs we committed through our ignorance." Esmeralda's mind slipped back to a teaching she'd learned years before. But many were not privy to this knowledge. She understood the Christ when He said "Love your enemies." Because that is the only way you can overcome them.

Many years ago, her father tried to teach Esmeralda the story of life, as his father had told him. After a string of hardships, she'd struggled with the same questions. Now, sitting in front of Rhoda, her father's words came flooding back to her. The story of good versus evil and how it came to be. Decades ago, she sat in the kitchen, listening to his words.

Slowly, he began to unravel the mystery of life for her. "You see," he started as he held his pipe in his weathered hand. The smell of burning pipe tobacco always reminded her of her father. "Before man fell from Grace, the Garden of Eden was spiritual Paradise. It was a place of unity, purity and innocence. Yet the Children of Yahweh were not compelled to learn His spiritual teachings. As the holy Father, Yahweh breathed in the Living Energy of Life and blew it into the handfuls of Earth from the heart of the Mother Gaia. From that pure, fertile soil, He formed His children. With his own breath, he blew the Breath of Life into them, which is their Spirit. In the days before He created man, the Holy Father created a paradise for them to live. As their Father, he gave them everything they needed for them to become Masters of Life."

In her memory, Esmeralda could still smell the deep aroma of the fresh coffee, which brewed in the kitchen at the time. Within her mind's eye, she saw her father's gnarled hands, from working so many years in the fields. Fresh pipe smoke curled through the air, as he exhaled the drawn in smoke. Together they sat at the kitchen table so he could tell her these stories.

In a slow, melodic timber, his gentle voice continued. "One day, out of frustration, Yahweh, the creator god of Earth, sought guidance from the Grand Counsel. You see, my dear," he said patiently. "Earth was a great class room, created for learning. Yet Yahweh's children were not inspired. How could they be? They wanted for nothing. After hearing of Yahweh's dilemma, the Great Counsel sought a suggestion from the Light Bearer. By then, this great Cosmic Being and his band of Angels had ascended many levels of Spiritual teachings."

Lighting his pipe, he took a moment to reflect, before he went on. "One look at Yahweh's dilemma, the Light Bearer saw the obvious flaw. In the Garden of Eden, there was no polarity. There was no free will or choice. There was nothing to compel the Children of Yahweh to learn, in order to gain mastery and ascend. And so the Grand Game was set up," his eyes twinkled as if he were letting her in on a grand secret.

"It was then, at that moment that Duality and the Laws of Cause and Effect were put in place on Earth. Now, the Children of Yahweh would know good and evil. The Grand Counsel requested that the Light Bearer and his Angels take on the roll of Adversary. The Light Bearer accepted. As a Great Cosmic Being, he was in service to help others learn the Great Spiritual Truths." Taking a few puffs on his pipe, he let the words percolate into the ground waters of her mind. He wanted her to understand how to be victorious in this great game, rather than sink into the bowels of temptation.

"As their Father," he slowly continued. "Yahweh completely believed that His Children would not fall prey to the traps and snares, laid by the Light Bearer and his Band of Angels. But, it only took one bite from a forbidden apple and His Children were banished from the Garden of Eden. You see, my sweet girl," he smiled. "It takes a great Adversary to make a Master. Yet, how many of Yahweh's Children would become Masters?" He left her always with this question. It gnawed on her, causing her to look deep into herself.

Before he died, he called her once more to his bedside. In those long days of suffering before his last farewell, he had a realization. It came to him in the many times he slipped in and out of consciousness. Often the Spirit of his his favorite uncle sat beside his bedside, feeding his mind tender thoughts of reassurance. With a tired gasp, he barely whispered this last thought into her ears. "My dear," he said as grasped her hands in his. To hear him better, she leaned over his frail body. "This is a dark world, my love. But we come here to bring Love into this sad world and ease another's suffering."

"Oh," she responded. At that moment, she knew he'd be traveling soon. Holding tightly onto his frail hands, she fought back the tears welling up in her eyes. As she pushed the long strand of hair from his eyes, she was overcome with a deep sense of love. "Papa," her voice sounded gently. "From the time I was a little girl, you told me the whole purpose of life, is to transform the darkness into the Light." A smile crept across his lips.

"I never believed you were really listening to me," he cried softly as he found his words had carried some weight.

"Of course I listened to you Papa,"she admitted as she looked deeply into his tired eyes. "I had no choice," she chuckled a moment thinking of all the spiritual conversations they had in the kitchen while he read her Tarot cards. "You said it so many times. How could I forget? When we bring this Great Love here, the darkness will no longer have power over us and then we will be free."

Hearing her words, a peace enfolded him. With those last thoughts, he passed the torch to his daughter, for her to carry forth and bring the Light into the lives of others.

While Esmeralda's mind wandered off, reliving this long ago time with her father, there was a long moment of silence. During this pregnant pause, a mountain of guilt washed over Rhoda. It was almost overwhelming. When things got rough, without family or loved ones, she had nowhere to turn. In her desperation to survive, she made stupid mistakes. With her error in judgment, she needlessly put her life and her daughter in harm's way. Lacking a family to take care of her daughter, she left her baby with friends. It had been years since she'd seen her little girl. She pushed the heavy thoughts right out of her mind and tried to change the subject.

"Hey... What's the last card mean? Is there a prince coming in my life?" Rhoda looked at the Six of Wands, who had a man riding a horse with banners of success all around him.

"Well, it means have faith and you will win," Esmeralda said as she shuffled through the deck looking for the Five of Wands. "See here, the Five of Wands is where the battle is. You have already pushed through the hardest part in your life and now you are ready for the Victory. You must keep trying and not slide back into the troubles of the past. Maybe you will even write a book."

"Yeah, if I could learn how to spell," Rhoda laughed. "You know the hardest part about growing up in the system?"

"No," she sighed. "I can imagine that it all of it must have been hard."

"You get shipped around to so many homes, packed full of throw-away kids and you're always changing schools," Rhoda laughed. "I never made it through high school. I got pregnant at 17 and gave that baby up for adoption. Then, I wanted a family so much, I found some guy, who said he loved me. He was some charmer. But when I got pregnant, he only stayed until Clarissa was 2. That's when I bottomed out. I got desperate. I bought groceries and diapers with bad checks and shoplifted her clothes."

"Hmm," Esmeralda agreed. "Yes, it's very hard to not have any stability or people around who love you."

"Well, it's not like no one ever loved me. The old gypsy woman, who told me about my mom, she'd bake the best maple and brown sugar cookies I ever had. I was there every day after school when I was a kid. She was like having a grandma. I never knew my real family," Rhoda sighed.

"Well, perhaps you could find them now," Esmeralda suggested.

"I thought about that, but all I have to go on is my mom's last name. She came from some small town in Ireland. It never mattered to me much before," Rhoda said out loud. "My gypsy grandma said she saw my mom trying to escape from there. So I put it out of my mind."

Stories of escape were familiar to Esmeralda. Before World War Two ended, her own mother and grandmother escaped from the Eastern Block in war-torn Europe. They left their home, family and their country, carrying only a small suitcase. "Yes, my mother and grandmother told me many stories of escape. They were terrified when they crossed over borders guarded by the Gestapo. The border police would throw them in jail, if they found out they were leaving eastern Europe during the war. All they could carry was a small suitcase," Esmeralda recalled.

"Yeah, well all I got to my name is in this trash bag," Rhoda chimed in. "By the time I was seven years old, I'd been raped and beaten. And it's never gotten much better." Even though she'd been a fighter most of her life, there was a sad sound of resignation in her voice. These well engrained patterns, which formed the construct of her life, seemed sadly unchanging.

"You've been in bondage by dark forces for many years. That's what the first card is telling you. Just like my mother, during the war. They went through much torment. But it made her a strong, formidable woman. You are resilient. You survived. That is the most important part," Esmeralda stressed.

"I don't know if I survived so good," Rhoda's thoughts went back to the courthouse. Inside the courtroom were all the reporters. It still gave her chills. The judge released her after finding out that the corrections officer had raped her many times. "I didn't have an easy time of it in the Penn."

"Do you want to talk about it," Esmeralda asked tentatively, knowing that this was a delicate subject.

"When I got out, I went in the grocery store. I wanted some fresh fruit and water that didn't taste like soap. You can't believe what I saw. My face was plastered all over the magazines. I was shocked. It was so embarrassing that I wanted to hide my face. I couldn't look the cashier in the eye. I felt so humiliated," Rhoda shook her head. "I'm sure the whole world knows what I did." The humiliation she felt went deep. "You can't imagine how bad a place can be. And then it can get worse."

Esmeralda waited for Rhoda to go on. It was important to allow her to feel this horrible emotion. In order for it to heal, the emotional charge needed to be released. Then the healing could begin. Tears welled up in Rhoda's eyes. Tears she hadn't allowed herself to shed. Because the horror of it all, would just destroy her. But now, in this little room, with the candles lit, it felt like her guts were going to explode.

With her head hung low, Rhoda muttered under her breath. "He raped me." The tears rolled down her face. Esmeralda's hand reached across the table. She cupped Rhoda's creamy white, freckled hands in hers. Slowly the sobs came. Rhoda bent forward and put her head in her lap. Esmeralda rubbed her back gently, feeling the waves of emotion course through Rhoda's body. "There are many dark spirits living within prison walls. Some of them have bodies and some don't," Esmeralda quietly spoke. "Only the pure love of Christ can overcome them."

Long moments passed as the two women sat there together. The revulsion of those many nights rose up inside her. Rhoda could still taste the blood in her mouth, how it oozed down her chin. Those painful memories still haunted her. After dark, there were certain sounds, like boots walking up metal stairs, which still made her heart stand still. When she heard a certain tone of a man's voice, she froze like a deer in head lights. Some things she couldn't shake off.

As Rhoda's face emerged from her lap, Esmeralda reached across the table for a tissue. Long trails of tears and snot covered Rhoda's face. Every hurt she ever had boiled up inside her. The long, drawn out sobs were followed with a feeling that she wanted to throw up. But there was nothing in her stomach. Esmeralda pushed the waste paper basket over, just in case.

"You have too much darkness accumulated in your aura," Esmeralda said as she stroked Rhoda's back. "It is like a magnet, which is what draws more evil to you. You must cleanse it from you, so you don't attract it anymore."

"Oh yeah, how do I do that?" Rhoda asked, wiping the snot and tears from her face.

"Every culture has their way of cleansing off the evil which we draw to us here on Earth," she began. "Some use fire, others go to the ocean or cleanse at the river."

"I don't know how to do that," Rhoda sniffled.

"Well, I found a simple way to do this," she began. "For a simple cleansing, you take a bath. Inside the bath, you put 2 cups of Kosher Salt and 2 cups of baking soda. It is good to have 3 white candles anointed with olive oil. Then, call on the Father, the Son and the Holy Ghost."

"Hmm," Rhoda contemplated. "The old gypsy woman said something like that to me once. She said that when we were born, we were pure, like snow. But after a while the snow got dirty, muddy, slushy and it needed to get cleaned. So when the snow melted, the waters found themselves again, and formed into the rivers, which went down to the ocean. Then the heat of the sun made the water evaporate, going up into the sky and then came down again in the rain. During the winter, it came down from heaven from snow and started all over again."

"It sounds very much like the cycle of life," Esmeralda commented.

"Listen, it's getting late. I wonder if you know about a cheap motel. I don't think the bus is going to come anymore today. It drove right past me. I think that was the last one," Rhoda changed the subject, knowing she needed to find a place for the night. Living on the street was tough on a woman.

"Well, there is a motel about a mile from here," Esmeralda started. "But, I have a room in the back you can have for a few dollars. I rent it out once in a while."

"Really? That'd be great," Rhoda sighed with relief. "I won't be any trouble. Promise."

"Oh, it's no trouble," Esmeralda said as she put the deck of Tarot cards back together. "After a good night's sleep, you'll feel better in the morning. If you're ready I can show you the room."

"Oh, sure," Rhoda paused. "So how'd you learn how to do this?" Rhoda asked, pointing at the cards.

"Oh, that's a long story," Esmeralda reflected.

"Did your mother teach you?" Rhoda prodded.

"No, she never believed in the spiritual. It was my father..," Esmeralda's voice trailed off as she made the sign of the cross. "May he rest in peace."

"How long ago did he pass?" Rhoda inquired.

Esmeralda paused, as she put away the Tarot cards. "It was Christmas Eve, 1993. He fell into a coma for about 8 days before. But he knew years before that he was going to get sick. He saw it in the cards."

"Oh, so he was a card reader too?" Rhoda was curious now.

"Yes, these are his cards. I've kept them all these many years." She packed them up in a blue silk cloth and put them back in a small cedar box.

"So it was a family thing?" Rhoda persisted.

"No, he learned it from a gypsy during the war," Esmeralda replied as she placed the cedar box in a drawer.

"Hmm, a gypsy, huh," Rhoda thought. It seemed to be a theme of her life, that some gypsy was involved.

"Yes, during the war, he was a cook on a hospital ship sailing above Norway, in the Arctic Ocean. One night my father went to his bunk. The gypsy who slept in the bunk above him, was reading cards. My father said that the gypsy was crying while he wrote letters to his family. So my father, who was just a young man of 17, asks him what was the matter. The gypsy said that the ship was going to sink and there would only be a few survivors."

"WOW! The cards told him that?" Rhoda had a look of disbelief.

"Well, I wasn't there. But a few days later, the hospital ship was torpedoed. My father was in the kitchen with 3 other men when the alarms went off and the ship started to sink. But they were smart!" she exclaimed. "They packed their clothes full with lard to keep from freezing when they hit the frigid waters. He was lost at sea for 10 days in a small life raft."

"TEN DAYS!" Rhoda exclaimed. "How do you survive for ten days?"

Esmeralda's eyes filled with tears, as she looked up at the ceiling. "Well, from what he told me, he had almost lost consciousness, after being out on the ocean so long without food or water. Then, rising from out of the water, came the spirit of his sister. From what he said, his sister's spirit made such a fuss, demanding that he wake up! When he came around, he and the other men saw another ship sailing close by. That's how they were rescued."

"So if his sister's spirit didn't wake him up, they wouldn't have seen the ship," Rhoda gathered.

"No, perhaps not. Yet the Spirits are strong," Esmeralda admitted. "But by that time, the Navy had already told his mother, my grandmother, that he was lost at sea. The poor woman thought he was dead," Esmeralda exclaimed. "But thankfully, he was in the hospital with amnesia. He didn't know his name. So months later, when he finally came home, he stood in the doorway of the kitchen. His mother was cooking at the stove. The poor woman thought she was seeing a ghost, when he started singing to her his favorite song, La Paloma. It wasn't until he asked her to make his favorite fried potatoes, that she knew he was alive."

"That's a story," Rhoda thought out loud.

"It was a very hard time," Esmeralda explained. "After the war, there was no home to go back to. Everything, even the churches, were bombed out. So to stay alive, he became a black market smuggler. Under the cover of nightfall, he helped people escape from the Eastern Block of Europe and get across the border. In their gratitude, they gave him mink coats, all their jewels, whatever they had to just get away from those black-hearted monsters."

"So, that's how he got into card reading?" Rhoda asked. The whole story fascinated her.

"Well, when when I was a little girl, I remember he studied everything he could about the spiritual, about the occult. He became very good at it." As she opened the door to the main hallway, the smell of garlic, paprika and searing meat lingered in the hallway.

"Oh, that smells so good," Rhoda's stomach growled.

"It's my mother's goulash. You may come to dinner or I can bring you a plate to your room." Esmeralda turned right down the hallway. At the end, was a single door. From her pocket, she pulled out a key ring and opened the door. Inside, was a simple guest room. Over the small dresser hung a picture of Jesus knocking at a door. Along the wall was a single bed covered in a feather bed and large feather pillows. On the dresser was an old television with antenna.

"I don't want to be a bother. I can get my plate and bring it in here," Rhoda offered as she flopped on the bed. The mattress was firm, but cushy at the same time. Sleeping on a real bed would be a treat.

"As you wish," Esmeralda responded. "I'll let you know when dinner's ready. In the meantime, you can take a salt bath and soak your troubles away."

And there, off to the side, was a bathroom with a full bathtub. It had been years since Rhoda relaxed in a hot bath. The showers in prison were gross. With a small trickle of water coming from an ancient shower head, it was hard to get clean. Inside the bathroom, Esmeralda went to a small wooden cabinet and opened the door. In the cabinet were towels, wash cloths and a box of Kosher Salt and baking soda. In a small drawer were white candles.

"If you like, I can make you a cleansing bath. It will help wash off much of the negativity that you collected from this last time. Granted, you won't be made pure as snow, but it will clear some things away," Esmeralda suggested.

"Oh, anything that'd help me out, would be appreciated," Rhoda cooed. "I can't thank you enough for your kindness."

With that, Esmeralda anointed the 3 white candles with olive oil. Before she struck the match, she passed it over the candles, making the sign of the Cross. Rhoda heard her invoking the "Father, Son, and Holy Ghost." Esmeralda called on the Divine Trinity to bless Rhoda. While the water filled the bathtub, she measured out 2 cups of Kosher Salt in a container. Looking skyward, towards the East, she said this prayer. "Almighty God, we ask that You bless this salt, as You once blessed the salt scattered over the waters by the prophet Elisha. Wherever this salt and water are sprinkled, drive away the forces of evil. Protect us forevermore by the power and presence of the Holy Spirit . Grant us this blessing through the Love of Christ our Lord. Now and forever, Amen." Then she added 2 cups of baking soda and 2 cups of Kosher Salt to the bath, to purify Rhoda's guilt-ridden, wounded aura.

On the dresser were a few sticks of incense. Esmeralda took one and lit it from the candle, placing it in a holder. The smoke wafted gently through the room. Sitting on the toilet seat, Rhoda recognized the smell. It reminded her of the gypsy woman from the old neighborhood. Taking this all in, she wanted to remember every detail, in case she needed to do this again.

"I'll leave you a clean nightgown on the bed," Esmeralda said as she started out the door. "Dinner will be in a short while. You can get your plate if you'd rather eat in here."

From her tired eyes, Rhoda looked up in gratitude. Nobody had been truly kind to her in so long. It felt good. "Thank you."

Getting undressed, she folded her clothes and put them on the dresser. The tub was almost full when she turned off the water. Her bones felt so weary. Climbing in, her body collapsed into the hot steamy water. Being on the inside for years, it was the simple things that she missed the most. In the quiet, her mind raced back and forth, trying to figure everything out. She couldn't fathom how she was going to make it all work.

Nothing was harder than having to leave her daughter with friends these last four years. It nearly killed her. The woman's prison was too far away for them to visit. So Rhoda only talked to her daughter on the phone a few times. Nothing was so lonely as missing her child. It was a constant heartache which nearly drove her mad. At times, knowing her daughter was out there, was the only thing that kept her alive.

Sitting in the bath, it took a while for her mind and body to relax. Life in a jail cell, gave her no down time. The stress of always being on guard, made her feel hard and callous inside. It took a while to ease back in the warm water and let her mind drift. After dunking her head under the salty water a few times, she laid her head back on the edge of the tub and closed her eyes.

In the silence, an old song came into her mind. An Irish lullaby.

Bing Crosby sang it in a movie she watched as a child. When she felt lonely, she imagined having a mother to cuddle with and sing her that song.

Soaking in the hot, soapy water, her busy mind went round in spirals. Then, in the stillness, she heard a gentle voice. "Move into your heart," it said in her mind. Pushing her thoughts out of the way, she heard the Voice again. "Move into your heart," it repeated. Then she took three deep breaths. Moving her head from side to side, she heard a bone in her neck crack. Another deep breath. "Move into your heart," she heard it say again. Taking a deep belly breath, Rhoda closed her eyes and placed her hands over her heart. In her mind, she journeyed out of her head down to her heart. When she got there, her heart was surrounded by miles of razor wire. Seeing this in her mind's eye, she chuckled softly to herself.

"No kidding," she whispered, as she gazed inwardly at the razor wire. Covering her heart was a shield of porcupine armor. It completely encased it. Then from somewhere, came two hands. Delicately, the hands removed the porcupine armor. Underneath the prickly protective cover, it revealed a small, shriveled heart which lay there, barely beating.

Seeing this all in her mind's eye, Rhoda's heart welled with compassion. After all she'd gone through, how could this be any different? Then the same two hands took the shriveled heart and wrapped it in a white gauze. Rhoda followed the hands in her mind's eye. Around the hands appeared a Sacred Fire, which melted the razor wire from around her heart.

Then her inner vision shifted some. Sitting on the edge of the tub, was a woman singing the Irish Lullaby. With crystal blue eyes and the same fiery red hair, Rhoda knew it was her mom. Then the woman cradled Rhoda in her arms, singing that familiar song. With her hands, she gently removed the white gauze from Rhoda's heart. Now, her heart was vibrant, larger and strong. Holding the heart in her hands, the woman placed the heart in a golden orb of light.

"Expand this light, until it enfolds you," her gentle voice commanded. With her mind, Rhoda imagined the golden, white light growing bigger and bigger until her whole body and bathtub was filled with light. A peace filled the bathroom. Finally Rhoda just let go.

"I've never left you," the woman said. Tears streamed down Rhoda's face. It was like the gypsy said all those years ago. Her mom was always there with her.

Outside the bathroom window, Rhoda heard a scratchy AM radio playing. Bing Crosby's voice filled the airwaves.

> *"Over in Killarney, many years ago,*
> *my mother sang a song to me, in tones so sweet and low.*
> *Just a simple little ditty, in her good old Irish way.*
> *And I'd give the world to hear her sing, that song of hers today...*
> *Too-ra-loo-ra-loo-ral, Too-ra-loo-ra-li, Too-ra-loo-ra-loo-ral,*
> *Hush now don't you cry!*
> *Too-ra-loo-ra-loo-ral, Too-ra-loo-ra-li, Too-ra-loo-ra-loo-ral,*
> *That's an Irish lull-la-by."*

With her heart overcome with emotion, salty tears streamed down Rhoda's face. In an instant, the veil between worlds grew thin. She heard her mother's voice singing along with Bing. Not that Rhoda could know this, but while she was pregnant, her mother sang that song every night, sometimes twice, before she fell asleep. In the next verse, Rhoda joined in. Her voice cracked a few times, rusty from the many years without song.

> *"Oft in dreams I wander, to that cot again,*
> *I feel her arms a-hugging me, as when she held me then.*
> *And I hear her voice a humming, to me as in days of yore,*
> *When she used to rock me fast asleep outside the cabin door.*
> *Too-ra-loo-ra-loo-ral, Too-ra-loo-ra-li, Too-ra-loo-ra-loo-ral,*
> *Hush now don't you cry!*
> *Too-ra-loo-ra-loo-ral, Too-ra-loo-ra-li, Too-ra-loo-ra-loo-ral,*
> *That's an Irish lull-la-by!"*

While Rhoda soaked in the bath, Esmeralda quietly snuck into the room. She laid a clean pair of pajamas and some slippers on the nightstand next to the bed. Lost in song, Rhoda's rusty voice sang along with her mother, in the Spirit World.

> *"I can hear that music, I can hear that song.*
> *Filling me with memories, of a mother's love so strong.*
> *Its melody still haunts me, these many years gone bye,*
> *Too-ra-loo-ra-loo-ral, Until the day I die."*

The radio station went to commercial, as Rhoda was slowly brought back. Dunking herself under the water again, she felt all these years of hurt just melt away. Nothing could have prepared her for meeting Esmeralda. Between the card reading and the cleansing salt bath, her life felt completely changed. For the first time, she finally understood the gypsy woman's words, "Your mother is always with you."

With her toes, Rhoda moved the drain stop and the water started to run out. Her hands and feet were wrinkled like prunes from sitting in the water so long. But she felt good inside, clean from all the dross she'd carried. Her hair was washed and she shaved her legs. It'd been years since she did that. Now if she could drop the fat from all the bad prison food, she'd be her fighting self again. But this time without the fight. She'd have to play it smarter this time. With her mom's Spirit beside her, Rhoda wasn't going back to prison ever, ever again.

On top of the dresser, was a spray bottle with ammonia mixed with holy water. Esmeralda instructed Rhoda to clean the bathtub out with that, when she was done. It would remove all the dark, psychic energy which collected in the tub. Squirting the tub with the ammonia, the fumes were enough to double her over in a coughing fit. But she felt like she was washing years of bad luck and bad decisions down the drain.

Draping a white towel around her body, Rhoda snuffed out the candles with some spit on her fingers. The heat in the wick burned her fingers just a little. If she had time, in the morning, she'd take that cleansing salt bath again.

Opening the bathroom door, Rhoda spotted the pajamas on the bed and the slippers. "Oh, there is a God," she said out loud. After she put them on, there was a knock at the door. "Yeah," Rhoda responded, opening the door.

Holding a tray of food, Esmeralda came into the room, placing it on the nightstand. "Here is some of my mama's goulash. She hopes you like it."

"Oh, man, that smells so good," Rhoda said as her stomach growled. "I haven't eaten all day." Quickly, she sat down on the edge of the bed and removed the lid on the plate. Gravy smothered the carrots, chunks of meat and special noodles which filled the plate. On the side were some home-made biscuits. It was heaven. She had died and gone to heaven.

While Rhoda settled in to eat her meal, Esmeralda stepped over to the television. "Now, this is an old TV, but it still works," Esmeralda explained. "We only get a few channels with the antenna. But you'll find something to watch."

Wolfing down her food, Rhoda looked up for a moment as Esmeralda turned on the TV and turned the few channels, searching for a good show.

"You know, that's quite a bathtub you got in there," Rhoda said over the squawk box.

"Oh, you liked the bath?" Esmeralda queried.

"It was magic. I think I saw my mother. She sang this song, that I used to hum when I was a kid," Rhoda's eyes got big. "You know, I closed my eyes and there she was."

"It's hard for a mother to leave her children, even when they go to the Spirit World," Esmeralda replied. "I knew a woman who had a deadly disease. She was in a coma for many days. The doctor told her family that she only had a few days, or maybe hours left to live. But strangely, she journeyed to the other side and her grandfather and best friend came to meet her."

"Oh yeah," Rhoda said, chewing with her mouth full. "I heard of something like that."

"This is quite interesting," Esmeralda went on. "Because you see, they took her to a beautiful place, filled with Angels. She was surrounded by this powerful love. A love so pure, full of compassion. There was no judgment there, just love."

"Yeah, I've never known that kind of love," Rhoda's lips smacked loudly. "I just got shoved from one place to another. I don't think anybody but that gypsy woman showed me a minute's worth of love."

"This is a hard world," Esmeralda agreed. "But, this woman was told by her best friend, "Now you see who you are. Go back to Earth and live fearlessly."

"Did the woman want to come back?" Rhoda's eyes were full of questions.

"Of course not!" Esmeralda exclaimed. "Surrounded by such powerful love, no one wants to return to a world filled with fear. But, she returned to her family, to her children."

"I wonder about my mother," Rhoda thought out loud. "I wonder how she lived. You know, I don't know anything about her. Just her name. I named my daughter after her."

After Rhoda finished her meal, Esmeralda took the plate and left. On the television, some movie was playing. It showed a mother going to visit her son in prison. The mother was a big woman, with her hair tied back in a tight bun. She had a pinched expression on her face. The mother picked up the black phone receiver hanging on the wall as her son sat down behind the glass partition in front of her.

"Hey mama," the son said as he looked down. Rhoda turned up the sound. Without any real family, she never had too many visitors come to see her when she was in prison.

The mother shook her head as tears welled up in her eyes. "What you doing in here? You know Jesus can't save you if you going to be messing in the devil's playground. Jesus can't get you if you done made a choice to hang out with Satan."

"Mama, I ain't hanging out with Satan..." the words eked out of his mouth.

"If you ain't hanging out with Satan, then what the hell are you doing in his house! Those ain't church bells I'm hearing!" the mother said, as the buzzer of electronic doors went off. "I already done talked to Reverend Michael. He's got the whole congregation praying for you!" Her voice grew shrill as she put down the receiver to get a handkerchief from her purse. Her son just hung his head. She blew her nose and wiped her tears. Then the show went to commercial.

"I'd say prison was the devil's house," Rhoda agreed as she settled back into her bed. The mattress was soft, unlike the cold metal bunks and thin mattress she'd slept on for the last 4 years in prison. After a while, her eyes grew heavy as she turned out the light, falling into a deep slumber.

CHAPTER FOUR: NATURE'S LAWS

ANGUS

Heavy, brutal, dark
A catacomb of love
Now grim and stark

Cold steel, metal edge
Hollow sound
No more to pledge

Banging now, stone on stone
How does it cut?
Oh... to the bone

Trouble, double, toil, struggle
Yet another day of Hell's jungle
Hidden behind veils of black
Eyes... no more softness do they lack

Hearts lay beating on the floor
As I crash through our bedroom door
Of what was once a humble home
Now a barren casket in love's catacomb

My heart, into self, it caves
I struggle now, where I once was brave

And look into your hollow eyes
Please tell me no more lies

This rock has crumbled into sand
In pools of water, do I stand
For pools of tears, I have cried
As I stood and watched, while our love died

Deep... go deep, my heart still beats
As I walk down lonely Hollywood streets
Soul burns, heart yearns
Where now, show me, do I turn?

To find that gentle tenderness
We had it once...
In our kiss

Hope, sweet hope
Baby... please, no more dope
No more... to watch you
I just can't cope

    As they walked out of the detox center, Hal stopped and stood with Leroy in the late afternoon sun on Pico Blvd. Sweeping the hair from Leroy's face, a cool, gusty breeze came up from the ocean's shore. Blaring sirens and screeching horns honked down Lincoln Boulevard as the clattering helicopters circled overhead. The city had changed a lot since Hal was down here last. "See that building across the street Leroy?" Hal pointed to a building on the corner.

    "Yeah, what about it?" Leroy asked.

    "Well, years ago, that was a Teen Center," Hal said pushing his hat back from his head. "I used to work with the street kids who showed up from all over the country. Most were addicts and alcoholics. Back then, crystal meth was just hitting the streets. These youngsters were dropping like flies. I never seen such a hopeless mess," Hal shook his head. "Some of these kids fried their brains on that poison."

"Why'd they come all the way out here?" Leroy asked, looking around at the city and all its concrete.

"Well, I reckon, it's because the winters in California weren't as cold as back home. Most of them came from broken homes. Half of them had been in and out of jail. I volunteered there for about a year into my early sobriety."

"What'd you do there?" Leroy asked.

"Well, dang near everything," Hal started as he walked down Pico towards Lincoln Blvd. "We fed them, found them clothes, got them shelter for the night. Most of all, we tried to keep them alive, while they were going through rough times. We had AA and NA meetings. I gave a few talks down at the local high school. For the twelve hours that we were open every day, those kids had a safe place to hangout." Hal's mind flashed back to the softball games at the park on Saturday mornings, and calling shelters all day to find a bed. It was good work, but sometimes it broke his heart doing it.

"You've been doing this 12th Step work a long time," Leroy noted.

"Yup, I've seen a lot of people come and go. I remember once, I was talking to this kid who hitchhiked out here, all the way from Oklahoma. He was just a little squirt, maybe eleven years old when he left the throw-away home he'd been living in. After that, he'd been in dang near every jail between here and there. After listening to him for a while, I finally got up the nerve to ask him why he kept going back. You know what he told me?" Hal looked at Leroy. Leroy shrugged his shoulders. "This kid says to me, that all his friends were in there." Hal shook his head. "Not only that, but that it's safer in jail than it is out on the streets. At least, you get three meals a day and a bed. Somewhere, this country's gone deadly wrong, when a kid figures he's got to go to jail to get a meal."

"Yeah, I'm not sure what to say about that," Leroy said knowing the pain of addiction himself.

"I don't got too much hope for your buddy Daniels in there," Hal admitted. "Some drunks have less manners than a bunch of barnyard animals."

"Mike's all right. That's just all the locker room talk," Leroy dismissed what Hal was saying.

"I don't see any locker room here, do you?" Hal challenged. He didn't have much stomach for the way some men treated women. "He talked about her body parts like they were hood ornaments!"

"Yeah, I knew that bothered you," Leroy admitted, looking at all the cars backed up on Lincoln Boulevard. Parked right in front of them, was a black BMW with a dream catcher hanging from its rear-view mirror. For a second, Leroy wondered if the driver slept while he was driving.

"It's a simple lack of human decency, little buddy," Hal shook his head. "What bothered me, was that he had no shame. You might not know this, but shame is the yardstick of a man's moral compass."

Most of the time Hal was compassionate when it came to alcoholics, especially veterans. But Leroy knew from experience that Hal had no use for those who abused others. "Hmm," Leroy sounded. "I don't know if you ever said that before."

"Well, maybe not," Hal started. "I haven't run into that in a while. But shame is a natural consequence when we do something that goes against Creator's laws. The greater the shame, the higher a man's moral compass."

"Yeah, I can see that," Leroy agreed. "But what's got your panties in a knot about Daniels?"

"It just seemed to me that your buddy didn't seem to have any," Hal concluded. "Somehow he forgot, or maybe he never knew, the difference between right and wrong."

"Yeah, it seems easy to forget what's right when you're getting paid to destroy things and kill people for a living," Leroy admitted. War was a dark road where the lines between right and wrong got very muddy.

"Now, granted he was drunk and stumbling out of a bar, when we found him," Hal surmised. "He reminds me a lot of a man, Jose, who had a couple years sober before he went into the Marines. He got stationed out in Somalia right around the time they had the 'Black Hawk Down' incident. One night, standing sentry, he saw his buddy in the next guard post get his head blown clean off."

"I know that nightmare," Leroy added, staring out at the thundering waves of the Pacific ocean.

"I know you do. So do I," Hal admitted. "But I don't think Jose ever dealt with it. He'd talk about it once in a while. But after he served in Somalia, he got stationed in Japan. That's when the trouble really started. He switched seats on the Titanic and got hooked on going to them girly shows. Only over there, they do things on stage I don't want to talk about."

Leroy chuckled a little to himself. Hal had a really shy-bone inside him when it came to talking about the birds and the bees. "Oh go ahead and say it," Leroy chided, pressing into the uncomfortable spot in Hal's nature.

"If you think I'm giving you details, about what that man admitted to me, you can fly over there and find out for yourself!" Hal asserted, putting the matter to rest. "The only thing I will tell you, is that those girly shows stirred a sleeping dragon in him so bad, it almost destroyed his life. The spirit of lust is always hungry, Leroy. It preys on the weak by tempting them with honeyed words and empty promises. Jose got so addicted to computer porn and talking dirty to girls on the phone, the only woman who could stand him, was one of them working girls."

"You mean a prostitute?" Leroy asked, as Hal nodded his head.

"You see, Leroy," Hal started. "The nature of addiction is so cunning, it's like going into battle with a nine-headed snake. Every time you cut one head off, it grows another one. So basically the battle never ends, unless you surrender to a Higher Power. Only a Higher Spirit can conquer a lower one."

Switching addictions was familiar to Hal. There's an old saying, 'if you only belong to one 12 Step program, after sobriety, you're in denial.' It's not uncommon for many addict/alcoholics find themselves going to at least a couple 12 Step programs after they get sober. In order for a deep wound to heal, it has to be cleaned out first. For years, Hal smoked a pack of cigarettes a day after he quit drinking. But after a while, his addiction to nicotine impacted his lungs. Typically, most drunks switch from one addiction to another. Until one day, the body can take no more.

With their minds twisted up from the sight of dead bodies and the stench of rotting flesh, most wounded warriors do just about anything to shut off the memories. For a time, drinking alcohol will stave off the fits of depression and anxiety which continue to stalk him. Thankfully, the first sips of that burning poison will calm his nerves. But no one understands how much he needs to drink. There's no running away from a half-crazed, busy mind which is flashing pictures of unspeakable things. Oftentimes, certain smells and sounds will bring the paralyzing anxiety rushing back. Knocking back a few drinks will ease the death grip of fear and make it go away for a time. But eventually, the drink stops working. To distract his busy mind, he needs to find something else. And so begins the merry-go-round of addiction. Jumping from one to another, just to get through the day.

One of the last things Jose told Hal, was that "forbidden sex was always the most exciting." And that never ending longing for excitement finally did his marriage in. In his inner tormented world, he became reckless in love. The craving for naughty love affairs kept getting stronger, but it came with diminishing pleasure. For most people, these tantalizing sweet sins were the road markers down a gradual, gentle slope which lead toward an ever increasing pained wretchedness. His private obsession, marked by his sexual appetite, dominated his whole inner life. It stole away his best years. The unhappiness it caused was very lasting. At his lowest point, he was driven mad by lust, drunk and too blind to see he was ridden by hags.

"I NEVER FELT SO ALIVE!" screamed the daredevil with his heart beating out of his chest, as he careened off a sheer cliff. Shivering with fear, he taunted death with only a packed parachute on his back. Whether it be alligator wrestling, combat or skydiving, fear and testosterone coupled with the rush of adrenaline, often kept a man gunning for the next thrill. It is the creed of the thrill-seeker. The problem being, danger and excitement tend to lead to disaster. No matter how great the rush is, that feeling eventually fades. So the daredevil has to find other thrills, with greater and greater risks. Riddled with addiction, most daredevils often go down hill.

Feeling the salty, gentle sea breeze on his face, Leroy got quiet for a minute. Something had been gnawing on him the whole ride across the desert. "Do you think Daniels was trying to..." his voice paused, the thought was almost too hard to bear.

"You're wondering if he was trying to get his sorry ass killed!" Hal jumped in and finished Leroy's sentence. "Stumbling in front of an eighteen wheeler at 0 dark thirty!"

"Well, after that newscaster said 22 vets were offing themselves everyday, it got me wondering," Leroy admitted.

"Look, if we didn't show up when we did, I can't say he'd be alive this morning. He drank enough to drown a small village. I was afraid to ask the doctor what his liver looked like," Hal added. "I know he's in good hands. And if he wants to live after he gets detoxed, that will be another part of his story. Right now, it's looking pretty sketchy."

After driving the long highways across the California deserts, Hal's body and mind were plum wore out. This close to the journey's end, all he wanted was to get up to Roy's house on Point Dume and relax. It had been years since he'd been out on the Pacific Coast. The soothing, cool sea air felt good. "Look, after we get settled in, I'm going to call my buddy Nate and see if he's running a lodge. I could use some purification after this day. I know he runs one in the mountains here in Malibu."

"That sounds good," Leroy chimed in as they got back into the truck. Turning the truck west onto Lincoln Blvd, Hal made a left down to Pacific Coast Highway. In all her glory, the Pacific ocean opened up in front of them. Sail boats and windsurfers were scattered across the sparkling blue-green waters. Admittedly, this was one of Hal's favorite stretches of highway, looking out at the Pacific Ocean.

With the Santa Monica mountains on the right, and the ocean on the left, they were stuck in the middle of bumper to bumper traffic. High-priced dwellings cluttered the expensively landscaped hillsides. Packed like a can of sardines, other fancy homes bordered the coastline along Pacific Coast Highway. Covering every square inch of land,was the evidence of mankind, people, either in cars or buildings. After coming from the vast lonesomeness of the Great Plains, this was a completely different world. With his arm hanging out the window, Hal felt himself settle back into a peaceful place.

"Ya see, Leroy, what most people don't get about alcoholism, is that it's an 'EITHER-OR' LIFE," Hal started to explain. "Either we live by Spiritual Principles or we die an alcoholic death. It's all laid out right there in the Big Book. But most people don't even understand how powerful the 12 Steps really are."

"Yeah, so what are you trying to say?" Leroy asked, curious where his mentor's thoughts were going.

"Well, it's like this," Hal started. "When you understand something, like Nature's Laws, you tend to obey it. Otherwise you might not get a good result."

Leroy gave Hal one of his looks. "Yeah?"

Hal's mind whirled around for an example. "Okay, take the Law of Gravity, for instance. The first time I jumped out of a plane from 12,000 feet, I still didn't know enough about gravity to appreciate its laws and how un-bendable they are. But when you're standing at the open door of a plane, looking down at Mother Earth, as she's falling away, well, you get a different sense of appreciation." Hal chuckled a little, thinking back to his first jump. "Now thank God, I wasn't an idiot. I took great care packing my parachute the right way. But after I jumped out the door, 12,000 feet up from the ground, well gravity pulled my sorry ass down like a lead balloon."

"Yeah, after you jump out, there's no turning back. You can't change your mind," Leroy chuckled knowingly.

"Well, not only that, but once you're in a free fall, you can't renegotiate a deal with the laws of Gravity," Hal chuckled. "The laws of Gravity are UN-BENDABLE! And that's true for all of Creator's Laws."

"Hmm," Leroy pondered Hal's last comment.

"The way I see it, Leroy, is there's one sure-fire way to know if you're in Creator's Will or not," Hal postulated.

"Oh yeah, what's that?" Leroy asked, taking the bait.

"Well, if you're doing something "CONSTRUCTIVE", that is, not hurting anybody else, I'd say that's living in accordance with Creator's Laws," Hal put forth. "But if your doing something DESTRUCTIVE, well I'd say you're siding with the other guy."

"You mean Ol' Mephisto?" Leroy chuckled.

"Go ahead a laugh, Leroy," Hal warned. "But there are a lot of mean spirits in this town. Over time, I've met my share of people whose hearts were dead because they sold their soul for money."

"So you're saying all these people with fancy houses and cars are the walking dead. What, like zombies?" Leroy chuckled. "Are their eyes going to fall out when they look at you? Maybe their arms and fingers will fall off?"

"Hmm," Hal toned as his jaw set tight. Nothing bothered him more than a thick-headed numbskull, who because of his own arrogance, was difficult to teach. One thing was for certain, traveling could bring out the difficult sides of people. Even the ones you liked.

Hal gave Leroy a hard look before he finished what he was going to say. Having made a few mistakes out in the land of Lost Angels, he knew from experience what a painted-on smile was hiding. But it's hard to explain that to someone, who hadn't had that experience.

Hal composed himself before he came up with a response. Being road-weary, he didn't want his irritation to be louder than his words. So he took a deep breath and sat there a moment, letting the ocean breeze wash over him. Taking another deep breath, his thoughts were clear and he knew what he wanted to say.

"Out in these parts, Leroy," Hal started. "If a man loses something he loves, something he worked his whole life for, he tries to fill that empty place inside with stuff. The problem is, you can't fix what's broken inside, with stuff from the outside. It only makes the hole inside bigger. Pretty soon, you can drive a Mack truck though that empty place inside, with room to spare."

A light went on in Leroy's mind as he looked at the cluttered hillsides, packed full of expensive houses. "So you're saying they put their faith in material things?" Leroy asked.

"The emptier they feel, the more toys they got," Hal answered. "I knew a guy, a stuntman, who was having the worst day of his life. He had a pretty hefty pocketbook, so money wasn't the issue. But on that day, he decided to buy something to make himself feel better. He wanted a truck. Not just any truck, but the biggest he could find."

"That must have been some hole in his gut," Leroy commented.

"Well, I'm sure it was," Hal agreed. "Because he drove out of the dealership with a mammoth-sized, rock-crawler."

"What? Like a Hummer? Leroy asked.

"Yup," Hal affirmed. "He didn't care how much it cost or what the gas mileage was. He just didn't care."

"I wonder how long that lasted?" Leroy questioned.

"Well, when I knew him, he was worth a few million. He had a fourteen acre spread on the East Coast, plus a few rental houses, a BMW, a Hummer and a mountain of dirt bikes," Hal added. "He never smiled much, even with all that stuff. If you take a gander out at these hillsides, you can probably make out how many empty souls live here."

It took a minute for Leroy to take in what Hal was trying to explain.

"Okay, let me put it to you this way," Hal asserted once more to drive home his point. "If stuff made people happy, why would the rich and famous commit suicide? From what I've seen out here, the money god is fickle. He don't guarantee smarts or happiness, if you know what I mean."

If a person looked closely, it wasn't hard to see the confusion between what was true and what was false. Especially, here in the big city. Being divine, beauty was natural. It was radiant, like a baby's smile, a range of snow-capped mountains or the brilliant, neon colored skies of the setting sun.

Whereas, vanity or self-worship, was artificial, man-made and cost a lot of money. Like some kind of cancer, it ate away at the inner sacredness of life, invisibly destroying all those it touched. Across the globe, there were entire industries dedicated to achieving this obsessive, artificial perfection which vanity claimed to possess. Perfume, fashion, body sculpting, liposuction, diet pills, anything to glorify the body and exalt the ego, no matter what the cost. Billboards heralding its false promises cluttered the city's horizons. In the empire of narcissism, acclaimed self-love, was a wild West of lying snake oil salesmen who claimed to hold life's perfection in a tincture. But alas, with all the lures and lies, vanity came with diminishing returns. Artificial beauty became a handgun. Some of vanity's most faithful died under the knife.

Through this self-obsession, the once delicate desert flower of the West, in all her feminine beauty, became a skeleton with hollowed cheeks and sunken eyes. To appear lifelike and flawless, this walking corpse needed war paint and bodily reconstruction to disguise all the imperfections. This deadly demand to be flawless became all consuming. For some, this conceited self-love aggravated their knife-like fright of growing old and made them less willing or able to bear children.

Like a vampire, this empty false pride drained the natural feminine beauty from each delicate flower. It hid beneath the veneer of painted-on smiles. It festered with unspoken insecurity; the dreaded fear of being replaced. While vanity slithered like a snake through the fear-bitten dynasties, time was not its friend. Time brought wrinkles and made their bones brittle.

Down the streets of Lost Angels, city dwellers preferred a phony image to the reality of their true inner Being. Along this thorny primrose path, they paraded around like dressed up, painted dolls. Life was a masquerade, as they pursued happiness from behind a mask. Some were vainly beautiful, with ice cold, blue eyes and chiseled features. Whiles others bordered on the grotesque. But none of it was genuine.

For deep within them, at the heart of the matter, their spirit lie sleeping. While their souls cried for a Higher Love, it couldn't be purchased at the cosmetic counter. This spiritual slumber created an unquenchable, inner longing. Worse than a restless tide, this emptiness kept their spirits craving something which material things could never satisfy. Endlessly, they searched for anything to quell this yearning. Yet most were disconnected from their inner life.

After living life like every day was the weekend, their bodies rapidly grew tired, riddled with every ailment imaginable. These sleepwalkers resembled waterless clouds who were blown across an invisible wilderness, by a continuously shifting and restless wind. Their disgruntled expressions gave face to the stormy weather of their inner world. Puffed up with pride and ambition, some trampled over the lives of others to fulfill their skin-deep desires. With every bloody, hard-won success, they believed they were gods themselves. Others only had faith in the fickle gods, a golden calf, whom they had formed with their own hands. Yet, a person's soul cannot be saved by gold and silver.

This meaningless pursuit of an unnatural life, mostly make-believe, forced them to self-medicate. Many waited long hours for the warm magic of the pre-dinner cocktail to flow through their veins. This spiritual thirst created an ever-increasing distance between their outer life and their true inner nature. As they frittered away their lives on things rarely worth mentioning, a large chasm opened between their heart and their mind. After a while, this chasm appeared incapable of being bridged. To make matters worse, many spent their lives doing things which went against their true nature. This created an inner conflict and compounded the emptiness. Because they didn't feel that what they were doing was right.

True Love is never shallow. It stirs the fire within the soul. From within, it emanates a sense of peace, the ability to weather every worldly storm. It graciously thaws the cold, wintery frost from the once hard-bitten hearts. With sparkling eyes, it works its way like ivy into every crevice of the old fortress walls, crumbling them to their depths. Its roots run deep and where the roots are holy, so are its branches. Only the search for Truth could still the soul, allowing the spiritual thirst within to be quenched. The true house of prayer, the divine mystery, was always love.

But for city dwellers, love was often jealous and petty. Shackled in an oppressive, spiritual darkness, it was difficult to breathe. To satisfy their freakish whims, some gold-digging, apple polishers used a false love as a manipulation to get what they wanted. Far from divine, they bared their adorned breasts, which only attracted wolf-eared, power hungry, money-men. This shallow love became an endless power struggle, riddled with betrayal and staggering guilt, a consequence, when actions are less than loving. Where real love was missing, the heart grows callous and cold. Without the sunlight of the Spirit, there was no true life. Everything inside was dead.

Like a cherished shield, vanity was the mask for all of their shortcomings. Its painted-on beauty covered an utterly empty way of life, lived without true value or purpose. Since they lived solely to find momentary pleasures, their happiness shifted ceaselessly like the wind. Parading as one of the deadliest of the Seven Deadly Sins, vanity was a powerful poison to the soul. It robbed the spirit of its sense of true purpose. It was the root to many evils, such as hatred, envy and slander. Everything ugly was anchored in self-worship, vanity.

Looking out at the waves breaking along the shoreline and the mansions cluttering the hillsides, Leroy couldn't help but wonder how easy it would be to sell out for all this stuff. "Yeah, I can see what you're saying," Leroy agreed.

"Did I ever tell you about Henry G., a fella I met out here in the Program? Back now maybe 15 or so years ago?" Hal queried.

"Naw, I don't think so," Leroy didn't seem to recollect.

Hal chuckled thinking about Henry's old stories. "Now, ol' Henry grew up in the South, on a plantation. His family had quite a bit of money. So, growing up, he got used to the good life. But trouble showed up when Henry was just a young pup. He started drinking around the age of 9 with the sharecropper's daughter. After a while, those whiskey demons played tricks with his mind and he wound up doing some crazy stuff. It must have been '55 or '56, when he enlisted in the Marines and ended up becoming a sniper, Special Forces."

"He must have been pretty good," Leroy commented.

"You could say that. He got sent to Southeast Asia and had over 100 confirmed kills to his name. But, that's not the part I wanted to tell you about. When he got out of the Corp, he started working in the Financial District, as a stock broker, doing heavy trading. Well, he got this notion that they weren't paying him enough money. So he started skimming a little extra off the top from some of his bigger clients, thinking they wouldn't notice. Well, of course, the Feds caught on and he got accused of embezzling. The problem was, old Henry had a slipshod way of skimming this extra cash. Since the Feds couldn't find a pattern, they couldn't pin it on him. So he never went to jail."

"Lucky," Leroy commented.

"Well, yeah, you could say that." Hal paused for a moment to recollect the whole story. "Now, by that time, ol' Henry was working on his second or third marriage. He had wives and kids to support. So he put all his stolen booty in a Swiss bank account, so no one would know,"

Hal laughed.

"Now here's the kicker," Hal went on. "After the heat wore off, he goes to Switzerland, or wherever that money was kept, and pulls it all out of the bank. When he walks out, he's got over four million dollars stashed in his briefcase. Then, he gets on the train headed for France. Of course, he fancies himself as a high rolling, ladies man. I never knew Henry to pass up a good time. So on the train, he meets two cute Dutch girls and they decide to get a hotel room. Well, as luck would have it, ol' Henry got all liquored up and passed out. The next morning, when he came to, the two girls were gone and so was the briefcase with all that money!" Hal howled. "Being that the money was stolen, he couldn't really go to the police. I'm not sure which one of Creator's laws it is, but you never get to enjoy stolen goods."

"That bites," Leroy laughed.

"Well, think about," Hal went on. "When we live according to Spiritual Laws, it's a form of humility. It's not hard to follow directions once you understand how something works. But even humility has its pitfalls."

"Yeah, what do you mean by that?" Leroy asked.

Hal thought back to a man he met here years ago. "Well, it's like this sun dancer I knew who got too big for his britches. He thought he was too good to keep fire for a lodge we planned to build up in the canyons. Of course, he was a white guy," Hal chuckled. "He probably saw the Red Road more like a corporate ladder, than a spiritual path."

"Hmm," Leroy toned seeing how a man's ego could get in the way.

"But then, I met Ohiya," Hal remembered as he looked out towards the ocean. "Now, he was a Sun Dance Chief. Even after he sun danced for 35 years, he still chopped wood, kept fire and built lodges for people, who might otherwise never come to ceremony. When it came to the Red Road, he was a truly humble man. His humility never got conceited like that. He never saw himself too good to do what was necessary to get the job done."

"Conceited humility?" Leroy laughed.

"Yeah, conceited humility. It's when a sun dancer forgets that he's a humble servant to Creator. And that every good turn we do for another, we do for our Higher Power," Hal agreed.

"The problem with most drunks is," Hal went on as he thought back to Henry. "They live according to their egos and their wants. Half of them are lazy and don't want to do the work it takes to get well. And the other half are so driven by ambition, they do a shoddy job because they got too many irons in the fire. Since most don't have a lick of humility, they butt heads against these un-bendable spiritual laws. Eventually, it breaks them in half. After you get sober, and come over to the winning side, humility keeps your head right-sized. It helps you work with the laws of Creation instead of against them. Can you see the difference?"

"Yeah, I can see that. So you don't think there's much hope for Daniels?" Leroy asked quietly.

"That's between him and the Creator, Leroy. The way I got it figured is, he's at the crossroads between HOPE and HELL. Only he can make that choice," Hal responded in a somber tone. "But sometimes a piece of metal is so bent and twisted, it's got to get completely melted down before it can be useful again. I've seen worse drunks than him get sober. The problem with him is, I don't know if he wants sobriety. I think he just wants the pain to stop."

"I can't say I blame him," replied Leroy. "Isn't that why most of us drink, because we want the pain to stop?"

"Pain shows up when there's something wrong, like a guilty conscious," Hal schooled. "And don't forget, alcohol is just a symptom, like it says in the Big Book. You gotta get down to the causes and conditions, for there to be a healing."

"Not everyone can figure that out," Leroy rebutted.

"Okay. Well, then you break it down for them," Hal added. For a moment he paused to think up a good example of what he was trying to say. "Have you ever watched a plow turn up the soil?

Leroy laughed at that question. "I grew up in the Heartland, the Midwest, remember?"

"Oh yeah," chuckled Hal. "But have you ever watched the blade of a plow pass through the top soil?"

"Well, maybe from the road. But I never sat on a tractor, if that's what your asking," Leroy admitted.

"The blade of a plow is pretty ruthless, when it's cutting through the top soil of the Earth. It churns it all up, so you can see what's hiding underneath. Whatever is under the surface, like roots or hard, flinty rock, that plow blade is going to reveal it," Hal paused to see if his student was paying attention.

"Okay, I see what you're saying," Leroy followed along.

"Now say, if you take drinking, it's a behavior. It's what you witness a drunk doing. But what you don't see is the twisted, inner turmoil that hiding underneath. Usually he had a thought before picking up that first drink. Most of the time, it's something like 'I can't handle this crap. I need a drink.'" Hal paused a moment. "Are you following me so far?"

"Yeah," Leroy agreed. "Life sucks sometimes."

"I never got promised a bed of roses," Hal added. "But underneath that thought, is a BELIEF. It's something we think that is true about ourselves which we don't have the power to change. And this is KEY, Leroy. Once you uncover a drunk's faulty beliefs, you might help him change the course of his life."

"So what do you think Daniels' beliefs are?" Leroy questioned.

"Well, I don't rightly know. Judging from his condition, he might feel pretty worthlessness. Didn't he say his wife kicked him out?"

"Yeah, and his mother. He said he's been bumming the railroads, living in the wild for a while. I think he drank so he wouldn't commit suicide," Leroy added. "He said he drank because he was lonely."

"I'd say he was lonely because he drank," Hal surmised. "That double-edged sword cuts both ways, Leroy. It goes both ways. Some of us move from one disaster to another. I can't tell you what Daniels thought of himself, but I can tell you what my rock bottom beliefs were," Hal answered. "Most of my life, I felt like a dented can. The kind you pick up, and put back down on the shelf at the grocery store. I believed I was second class, unlovable, worthless, not good enough and that no matter what I did, nobody cared. Hell, even the nun at Catholic boarding school told me the best I'd ever do was go to purgatory, and I believed her!"

"So you might as well drink," Leroy finished the thought.

"You got that right," Hal agreed. "And drink I did. But after I worked a good Fourth Step, Harry asked me a question which ripped me wide open." Hal paused remembering that 'breakthrough moment' all those years ago.

"What was the question?" Leroy wanted to know.

Coming back to the present moment, Hal looked at Leroy. "Well, Harry asked me if all those unfriendly beliefs of mine were true."

"What'd you tell him?" Leroy asked staring out the window at the passing shoreline.

"Well, on closer examination," Hal began. "It was all pride in reverse. People said mean things to me and I believed they were true. Now today, when that old false pride rears its ugly head, instead of beating the crap out of myself or someone else, I look for an opportunity to do something right. I ask myself what would love do now and change the behavior."

Glancing at Leroy, Hal could see the troubled expression on his face. He knew that look. It was heartbreaking to watch a man self destruct. "You know Leroy, that last mile, before a man's gets sober, is usually the roughest. It has to be."

Looking out the window, the sound of the ocean's breakers were in their ears. Hal noticed how the sunlight glistened on the ocean waves as they rambled along Pacific Coast Highway. There was nothing like fresh ocean air to clear a man's mind from the torment of the early morning. Hal was grateful for a space to just breathe.

It took a little less than an hour to make it up to Point Dume, a beach-side community along the Malibu coast. Driving through the neighborhood, most houses were hidden behind tall, electric gates. Hanging overhead was a lush, leafy green canopy from the tall trees which lined the streets. Tall shrubs along the walkway kept out the wandering eyes of passersby. Finally at Roy's house, Hal pulled in the driveway. He let out a huge sigh of relief. The long drive was finally over and he could get a good nights sleep.

It was an old ranch style house. A wooden white fence framed a sprawling front lawn and a big front porch. Dry and dusty, Hal and Leroy walked in the front door. The inside of the house was nice and cool. Albert, the caretaker, had the refrigerator stocked with cold water, fresh fruit and vegetables to snack on. Walking through the front room, Hal opened up the sliding glass door which went out to the backyard. Under the vine covered awning, was a wooden table with a few chairs. Before him was a 180 degree view of the ocean. Road weary, Hal sat down on the swinging chair. As he rocked back and forth, he felt nothing but gratitude. They had made it safe the whole way.

"Whoa," exclaimed Leroy, as he walked out in the backyard and took in the view. "How do you leave this? Why would you leave this?"

"Hmm," Hal toned before he responded. The sparkling ocean, with the cool sea breeze, was replenishing. Their surroundings were beautiful.

But there was a cold reality which came with fortune. "Emma...," Hal took a deep breath, realizing the gravity of the situation. "Roy found Emma with a needle in her arm. If he hadn't walked in the bathroom when he did, she'd be in her grave. He couldn't let that happen again."

"Wow, even with all this money, drugs can still take you out," Leroy thought out loud.

"Yeah, money offers no protection from the insanity of addiction," Hal offered as he thought back to the actors and musicians who died intoxicated. "Like that one actor, who had 23 years clean and sober. I think he won an Academy award," Hal shook his head. "He stopped working the program and died with a needle in his arm. Money don't exempt anyone from the consequences of poor choices Leroy," Hal went on. "The problem with most drunks is, they want the gift of sobriety but don't want to do the work."

"Surrounded by all this stuff, it'd be easy to forget that it's a daily reprieve," Leroy pondered.

"Yeah, there's the rub," Hal agreed. "Most folks don't understand the principle of temptation. Money is a great lure. And there's a lot of money out here."

"I wouldn't know," Leroy scoffed. He grew up in a government-issue house on the lone prairie.

"Well, you see," Hal started to explain as he rocked back and forth in the swinging chair. "All of life is an echo, Leroy. What you send out comes back to you. And if you don't clean up the mess you made, it will find you and knock you on your ass. We all have to clear our accounts with Creator, Leroy. And He don't take credit cards. So even the rich have to settle their debts by making better choices and being of service. Getting Emma outta here was the best choice Roy could make at the time."

"So Roy gave up all this to save Emma. I never knew. She never really talked about that part, except for the first day I met her," Leroy remembered back to his first day shoveling horse shit in the stalls of the barn.

"Yeah, that little chipmunk dang near broke his heart," Hal shook his head. Truth be told, it would have broke Hal's heart too. "You see, all over these hillsides are empty mansions turned into drug rehabs for the rich and famous," Hal's arms swept across the panorama. "It'll run you between $60,000 to a $100,000 to stay in one of these fine establishments."

"And we did it in a teepee," Leroy shook his head.

"Well, to each his own. Some people won't live without their creature comforts. But most great ideas are simple, Leroy, most great ideas are simple," Hal stifled a yawn as he closed his eyes. "Why don't you see what they got on viddles in the frig. I got a hankering for some good home cooking. I'm plum wore out from all that road food. I got to just close my eyes for a minute."

It didn't take long for Leroy to hear that familiar log sawing Hal did, after a hard day. Finding a pillow, Leroy stuffed it under Hal's leaning head. Hal grunted a little and Leroy walked into the kitchen. It was the little things that revealed a man's true character. The small acts of kindness which mattered most in life.

Inside the kitchen, Leroy went searching for some good eats. There was a big stainless steel refrigerator, with a full ice maker and cold water on the outside of the freezer door. In the pantry, he found different kinds of pastas and sauce. The freezer was packed with garlic bread, ice cream and some frozen chicken pot pies. There were salad fixings in the frig.

Then Leroy went outside to the garden. The hum of buzzing bees sounded as he smelled the sweet fragrance of citrus blossoms. Lining the backyard fence, he found all kinds of fruit trees. They hung full of oranges, avocados, lemons, grapefruit and apricots. Watching him from the pillars of the fence, were two yellow tabby cats. Their keen eyes didn't miss a move Leroy made. Another yellow tabby watched him from between the tall stalks of Swiss Chard. Flying across the tall tree branches, were chattering squirrels who shook their tails at the three yellow cats, taunting them from high above. Blue scrub jays landed in the fig tree, pecking at the sun-ripened fruit. Humming in the rosemary and lavender flowers were more honey bees. The garden was alive, full with ripe tomatoes, carrots, cucumbers hanging from a vine, green and red peppers, Swiss chard, squash and snap peas. Hal always talked about planting a garden, or getting a green house. Now Leroy knew where he got the idea.

In the cabinets by the stove, Leroy found the pots and pans. He filled one pot with water and set it on the stove to boil. Then with a colander and some scissors, he went into the garden and cut some Swiss Chard, tomatoes, a couple cucumbers and a few red peppers. He didn't realize it until then, but he liked cooking. After chopping, slicing, dicing and cooking, he put out a spread of pasta with red sauce, sauteed Swiss Chard, toasted garlic bread and a dinner salad.

Outside on the porch swing, Hal got a strong whiff of the garlic bread toasting. It drew him right into the kitchen. "Man that sure smells good," Hal said as he moseyed up to the counter.

"It's ready, let's eat," Leroy said as he put it all on the table. "I think the plates are in that cabinet over there."

Finding the plates, forks and knives, Hal set the table. "I can't remember the last time we sat down like this."

"It's been a while," Leroy added. "I think the last time I sat at a dinner table was at Roy's just before we headed out."

"You're right. It's been a while." Hal stomach growled as he pulled out his chair and sat down.

Hours later, back at the detox center, Daniels was just starting to come around. After Hal and Leroy dropped him off, he lay there passed out like a lump on the hospital bed. The counselors and nurses continually checked on him. With his body dehydrated, the alcohol poisoning was still in a dangerous place. As Daniels started to come to, one of the counselors was at his bedside.

"Ah," Daniels groaned. His head was pounding. He started to jerk the IV out of his arm.

"Hey! Hey, don't do that," Miles, the counselor, warned sternly. Looking into Daniels' bleary bloodshot eyes, he asked, "Do you know where you are?"

"Argh...." Daniels groaned in pain. "Naw, I don't remember anything." Exhausted, Daniels collapsed back down on the bed.

"Do you remember who brought you here?" Miles asked.

"NO!" Daniels growled. His head throbbed with sharp, stabbing pain. He was disturbed by what he saw. "Where am I? I don't remember anything."

"Two men, Hal and Leroy dropped you off. They said you were crossing the interstate in the middle of a hail storm and almost crossed paths with an 18 wheeler," Miles let that sink in for a minute.

"Leroy? Ya mean Sarge?" Daniels grappled with that for a moment. Tidbits of the last 24 hours came into his mind like a blur. "Did Leroy say we were in the Marines together?"

"Yeah, he mentioned that. He said that he got hit real hard and was sent home. And you went back for more," Miles filled in a few details, waiting to see how much Daniels remembered.

"Oh man, I think I kinda remember that. But it's sketchy, ya know," Daniels looked up at the ceiling to search his memory. "I can't believe Sarge found me and brought me here. He was a great Sarge, ya know. He always cared about us guys. Just like we were brothers."

"Yeah, they both seemed like good guys. Look, you got some family I can call to let them know where you are?" Miles queried.

A pained look crossed his face. Daniels shook his head. "Naw, I burned all them bridges. Even my mom threw me out the last time I tore up her house. My wife is scared of me. I can't say I blame her. After I woke up in the middle of the night choking her, she took the kids and moved in with her mother. Naw," Daniels hung his head. "I burned them all."

"PTSD will kill you and everything you love along with it," Miles started, knowing full well the lingering paranoia which came from a failed military operation. Conquering that phantom of fear and all its tentacles, took everything he had. The night could be as troublesome as the day. There were times, in his dreams, he saw himself being dragged down by a thousand arms of death, where bodies were flung into a mass grave of souls. "It's not easy to come back to civilian life, after being deployed a few times." Miles rolled up his sleeve. USMC was tattooed on his forearm. "Sometimes, it's not easy to be the one who survived, the one who came home."

"So you know," Daniels said looking relieved. One of the hardest things about coming home, was that no one understood what he'd been through. Having lived with the constant threat of danger, his mind was always on HIGH ALERT. He paid close attention to everything. While he was on the battlefield, surges of adrenaline pumped through his body almost everyday. When he jumped out of airplanes, every moment was a rush. But after he got home, different sounds and smells triggered his gruesome battlefield memories. Playing like a movie in his mind, he relived the exploding bombs and raining bullets all over again. The problem was, he couldn't shut it off.

It's one thing to watch a war movie, where the hero victoriously pumps the enemy full of ammo. But nothing compared to living it. One time chunks of his buddy's guts blew up in his face, after he stepped on a land mine. Then came the night, they were running for cover from enemy fire. Under his feet, he felt the crunch a dead man bones after he'd stepped on him. His mind flashed back to the endless hour he cradled his friend, watching the blood ooze from his chest, knowing he couldn't save him. That night Daniels' only comfort was that his buddy didn't die alone.

No, most people, who spend their days shopping at the mall, can't understand what he lived through, out there in the war zone. Out of pure survival, combat forced men to get close to each other. For a short time, they became closer than brothers. And now he didn't have that anymore. He didn't have anything. When people looked at him, they saw his dirty clothes and bloodshot eyes, and turned away. They couldn't see him. Now, he was alone, seriously broke and basically unemployable.

"Yeah, I know," Miles confessed, knowing the pain of being misunderstood. "That's how I got to be a drug and alcohol counselor. For the most part, I drank because I was just too damn sensitive for this world," Miles admitted quietly. "I drank to erase what I saw and did out there. But honestly, I had to get sober myself, before I killed myself or someone else. It took doing a stint in jail for assault with a deadly weapon, before I could surrender."

There's nothing more noble than fulfilling one's duty. It's always been considered one of man's highest virtues. Men risk their lives to fulfill this sacred contract, the love for the cause. During Miles' time in prison, something inside him clicked. Watching as more and more veterans were hauled off to jail for violent offenses, Miles knew something was very wrong with the way things were going. Then one day, a panel of people from AA came to the prison and told their stories. They talked about how Bill W., one of the founders of Alcoholics Anonymous, was a veteran from World War One. They shared how a suicidal Bill W. nearly drank himself to death.

Nearly ninety years later, it was still the same. Veterans came home from battlefield and drank themselves to death. But that day, one of the speakers told Miles' story. From that moment, he knew something inside of him had to change. The love for the cause became about holding out his hand to his fellow sufferer. Looking at Daniels, he was glad he made another choice. One that would help save lives.

"Oh man, I can relate to that." Daniels paused before he went on. "I can't even go to the gas station," he admitted. "The smell of diesel fuel sends my mind right back there." His voice trailed off. At that moment, the reality of his life was so stark. It took all he had to let it sink in.

"There's a lot of us you know," Daniel's voice trailed off as he realize he'd lost his grip on the world. His eyes darted around the hospital room. "Wandering around out there. Not sure what we're supposed to do. I met some of them when I was bumming the railroad. They got homeless camps. Most of us are living with those nightmares every time we close our eyes. The war never ends. It's in my head," Daniels shook his head.

"From my experience," Miles started. "There are two men you lose when you pull the trigger." His voice was solemn as he stared at the floor. "The first guy is the life you take and his face is hard to forget. But the second guy is the man you were before you pulled the trigger. Once you got blood on your hands, your innocence is gone. You can look for it all your life, but you'll never get it back. It'll haunt you like a ghost."

The truth of Miles' words hit Daniels like a brick. There was something on his mind, something he needed to confess and let go of, before it strangled him. Miles sat there patiently, waiting for Daniels to go on.

"What is it?" Miles finally asked after a long moment of silence. It took a few moments, but Daniels finally spoke.

"A few weeks ago," he started, staring off into space. "I took my dog Chloe up skydiving. She's all I had left." Deep emotion stirred up inside him, as he realize what he was about to confess. His life had become a nightmare, careening towards death. "Somehow I managed to come up with the cash for one last run. Only this time, I wasn't going to pull the chute. She'd gone sky diving with me before. But as that bi-plane climbed to 12,000 feet, I knew I couldn't do this life anymore. When I jumped out of the plane, I held on to her so tight," Daniels' eyes teared up when he realized he was embarking on the final frontier.

"But, then something happened," Daniels went on. "I don't know what. The ground was coming up so fast. I knew, in a few seconds, we'd be dead. That's when she started crying and licked my face. When I looked into her deep brown eyes, I knew couldn't do that to her. I couldn't take her life. I'd killed so many out there, on the battlefield. But I didn't have the guts to hurt my girl," Daniels started to shake. "Down on the ground, the emergency vehicles were screaming across the runway. They must of seen me falling out of the sky like a lead balloon. But just in the nick of time, my hand reached for the pull chord, and the chute flew open. It swept us up, out of harm's way, before we hit the ground."

Talking a man off the edge of a cliff was never easy, especially when he felt his life meant nothing. It wasn't the first time Miles heard a vet confess about trying to commit suicide. The gravity of it all, weighed heavily on them. "Did something happen before, that made you take that route?" Miles asked, not wanting to pry but to give Daniels a chance to sort this out.

The guilty look on Daniels face said it all. The staggering burden he carried deep inside rotted out his soul. "Not long after my wife kicked me out, a buddy of mine, Jamie, asked me if I wanted to go camping with his wife Kay and a group of their friends. I said sure, since I was couch-surfing at my moms. I just needed to get out and clear my head. Well, on the way there, Kay and Jamie got into a big fight. She threatened to leave him and he went nuts. He was driving crazy, talking about committing suicide if she left him. At first, I thought he was just being dramatic. But after we got to the campground, she threw a rock at his head and said she never wanted to see him again. And that's when he stormed off." Daniels took a drink of water that was sitting on the bedside table. This was the first time he'd told this story. It really weighed heavy on him.

"Then what happened?" Miles asked, knowing that wasn't all.

"Me and Kay got drunk," Daniels started. "I didn't think anything of it. She was furious at him, and kept taking shots of tequila. Next thing I know, she's curled up in my lap. Well, one thing lead to another…" Daniels paused. The guilt of this confession was crushing him. "I didn't say no."

"Did Jamie catch you?" Miles asked tentatively.

"I don't know," Daniels looked up catching Miles' eye. "I've been over and over it in my mind, but I don't remember if Jamie came back. If he did, I'm surprised he didn't shoot me."

"Or his wife," Miles paused. He just seemed to understand. He saw Daniels with the eyes of his heart, rather than the cruel, faultfinding, narrow view of his mind.

"He never came back as far as I could tell. But four days later, when I dropped Kay off at their house, we found Jamie hanging from a rope in the garage." The room went completely silent for a long moment. "If he saw me with his wife," Daniels shook his head. "Maybe that's what pushed him over the edge."

"You can't know that," Miles offered. "Sounds like he was already unstable."

"Yeah, but I had a hand in it," Daniels admitted. With one thoughtless act, he let himself fall lower than the stones on the ground. "When I close my eyes, I see his face, his burning eyes. It keeps me up at night."

"Look, I know how you feel," Miles said. "I made some idiot moves before I got sober. One night, I stopped at a bar on my way home from work. It was just downstairs, off the lobby of my office building. So it made it easy to rationalize needing a drink after the day I had. Just as I sit down, this pretty woman steps up next to me and orders a drink. Well, it didn't take long for me to strike up a conversation. After about an hour, she invites me back to her place, a beautiful home, right here in the Marina. I follow her home. She leaves the front open, with a trail of clothes for me to follow back to the bedroom."

"Oh, I can see where this is going," Daniels groaned.

"Well, I'm just pumping away, when the bedroom door busts wide open. I look over my shoulder and my wife is standing there. I can tell by the look in her eye that she's pissed off. Then she says, "ARE YOU DONE YET?"

"Oh man," Daniels bursts out in a knowing laugh. "What'd you say?"

"I said 'No, not yet," Miles admitted, shaking his head. "When I didn't come home for dinner, her woman's intuition kicked in. She drove down every city street until she tracked down my car. That woman had brass balls, coming into that bedroom and seeing me like that."

"Yeah, but you didn't kill her," Daniels sighed.

"There's more than one way to destroy someone," Miles admitted. "When I met Syd, she was maybe 120 pounds. By the time we got divorced, she weighed close to three hundred." Miles knew inside he'd caused some damage. "Truth is, I don't know how many people I killed," he admitted.

"What in combat?" Daniels asked.

"No, I was dealing heroin before I got locked up," Miles admitted. "One day, I'm doing my rounds, and I had some good shit. I get to this house, crowded with people. They all knew I was coming. I walk inside to sell my goods and tell the guy, go easy on this stuff, it's that good." Miles paused a moment as the memory of that day crowded into his mind. "But the guy drops two balloons of high grade heroin into a spoon and heats them up. Then he fills the needle and shoots up. Next thing I know, he drops dead right there at the table. So I packed up my goods and left."

"Man, how do you set that right?" Daniels asked.

"It's progress, not perfection," Miles confessed. "Even now, some days, it takes all I got to fight my way out of this wet paper bag. But I got a different set of tools now," he said as he reached across the desk for a big blue book. "The man who wrote this book, was a World War One vet. And he got sober and helped a lot of other people do the same." Miles put the book on Daniel's bed as he remembered Daniel's dog. Sometimes having the unconditional love of a dog can make all the difference. "Where's Chloe now?"

"She's with my mom. I've been on the streets. I didn't want to do that to her," Daniels said as he reached for the book. "Alcoholics Anonymous was started by a World War One vet?"

"Yup," Miles said. "Him and a doctor."

"Ya know, they put me on all kinds of meds, when I got home. But that just made it worse. Most of the guys I came home with aren't doing so hot," Daniels confessed.

"Yeah, putting Band-aids on bullet holes don't work well. Meds don't make the nightmares go away," Miles paused. "Or the guilt."

"Yeah, there's no getting rid of guilt," Daniels admitted.

"Well, this old timer in AA put it to me this way after I messed up my life," Miles went on. "He said everything I experienced became knowledge which no one can take away. And what I know in my heart, turns into wisdom. That wisdom becomes the power to make a better choice. Without the power of choice, I'm up a creek without a paddle. So let me ask you this," Miles postured. "Do you have trouble with alcohol?

"What, is that a trick question?" Daniels scoffed as he shook his head. "Last night I was too drunk to fight old crooked nose, the bouncer."

"Look," Miles leaned forward in all earnestness. "Let me explain it to you this way. If you got a well-oiled machine, and it gets grains of sand in the moving parts, it's going to choke."

Having worked on trucks in the desert of Hell, Daniels had experience with this. "Yeah, I see that."

"That's what alcoholism is," Miles sighed, relieved he found an example Daniels understood. "It's the grains of sand that choke the machine. Now, the only person who can decide if you need help with alcohol is you. I found some things that helped me. If you decide you want some help, we got classes you can take right here in the facility. But we can talk about that after you get some rest. I'll be right down the hall if you need me."

"Thanks," Daniels whispered. Miles' simple message was like a promise of life to a doomed man. Everything real is simple. Before he rolled over to go back to sleep, Daniels cracked that Big Book open to Chapter One. The first words were "War fever ran high..." Somehow, just knowing that someone else understood how he felt, gave him peace. It was the first time, he didn't feel completely alone.

CHAPTER FIVE: TO BE OR NOT TO BE

COWBOY LULLABIES

Looking out at the smoke filled skies
I hear your cowboy lullabies
The ones you sang to me at night
That chased away my little boy fright

But now the sky is raining fire
I can't help feeling oh, so tired
I wish I could just hear your voice
What I'd give for another choice

The Stars and Stripes are flying high
As I let out my battle cry
Tell those back home I love them so
The war planes are flying mighty low

My heart is beating out of time
Adrenaline's rushing at the Front Lines
It's hailing rockets from over there
Rocky's got a 1000 mile stare

We waste our genius on these wars
Trying to settle another man's score
April Fools always know what's best
They think they're better than the rest

The war cries keep me up at night
I don't know whose wrong or whose right
I wish that you could calm my fears
My eyes are burning with unshed tears

My buddy Rocky's laying next to me
Says he's hurting, he just can't breathe
I hear him take one long last breath
Beside him sits the Angel of Death

His body shudders, a tough guy cries
I sing him a Cowboy Lullaby
Home to the Angels he will go
At least the preacher told me so

Rocky's being shipped home today
Putting an end to his warrior ways
His body will be laid to rest
Oh Mamma, he did really do his best

Oh mamma, I do miss you so
Even when I'm on the go
I hear your lullabies late at night
They still ease my little boy fright

Come morning when the sun gets bright
I'll thank the Lord I'm still alive
I know you're praying, I am too

I just can't wait till this war is through

Looking out at the smoke filled skies
I hear your Cowboy Lullabies
The ones you sang to me at night
That chased away my little boy fright

After dinner, Hal got on the horn and called up his buddy Nate. He was hoping that there'd be a sweat lodge in the near-about. With Hal's voice booming clear across the living room, Leroy overheard the whole conversation.

"Yeah, me and Leroy, we just pulled in a while ago. Oh, the drive, it was all right. Long but pretty. Mother Nature sure puts out quite a spread," Hal paused a minute. "Hey I was wondering, you gonna fire up a lodge here soon? I got need of some purification," Hal chuckled. "Oh no, it's nothing like that. Last night, we found a buddy of Leroy's wandering, drunk as a skunk, across the interstate in a hail storm. Dang near got himself killed by an 18 Wheeler. We dropped him off at detox this morning after we rolled in. Tomorrow, 6 O'clock? Yeah, sure, we can make it. Is it in the same place, up the canyon? Yeah, I remember how to get there. Just tie a red cloth on the gate so I don't get shot at," Hal chuckled. "I never liked coming face to face with twin barrels." Hal laughed. His memory went back to one night when he couldn't find the right gate. He came face to face with a shotgun and a growling Rottweiler. "Naw... I'm not holding that against ya," Hal laughed. "Just put a marker on the gate, and we'll be there tomorrow. Talk to ya later!"

"Well, that's settled," Hal called across the living room. "We're set for a lodge at six tomorrow night."

"Sounds good," Leroy answered.

"TIGERLILLY! TIGERLILLY!" a woman's voice called outside in the front yard. Curious, Hal got up from the couch to have a look-see. "TIGERLILLY! TIGERLILLY!"

"Is that my favorite crazy cat lady?" Hal called out over the front yard as three cats came running out of the bushes. Along the tree lined street, an older woman dressed in a house dress and apron, was carrying two plates of cat food in her hands.

"Oh Hal," the old woman cooed. "My son calls me the "Awesome Kitten Whisperer.' I like that much better than 'crazy cat lady." She laughed as she walked across her driveway and put the plate of food down on some step stones. "When did you get in?"

"Just about an hour or so ago," Hal walked up to Ester and gave her a hug. "You still feeding all the strays in the neighborhood?"

"Oh these three were abandoned by a woman who used to live across the way," Ester explained. "They found their way into my backyard. But you know Merlin, he's pretty territorial. So I feed them out here. What brings you back out West?"

"Roy sent us out to fetch a horse," Hal offered as he watched these three grateful cats gobble up their food. "They're lucky to have you, Ester."

"Oh, I don't mind," Ester started. Hal noticed her arms were full of scratches and there was a nick on the tip of her nose. "How's Roy and the family? Is little Emma doing better now? She gave Roy quite a scare."

"Hmm," Hal toned. "Yeah, the family's doing much better. I ran into them at WalMart of all places. I hadn't seen them in quite a while, after I stopped working at the ranch."

"Oh, that's right. I remember now. You started working at that alcohol rehab up the street, once you got your counselor's credential," Ester recalled. "How'd that work out?"

Hal burst out laughing. "I finally understood why, in AA, we do things for fun and for free."

"OH," Ester exclaimed.

"Yeah, when you get a bunch of ex-drinkers in charge of the cash-cow, all kinds of strange character defects show up!" Hal laughed. "I had to get out of there, before I hit somebody."

Ester laughed. "You know, I celebrated 32 years a while ago."

"AH! GET OUT! Heck, you don't even look 32 years old," Hal schmoozed. "But what's that all over your face, Ester. It looks like you got in a fight with a feather duster!"

"Oh, that's just flour. I got two berry pies cooling in the window," she said with a smile.

Now she had Hal's full attention. There was nothing better than Ester's berry pies, with a little vanilla ice cream. "You got any vanilla ice cream in the freezer?" Hal asked, knowing the answer.

"Of course," she smiled. "Can I interest you in a slice of pie?"

"I thought you'd never ask," Hal's mouth was salivating. "Hey, what's that nick on the end of your nose?"

"Oh, that's from my Wiley," she cooed. "He's a little feral kitten a friend found starving in a trucking yard. Well, knowing how I am with cats, they brought him to me." She showed Hal all the scratches on her arm and a small scratch right under her eye. "The first few days, I had to hold him in a towel. He was so wild. His claws are razor sharp."

"How's he doing now?" Hal asked.

"Oh, he'll let me hold him," she laughed. "But sometimes he still gets that crazy look in his eye, and lets out a yowl that'll curdle your blood."

As they walked up to her front door, Hal could smell the pies cooling in the window. The true art of pie baking was lost to most modern folk. But Ester was an old soul. She knew some of the finer things in life. As she lifted one of the pies from the window, Hal caught sight of a picture of her son.

"Hey, ain't that a picture of your boy?" Hal asked.

"Oh yes," she smiled. "He was working at the Academy Awards that night, when they snapped that picture of him. It's hard to believe he's so grown up."

"Heck, I remember when him and Emma used to ride horses around the ring," Hal reminisced. "The time just flies by."

"Here, I got something for ya," Ester said as they sat down to the table. "I just read this book, written over 100 years ago. I think you might like it."

"John Barleycorn?" Hal read the title. "Alcoholic Memoirs by Jack London."

"It's his autobiography about his relationship with alcohol," Ester continued. "Go ahead, take it with you. It says he committed suicide at 40."

""Well, don't tell me the end of the book before I even sit down to read it," Hal laughed. "But man, he was still pretty young."

"He had his first drunk at 5 years old," Ester added. "But he would have died anyway from alcoholic kidney failure. He never believed he was alcoholic, but drank almost every day towards the end. He died just 3 years after this book was published."

"Well, 1913 was 22 years before AA got founded," Hal added. "He didn't have the benefit of knowing Bill W. and Dr. Bob. John Barleycorn is mentioned in the 12 and 12, isn't it?"

"Yes, I think in Step One," Ester thumbed through her bookshelf and pulled her Twelve Steps and Twelve Traditions out. "Here it is, on page 24; 'John Barleycorn himself had become our best advocate.'"

As it turns out, the reviving effects of drinking the blood of a Spirit named John Barleycorn were written about in English poetry and folk songs since the 16th century. A ballad titled "A Huy and Cry After Sir John Barleycorn" was written by Alexander Pennecuik in 1725. Barley was the grain from which beer and whiskey were made. Many have sung songs about John Barleycorn, and many have died at his cunning hand.

After a good talk, Ester wrapped up half the pie and sent it home with Hal. She missed her neighbors, but understood why Roy made the decision to leave. More and more she heard stories of young people dropping like flies. Heroin and meth were taking the lives of so many people in the city now.

"Hey Leroy!" Hal called as he walked in the front door. "Leroy!" Hal set the pie down on the kitchen table. Glancing down the hallway, he saw a light coming from one of the bedrooms. He ambled down the hallway to investigate. Sitting in a chair in Emma's room, Leroy held a picture of Emma riding a white steed. "What do you got there?" Hal asked.

"Would you look at this room. It's like a time capsule," Leroy exclaimed as Hal looked over his shoulder at the picture. On the white canopy bed were stuffed teddy bears and a big green toad. Pink frilly curtains covered the windows. Hanging on the wall were pictures of Emma riding horses and plaques from riding competitions.

"I remember that day," Hal said. "Emma finally got Snowball calmed down enough to ride him around the ring. She worked him hard and wasn't going to give up until she could ride him."

"SNOWBALL! That's what she named him? I wouldn't let her ride me either, if she gave me a name like that!" Leroy huffed putting the picture back down on the desk.

"Well, she was just a kid. Maybe 12 or fourteen. I can't remember exactly. But Roy never meant to keep that horse. Well...," Hal shook his head. "That was until Emma fell in love with that feisty steed. Then he couldn't rightly say no. He always had a soft spot when it came to Emma."

"Look at this room. It's so girly," Leroy said abruptly as he pointed to the frilly canopy bed, fluffy pink pillows and pink feather-bed duvet. "I never thought of her like this."

"But you didn't know her when she was little. With her big eyes, she had old Roy wrapped around her little finger. Granted, he clamped down, after she nearly killed herself. But make no mistake about it, she was daddy's little girl, through and through," Hal laughed. "Listen, I got some homemade berry pie on the kitchen table. Fresh baked."

"Thanks, I'm not hungry just yet. Maybe in a little while," Leroy said thoughtfully looking at her picture. Not that Leroy would admit it to himself, but he had a soft spot for Emma too. After all these years of working on Roy's ranch, he'd grown mighty fond of her. Most days, after Leroy finished training horses and cleaning out stalls, both of them would ride the horses down by the river. She was a fine horse woman. Hal had taught her well.

"Well listen, I'm thinking of taking the golf cart down to the beach to say hello to the ocean," Hal nudged. "You want to go?"

Leroy looked up, "Sure, give me a few minutes."

In the backyard, Hal went out to the garage, where the golf cart was parked. After he checked the battery to see if it was full, Hal pulled it out into the front yard. A slight sea breeze was kicking up in the long of the afternoon. It felt good to be out in the California sunshine. There was something special about the Pacific Ocean. It just made him feel good inside.

"Come on Leroy! We're burning daylight," Hal hollered through the front door. Grabbing his hat out of the truck, Hal made sure he had the house keys in his pocket. He didn't want to get himself locked out. It was different out here. Everything had a lock and key.

"Make sure the door's locked," Hal instructed as Leroy walked out the front door. Leroy checked the lock and pulled the door shut with a thud.

"You wanna ride this thing down to the Ocean?" Leroy scoffed, looking at the golf cart.

"Aw, hell Leroy! Just get in! The ocean's just a couple blocks and everybody rides golf carts around the neighborhood here," Hal laughed at the thought of two Indian warriors riding around in a golf cart. It did seem pretty comical. Leroy slid into the front seat, giving Hal a scowling look.

So the wind wouldn't blow it off, Hal pushed his hat down on his head and off they went cruising through the Malibu neighborhood. Lingering in the air was the scent of sweet jasmine which climbed along the fence posts. Cascades of bright fuchsia bougainvillea draped the tall neighboring fences. Groomed towering shrubs prevented passersby from looking inside the front yards. As they tootled along, Leroy counted almost three chimneys for each house. Tall pine and eucalyptus trees lined the streets. Manicured front lawns, rose gardens, and flowers of every kind decorated the front yards. Security gates with pass code boxes stopped strangers from walking up to any front door. For the few houses which allowed a view of the front yard, surfboards lined the front walkway. Along the shoreline, were some of the fancier mansions. One sprawling domicile caught Leroy's eye. Painted canary yellow with white trim, it was a two story farmhouse with a red tile roof. "That's nice," Leroy thought out loud.

"I think that's Goldie Hawn's old house," Hal reflected. "I don't think she lives there anymore though."

"Hmm," Leroy toned, caught in the view of so much wealth. "I don't know if there's a town across the whole prairie that has houses like this."

"Aw, you ain't seen the half of it," Hal chuckled. "Just wait until we blow through Beverly Hills. They got some houses there as big as city blocks!"

"How many people live in there, you think?" Leroy pondered as he spied through the windows of one mansion revealing the ocean view.

"Heck if I know. Maybe one or two," Hal responded as he steered the golf cart down the seashore lane.

"You mean, they have all those rooms for one or two people?" Leroy said in disbelief.

"Not everybody likes each other, Leroy. Wealth has a funny way of turning friends and family into leeches and spongers, making many rich people get pretty isolated," Hal explained.

"You can get lonely when you're poor too," Leroy shot back, knowing the hard-bitten truth of homelessness.

"The difference is, most people don't envy the poor," Hal volleyed.

"They got nothing to steal. There's nothing to be jealous of."

"So what are you saying? Poor little rich kid," Leroy scoffed.

"Well, think about it," Hal continued. "True friendship is usually between equals. People with money like this, don't have a wide selection of peers to choose from. Some of these big houses sit empty most of the year. They're just kept up by a grounds keeper."

"Where do I get that job?" Leroy mused, looking through the impressive iron gates that shielded the owners from the outside world.

Winding down the back road to Zuma Beach, the cool, salty sea breeze kissed Hal's face. "Oh, I missed this place," he finally admitted. Cars, trucks and surfer vans were crammed together, parked on the beach-side lane. Along the crowded street, Hal found a small place to park the golf cart. "See, if we brought the truck, we'd never find a place to park," Hal offered as they got out. Standing on the ocean's shore, the wind blew Leroy's long hair back from his bronze face. Leaning on the golf cart, Hal was already pulling his boots off to walk across the sand.

Under the dome of the bright blue sky, lay the Pacific Ocean, opening up in all its grandeur. Beyond the breakers, small pods of surfers waited for the next great swell. Speckled along the shoreline, were blankets full of people, kids with a Frisbee and girls in small bikinis. It was a feast for the eyes in every direction. Thunderous waves crashed along the shore. Between the breakers and the beach, a few guys threw down round planks of wood and jumped on to glide across the receding foamy water.

"What do you call those," Leroy pointed to the guys gliding across the water from the outgoing wave.

"Don't quote me, but I think they're called Skim Boards," Hal shoved his socks into his boots and rolled up his pant legs.

"They look fun," Leroy thought out loud. "I don't know if I'd try surfing, but I'd try those."

"I'll just make sure to get you some floaties the next time you go in the water," Hal poked, remembering the sea pony incident on the Colorado river.

"Oh shut up," Leroy poked back. "At least I can swim." Leroy's eyes rested on a small group of girls wearing the most revealing swim wear. Hal followed his eyes, and saw what Leroy was staring at.

"Look all you want, Leroy, but the smaller the bikini, the greater the heartache," Hal commented.

"Leaning over, Leroy whispered. "You mean the greater the hard-on."

"Yeah, that too," Hal laughed, knowing from experience. "The heartache just lasts longer. There's a lot for the eyes to feast on in L.A. But from what I know, some of them gals, well... they might polish your apples till they shine, Leroy. They're just not the marrying kind."

"You're just gun shy," Leroy shot back.

"Oh, it's not that Leroy. You forget, I got sober in this town. I've seen most of what there is to see, the good and the not so good. When it comes to lust and love, what you gotta know is, they don't run on the same train track," Hal finished.

"What do you mean by that?" Leroy asked, not letting Hal off the hook so easily.

"Well, just because a girl gets your motor running, doesn't mean she's in it for the long haul," Hal came back. "Out here, in these parts, some of these gals use beauty like it was a power tool. Heck, besides the gallon of warpaint they got painted on their face, half their body parts are made out of plastic or some other chemicals. You never quite know what you're getting under the hood, if you get my drift."

Oh, Leroy just chuckled. He'd never seen Hal dance around a subject like this one. His copper-toned cheeks were almost beet red. "So what you're basically saying is, look out for temptation."

"Oh, boy howdy!" Hal agreed. "There's plenty of temptation out here. Back on the rez, you'd have to pay extra to have one of them funny channels and make sure your mom didn't find out. Out here, you can take a gander at the skin parade walking down the street for free. In this town, Victoria's got no secrets, if you know what I mean." Just then, an olive skinned man walked by in very revealing pair of g-string Speedo's. Feeling a little embarrassed, Hal averted his eyes not to take in the sight.

"Yeah," said Leroy, seeing Hal's expression. "I don't think Victor or Victoria have any secrets around here."

"You know, temptation takes all forms, some more pleasant than others," Hal surmised. "The sad thing is, most drunks get destroyed by their weaknesses and that Ol' Tempter, Mephisto just hates a weakness."

"Mephisto," Leroy laughed as he pulled off his sneakers and put them in the golf cart, next to Hal's boots. "Come on, old man! I'll race you to the water." Sprinting towards the water, the sand was blistering hot! Running on the balls of his feet, Leroy was in a full dash. Besides the pounding surf, all Leroy heard was Hal's laments.

"OUCH! THAT'S HOT!" Hal yelled as he pulled up the rear. When they reached the waves, Hal let out a sigh of relief. With his feet cooling on the wet sand, he admitted, "Life is good, Leroy. Life is good."

Nothing soothes the soul like the sound of the pounding surf. The waves glistened with sparkles of sunlight as the sun headed towards the western horizon. Reaching in his pocket, Hal fished around for some pocket change. "Oh, I almost plum forgot," he muttered to himself as he pulled out 7 cents from his pocket.

"What's that for?" Leroy inquired.

"Well, the last time I lived here, I met this Indian from Peru. He was a priest, of sorts," Hal explained. "He told me, in his religion, the Angel of the Ocean is called Yemaya and that I should offer her 7 pennies when I come to visit her. That she would bless me that way."

"You mean like how we offer tobacco?" Leroy asked.

"Yeah, I guess it's like that," Hal suggested. "I didn't really study a lot about his religion, but I picked up a few things here and there. You'll meet every kind of person out here, Leroy. Every kind. He did his ceremony at the ocean for purification and cleaning, just like we do in the Inipi. I brought him to a sweat lodge a couple times, so we shared some trade secrets."

"How do you use the ocean for cleaning?" Leroy questioned. He'd never heard of that.

"Well, from what I understand, it goes back to the times before Atlantis sunk," Hal recalled. "Apparently, the salt water of the ocean is a powerful cleaning agent. It has the same spiritual power we find in our ceremonies. He told me to just sit down by the ocean and scrub myself off with the sand, like this, in a downward manner. Then make my offering, and dunk myself in the water a few times. The Angel of the Ocean, Yemaya, would clean off any negative energy I picked up."

"People of the Earth," Leroy said out loud. "All the Indigenous people use the Earth Spirits to help them live."

"Glad you've been paying attention. Sounds like you learned a couple things," Hal joked, having mentored him for years.

"HEY! I'M A SUN DANCER!" Leroy said with all seriousness.

Giving Leroy the once over, Hal pointed his finger at Leroy and started laughing. "What's so funny?" Leroy demanded, but Hal kept laughing.

"Ah," Hal toned when he finally got over his belly laugh. "One time, I said that to my mom." In his mind's eye, Hal could still see the look on her face. "After four years of sun dancing and dragging buffalo skulls, I walked into the kitchen with my shirt off." Hal laughed, thinking back to that afternoon. "You'd have to meet my mom. She was darn tough. But I'll never forget the look in her eye that day. She gave me this burning look. If I was a blade of dry grass, she'd have lit me on fire. With my shirt off, you could see the scars where I pierced up to the tree. And I think I said it, just like you did. Kinda full of myself, thinking I deserved some sort of medal."

"Yeah, and...," Leroy prodded, knowing himself how easily humility can get conceited.

"Well, you had to know my mom," Hal started. "She was nobody's fool. By then, she'd gone to a few sun dances, so she knew the drill. But that day, her eyes turned on me like blazing lightning bolts!"

"Oh," toned Leroy, familiar with that look. "Kinda like she's frying your soul with her eyes."

"Yeah, just like that," Hal nodded. "Her eyes burned a hole right through me. And then, with her hands on her hips, she turned on me and said 'Well, I'm a Mother!' And she raised her hands over her head, and said, 'You see this body, this is my Tree of Life. And right here, in my womb is the arbor where you danced inside me, every day and night, for 9 months. When my water broke, this Tree of Life shook for 22 hours giving birth to you! Giving birth is painful and there was a lot of blood!' Then she pokes me HARD in the belly button and finishes it like this, 'Your belly button, Mister Sun Dancer is the scar that got left, when they finally cut the cord between me and you!"

"Oh man! You got TOLD!" Leroy laughed. "I better watch how I say that."

"Well, back in the day, women didn't sun dance. They gave birth and raised families," Hal surmised. "It was a different world back then. Now you got women who not only sun dance, but they want to go fight in combat."

In a thoughtful manner, Hal took those coins and held them over his head. He called on Great Spirit and the Angel of the Ocean to bless him and Leroy, in their travels along the West Coast. Remembering his mom, he asked for a blessing for her. She put up with a lot, raising him and his brothers and sisters. As he tossed the coins into the Ocean, a powerful wave crashed on the shore. With great force, it splashed Hal and Leroy, soaking their jeans. Pushed backwards by the sheer strength of the wave, Hal laughed as the Angel of the Ocean flooded him with Love. Under their feet, small sand-crabs scurried along, diving into the sand, leaving a trail of small bubbles. As the water went back out to sea, a hard current pulled the sand from under their feet.

Gazing at the peaceful ocean, a sense of gratitude washed over Hal. Crashing waves pounded the ocean's shore as the sea mist sprinkled through the air. The foamy water covered their foot prints as they walked along the sandy shoreline. Being here again, Hal's mind flooded with memories. He recalled the time he spent with Ohiya on the sun dance trail. Like a movie, it came flooding back to him. If he got quiet a moment, he could almost hear Ohiya's laughter splashing through the waves. Ohiya loved the ocean. She knew him well.

"Did I ever tell you about the time Ohiya wanted to build a school out here," Hal's voice broke the silence. "He wanted to call it 'Wakan-Kdi-Ska Tiospaye' and teach ceremony to the people."

"I don't think so," Leroy responded. "Doesn't that mean 'White Lightning extended family?"

"You got it," Hal affirmed. "Since he was Heyoka, his dream was to have a piece of land, put a teepee on it and teach people the Old Ways. After years of being a Peyote Road-man and Sun Dance Chief, he was plum wore out from traveling," Hal added. "He was always on a bus or a train, running ceremony up and down the West Coast."

"That's not an easy life," Leroy agreed.

"Well, being a road-man is a lot of work. People hand you tobacco for a prayer ceremony, and it takes a good month or more to set up. But personally, he didn't take peyote anymore. Said he didn't need to," Hal's voice faded a little. "When he first became a road-man, he and Grandpa Peyote got well acquainted. He took it everyday for a year."

"Wow, that's a lot. Wasn't he Dakota?" Leroy asked trying to jog his memory.

"Yeah, his people also came from Sitting Bull, if I remember right," Hal answered.

"So how did he get to be a Peyote Road-man?" Leroy asked. "He grew up pipe-way, right?"

"Yeah, if I recollect right, his father was a Dakota Chief. So Ohiya grew up with Sun Dance, Vision Quest and the Inipi. I'd have to check my history, but I believe Grandpa Peyote came to Sitting Bull through the Ghost Dance. It has something to do with that Paiute fella named Wovoka and his vision," Hal surmised. "So when Ohiya came out West, he got introduced to the Teepee ceremonies and carried that altar as well."

Compelled by the conversation, Leroy had to ask. "So did you ever take peyote?"

"Yeah, a few times," Hal recalled. "But honestly, I'd rather do 4 sweat lodges back to back, than sit up all night. Most of the time, by 2 am I'm plum wore out, and finished with whatever prayers I got. So sitting there until dawn, well, I just get grouchy."

"Didn't it mess with your sobriety?" Leroy wondered.

"You know, everything, every spirit has a dual nature, Leroy. They way I was taught, peyote is a medicine. You take it as prescribed. I'm sure there are people who disrespect it and use it like a drug. But I didn't want to become one of them 'peyote-heads' like Ohiya called them. He told me that most people only played with the medicine. They don't know how powerful it is," Hal explained. "But before I went to my first Teepee Meeting, I had a powerful dream. It told me what I needed to know."

"Oh... do you remember the dream?" Leroy inquired.

"Well, of course I remember," Hal laughed. "Why? You want to know?"

"Yeah, I'm interested," Leroy answered.

Along the cliffs, was an outcropping of big boulders which had fallen from the mountainside years ago. Hal walked towards the ones which were just right for sitting. "Come on, let's sit a spell and watch the sun go down," Hal offered. Listening to the thunderous pounding waves settled Hal's soul. Sailing over the crest of the waves, a V formation of pelicans caught his attention. Not far off, a gang of yammering seagulls were making quite a ruckus. The entire flock haggled loudly over some beachcomber's bag of corn chips and were dragging it all over the place.

While the sky turned various shades of crimson, with bright, neon orange clouds against a light blue backdrop, Hal gathered his thoughts. "Well, I had a few years sober, when I got invited to go to a Teepee Meeting. Out here, people do both pipe-way and peyote-way. But they don't mix it together. You might be sitting next to a fella at the Inipi one night, who also goes to Teepee Meetings. The West Coast has an interesting mix of folks," Hal began. "Now, I knew this guy from around the fire place. His family was going through a rough patch, so he invited me to support his prayer."

"Like they used to do with the Inipi," Leroy added.

"Yeah, most Teepee Meetings have a specific prayer," Hal agreed. "But, like you can imagine, I was a few years sober and didn't want to mess it up. So I talked to a few good people about it. But bottom line, it was my decision."

Beyond the breakers, a few dolphins jumped out of the water, making their presence known. Hal's soul smiled as he recognized his brothers of the ocean. Leroy leaned forward, just soaking this all in. The ocean was a mystical, powerful place.

"The night before we were supposed to go, I prayed about it," Hal continued. "And in the early part of the morning, a Big Horned Owl came to me in my dream time."

"An Owl?" Leroy was surprised. Usually, Owls are known for their foreboding omens.

"You want me to tell you this or not?" Hal asked sternly. Leroy buttoned his lip, knowing he'd better not interrupt Hal if he wanted to hear this story.

"Yeah, an Owl," Hal replied as his ruffled feathers settled down. "The only thing I can figure is, Teepee meetings run from sundown to sun-up, which is the Owl's time to rule the sky. But in the dream, I was standing at the foot of a driveway. In the yard, was a big Sycamore tree. Looking up, I saw a feather fall down from the top of the tree. That's when I spotted a Big Horned Owl sitting high on the top branches. I walked over to pick up the Owl feather, when something caught my eye. All over the street, from corner to corner, was every kind of feather you can imagine. Red, blue and yellow feathers from a Macaw. There were Hawk feathers. You name it, every kind of feather. That's when the Owl spoke to me. He said "There are as many ways to pray as there are feathers on this street."

"Hmm," Leroy toned as the sun dipped lower in the Western Horizon.

"Now, the funny thing is," Hal pondered. "When my buddy came to fetch me that night, he'd never been to the land where the Teepee meeting was. So when we got to the back road, this owl showed up and flew right in front of us. I told my buddy "Follow that Owl." And sure enough, we ended up in the right place. All night that Owl hooted outside the Teepee. And halfway through the ceremony, all the people brought out their feather fans. That's when I saw every color and kind of feather you can imagine. Just like in my dream."

"You didn't have a dream! You had a vision!" Leroy exclaimed.

"Yeah, no matter. The Owl was right you know. There are as many ways to pray as there are feathers. That's all I got to know. Finding the right one, the right path for me, was all I had to think about," Hal finished.

"So how was it?" Leroy wanted to know.

"You mean the ceremony?" Hal asked back as Leroy nodded yes. "The first one was like a hot air balloon ride," Hal recalled. "Once Grandpa Peyote took over, the fire spirits started talking to me. I saw the faces in the Stone People. But when I walked outside the teepee, I was struck with all the beauty of Creation. I'd never seen stars shining brighter than they did that night. I could hear them twinkling," Hal paused. What he couldn't describe accurately was the powerful sense of Oneness he felt with all life, gazing out at the twinkling stars that night.

"They got a particular kind of drum," Hal recalled. "It's called a water drum. It beats faster than a baby's heartbeat in the womb. It's different than the Big Drum. All in all, I'd say the ceremony was powerful."

Hal paused a few moments to recollect his experiences. "But then I got invited back a couple more times. Grandpa Peyote showed me some of the rougher sides of my life. It was all my unfinished business that I had to clean up. The last time I went, I welled up with this fierce anger. It was hard to contain. I thought I was going to explode. I told the Roadman I had to leave the ceremony. After Morning Water, he let me go. Otherwise I would have started hollering at everyone. So I took my prayer outside and talked to the sky."

"Hmm," Leroy toned. Within moments, the sun touched the horizon where the ocean met the sky.

With a grin on his face, Hal leaned over towards Leroy. "Do you hear it?" Hal asked.

"Hear what?" Leroy replied.

"The ZZZZZHHH," Hal hissed, trying to make a sizzling sound, as he pointed towards the sun sinking into the Pacific, at the ocean's horizon. "Look at the skyline. Can't you see the ocean boiling? Way out there where the sun hits the water," Hal chucked at himself, making a funny.

Shaking his head, Leroy chuckled at his goofball mentor. From the North, waves of dense fog began to gather overhead. Whipping along the cliffs, a mighty wind coursed over the water. After the sun went down, it got chilly fast. It'd be a quick hike back to the golf cart, and back up the hill to Roy's house.

****

Many days later, at the treatment center, Clarence, an old black man, stood in front of a group of men. He had a smooth, deep voice which most just liked to listen to. Back in the day, Clarence was a jazz musician. From one gig to another, he traveled through the shanty towns, along the back roads of the South, just to make music. But then the Korean war broke out. Being a young man, he was drafted into military service and became a sailor. As a sea rover, he learned hard and fast lessons about the enchantments of bars, loose women and the valor-filled smoking rooms. Through this bitter education, he became a slave to the skin-deep desires of the flesh. After he found himself rotting in a living grave for a while, Clarence finally surrendered.

Now his wrinkled hands held a piece of yellow chalk while he waited until the men got quiet before he spoke. After decades of sobriety, he was deep, wizened, soft and gentle-mannered. A sculptor of hard hearts, he employed a 'Velvet Hammer' to chisel away at the hard nature which men developed by living long in the dis-ease. With all he had inside, he helped these men get out from under the crushing boot which threatened to take their lives. He believed that things naturally came to order out of chaos. So he stood and waited. His humble, gentle eyes surveyed the room. After a time, he noticed those in the audience who saw him waiting. They began to quiet each other.

"Shut up Ese!" Clarence heard more than once, while he stood in front of the sea of men. Amidst this motley crew, were all kinds; tough, young, old, tattooed, White, Black, Red and Brown. Quite a few of them were thought dead. Others, whose eyes were cold and heartless, might as well have been. Bound by a double-mind, most of these hellions were haunted by the hoot owls of their past, their hearts were frozen and went numb. One crusty, bearded biker whose whiskers were rusty and coarse, flashed his twinkling dark eyes to another man as he pointed to his t-shirt which read: "Liquor in the front, Poker in the rear." Of course, there were the usual loud-mouthed liars, whose peccadilloes, a rap sheet of sorted misdeeds, they wore like a badge of honor. One fast talker with ruffled hair, wearing a wrinkled, plaid sports coat, was the house charmer who used flattery to get what he wanted.

When Clarence was just a young pup, his granddaddy once told him about these types of men. "Scrappers' is what his pappy called them. They were only good at three things; fighting, eating and mating. Though Clarence welcomed each one without judgment, he wouldn't want to meet any of them on the street these days. When it was his turn out there, as it was many years ago, the rules and the drugs were different.

Now, from the stories that he heard, the world raged and it raged hard. Clarence knew what it was like to be poor, colored, no dad, with a mom who was always working. Those times were tough. But now, gun shots came through those kitchen windows and little boys like him, died in the streets. Lord, it was a world he didn't want any part of. Young girls walking the streets, living afraid every day. A body grows old quick, living fast like that.

For years, he'd seen them come here, to the very last house on the block before death. Though some had big muscles, most lacked wisdom. Not because they were stupid, but they never learned from their mistakes. Most of their lives, they did the same thing over and over again, thinking it would turn out different.

While some had never heard of God, others had rejected Him. A few were ragged drifters, sea gypsies who were exhausted and scarred from hard years of wandering through all of Creation. Most lived for no other purpose than to amuse themselves. Through this tough living, their inner purity was corrupted. They clung to the chaos, because it made them feel alive. Some left and some came back, with even bigger stories to tell. Some left and died, doing the same stupid shit they were doing before their judge-ordered dry spell. And then there were a few he got letters from. They got sober, a good job, a new car. One even got himself a wife. Those were the letters he liked. He wished he'd get more of those.

Above the dusty chalkboard hung a poster stuck with push-pins on the wall. It had some of the worn out acronyms from the early beginnings of recovery from alcohol and addiction.

PRIDE: Please Remember I Direct Everything
EGO: Edging God Out

FEAR: Face Everything And Recover (or) Fuck Everything And Run

ISM: I, SELF, ME; I Sabotage Myself

FINE: Fucked-up, Insecure, Neurotic and Emotional

GOD: Good Orderly Direction (or) Group Of Drunks

The room got quiet. Some of the meth addicts were fidgety. Their legs kept bouncing while their eyes darted everywhere. "Too broke to pay attention!" his grand-dad would say. He did have that. One good man who taught him how to live. A boy needs one good man. There just seemed to be a shortage of them.

"I want to thank you for your respect," Clarence started, his rich, deep voice slowly gentled their wayward spirits. "Respect, honor and trust are some of the most valuable things a man loses when he embarks on a relationship with a controlled substance. Drugs, alcohol and violence become the way. And you quickly lose all that is good, especially yourself and your self-respect."

Daniels sat in the back row, which Clarence kindly called the Shoe-Rack. It held all the 'Slippers, Loafers and Sneakers' who walked in court ordered. But most had no interest in getting sober. Many suffered from other problems, which were just compounded when they drank or used drugs.

"Before I get started on the Twelve Steps, I wanted to read you something out of this holy book," Clarence started. "This small paragraph is hanging by the door on your way out. You might not have noticed it, but it's the way that alcoholics used to get treated for their problem. This is a passage in Deuteronomy 21:18. I don't know how long ago it was written. Quite a few years before Christ, I imagine. But they dealt with drunks in a much rougher way. It's called the 'A Rebellious Son' which I know describes a lot of alcoholics struggling with the dis-ease. Here goes..."

Clarence paused to look down at the bible passage he was about to read. "If a man has a stubborn and rebellious son who does not obey his father and mother and will not listen to them when they discipline him, his father and mother shall take hold of him and bring him to the Elders at the gate of this town. They shall say to the Elders, 'This son of ours is stubborn and rebellious. He will not obey us. He is a profligate and a drunkard. Then all of the men of his town shall stone him to death. You must purge the evil from among you. All Israel will hear of it and be afraid." Clarence closed the holy book and looked out at the men. By their dull, blank stares, he knew most of them weren't paying attention.

"Anyone here know what a profligate is?" Clarence took a chance to see if someone was paying attention. Sitting next to the book shelf, Saul reached for the dictionary. He raised it up to Clarence and caught his eye. "Go ahead Saul, what does it say?"

"Profligate: 1. very wicked, shamelessly bad 2. recklessly extravagant, a person who is very wicked or extravagant," Saul finished reading the definition.

"Shamelessly bad, um, um, um," Clarence shook his head. "I know from some of the stories I've heard round here, well, a lot of men would have been stoned to death. Back in those days, they didn't call alcoholism a dis-ease. They called it evil and would stone you to death to get rid of it. Which leads me to the Twelve Steps, which aren't quite as old as the Old Testament, but they have another solution for this deadly affliction."

"Now, in Step One of the Twelve and Twelve, it calls alcohol a 'rapacious creditor," Clarence paced the front of the room while he talked. "Does anyone know what the word rapacious means?"

Sitting next to the bookshelf, Saul went to grab the dictionary. He looked up the word while Clarence waited. Thumbing through the dictionary, Saul looked up at Clarence. Clarence nodded.

"Rapacious: 1. Feeding on live prey," Saul gave the answer from the dictionary.

"WOAH!" Clarence exclaimed as he scribbled 'LIVE PREY' on the chalkboard. "Did you hear that gentlemen? Feeding on LIVE PREY! A predator, an animal. What else Saul?"

"Ravenous, voracious, plundering," Saul finished and looked up at Clarence.

"Thank you Saul," Clarence said as he set the chalk in the tray. "Y'all didn't think you'd get a vocabulary lesson. But what I'm trying to tell you is, ALCOHOL AND DRUGS WILL EAT YOU ALIVE!"

Sizing up the room, he knew many weren't listening. Most of them had been lectured to by their mothers, girlfriends, wives, cops, judges, parole officers and social workers. Based on the dull, blank stares, he knew this was a tough audience. You can't force a teaching on a man who is not ready to hear it. But this is what he did, working with the 'down and outs' who may not get another chance at sobriety before they died.

For Clarence, the challenge was worth it.

"There's always a moment, a final decision in every addict/alcoholic's life," Clarence looked across the room. "To be or not to be," he chuckled a little. "That is the question in front of us today, gentlemen. Because alcohol and drugs will destroy your mind, body and soul. The pain will get so great, you will lose all that you have and IT WILL WIN!"

Before he started his classes, he always prayed to his Higher Power, the Almighty, to let his words fall on the one who needed to hear it the most. "I have seen this time and again for about the last 30 years. Not one man, who has walked in here, told me how great it was out there. Every man I ever met, who come up here on a court card, was twisted up, some were broken. Their lives were in ruins. Some were near dead. We did bury a couple. They brought that shit in here. They just couldn't give it up. Ya see, a man whose body craves alcohol, will drive him to it, no matter what the cost."

The heels of his shoes clicked across the cold tile floor as he paced back and forth. A passion welled up inside him as he remembered the funerals he attended when they found those two young men dead in their bunks from an overdose. "That was one of the saddest days I've seen yet. One kid was barely 18 years old. He had everything ahead of him. But the boney fingers of Death snatched his Soul, right here, in his bunk. The dis-ease was eating him alive, gentlemen. It was EATING HIM ALIVE! DO YOU HEAR ME YET?!" Clarence voice boomed across the room.

In the back row, Nick, the self-proclaimed 'Italian Stallion,' nudged Gus, a stoic Indian Elder from the Great Plains. They had seen each other around the facility a few times. "This guy is pretty dramatic," Nick chuckled under his breath.

Hearing a chuckle from the back row, his ears pricked up. Within seconds, Clarence stood in front of Nick. He might be older, but his hearing was still good. "STAND UP!" Clarence commanded. With a surly look, Nick gave Clarence the once over. Clarence reminded him of a Black drill sergeant, he knew from back in the Corp.

"You want me to give you ten?" Nick asked sarcastically as he slowly pushed himself up out of his chair.

"Oh, I see," Clarence shot back as he sized up Nick. "I got me one of them "Eye-talien" wise guys. One of the good fellas," Clarence paused for a moment. "No I don't want you to give me ten. I don't think you could as skinny as you look. But I want you to tell the fellas here, what you said to old Gus. He's our tribal leader. We got at least one of everything in this house. The dis-ease don't see no color. You better remember that! It don't see no pocket book either. No matter if you be rich or poor. It will eat you up. Just tell the boys here what you said."

"Well, ugh," Nick stammered. "I said I thought you was a little dramatic, that's all."

"VERY GOOD!" Clarence bellowed. "That's what I thought you said. Now I want you to tell these boys where the police found you before you got sent here."

Nick looked down at his feet. A rush of shame went through him.

"Come on boy! You tell them," Clarence commanded. "Or do you want me to. Maybe one or two of the guys here remembers."

Usually a haughty, silver-tongued devil, Nick's voice was barely audible as he choked out a whispered response. "In an abandoned building, over-dosed and almost dead."

"What did you say? Those boys back there, they can't hear you," Clarence wasn't going to let this one drop.

"IN AN ABANDONED BUILDING, OVER-DOSED, ALMOST DEAD!" Nick's furious eyes glared at Clarence as he shouted his reply across the room.

Clarence turned on his heel and looked at everyone across the room. "Now that's what I call DRAMATIC!" With his heels clicking on the tile floor, he walked back to the front of the room. "Now is there anyone here that doesn't see my point? Addicts and alcoholics will either wither and die alone, or we can conquer this thing together. Do I have any takers here yet?"

Marinating in their own sour juices, the men were stoically quiet. No one felt like being the center of attention today. As some of their faces turned to stone, Clarence felt the walls of indifference go up. There was nothing harder than scaling those hard granite walls, when a man closed himself down. It was never easy to get a heart that's turned to stone, beating again into a feeling heart, rich with flesh and blood.

Sitting next to Nick, sat Gus. By nature, he was a stoic Indian who knew well the intoxicating spirits in the whiskey bottle. He'd seen all the ways that demon whiskey tormented his people. That bad firewater, alcohol, embodied an Evil Spirit. Only a drooling fool doubted the power of its poisonous sway. Many moons ago, it was a lesson he had learned all too well. If a man didn't pray to the Higher Spirits, he'd be preyed upon by the lower ones. And from his experience, Evil Spirits were very real.

"Okay, sometimes I do this to illustrate my point. Now everyone who lost a car, got into an accident, DUI or whatever, when they were loaded, stand up," Clarence directed the men. About ten men stood up.

"Okay, now all of you who lost a house or apartment, got evicted, maybe your wife or girlfriend threw your sorry ass out, WHATEVER! Stand up!" Fourteen more guys stood up.

"Who here lost their woman, best friend, or family, STAND UP!" Clarence was on a roll.

Daniels found himself getting out of his seat. Looking out at the sea of men who shared his sorry lot in life, he didn't feel so alone. All but one stood now.

With his knees bouncing, Timmy sat there as all eyes slowly turned to him. Clarence finally noticed Timmy sitting down and walked up to him. With soft eyes, Clarence looked at him and didn't speak for a moment. "Now you mean to tell me, that you haven't lost any of those things I just mentioned due to drugs and alcohol?"

Butterflies fluttered in his stomach as Timmy felt everyone's eyes looking at him. He could barely get the words out. "I didn't have any of those things," Timmy started. "I got put into foster care when I was four. I got moved everywhere, so I never fit in. I'm only 19, but my last foster-mom dropped me off here because I was smoking pot everyday and shooting meth."

"Well son, it sounds like you lost everything to me," Clarence said softly, his eyes overcome with emotion, as he motioned the men to sit down. "When I was a young and stupid man, I thought I could master this demon whiskey by myself. My grand-daddy called alcohol by its formal name, 'John Barleycorn.' Barley is what they make whiskey out of and I drank enough of that. Back then, I had a wife, a house and my babies. But I was a drinking fool. And that dark magic of John Barleycorn, well, it kept whispering to me. Its songs got into the workings of my mind. That whiskey demon was slowly leading me down the road to death."

"Well there come a day, not long after that, when I never took a sober breath. My body was never free from that poison. I had the craving and that alcohol fire was mastering me. My mouth was always dry. I had a nervous stomach, retching my guts up every day, like a pregnant woman. Pretty soon, the only way I got to see my wife and my babies was through a thick, plate glass window. I watched my children grow up by getting their school pictures sent in the mail. The drunk that I was, I deliberately blinded myself to all the pain I caused them. Now I think I got a few fathers in here and I got to ask you one question. How do you want to watch your kids grow up? From a distance? From a few faded memories? Through pictures and plate glass windows? Or from a headstone? Believe it or not, you matter. You matter to them. How you live matters."

Looking down at his rough, grease-blackened hands, Daniels got an ache in his stomach when he thought about his wife and their two kids. The first time she came to see him in jail, with their new born son, he just about died inside. His heart was in turmoil, just remembering that day. Inside his cash-bare, empty wallet, he carried a worn out picture of them.

"There's a promise in the Big Book of Alcoholics Anonymous, gentlemen," Clarence went on. "And I am a witness to that promise today. It says 'No matter how far down the scale we have gone, we will see how our experience can benefit others.' Now, from what I gather, experience is the best teacher. Nobody can take that knowledge from you, once you walked through that alcohol fire. And that knowledge, which you earned by the seat of your pants, becomes wisdom. Wisdom, gentlemen, is the Power of Choice. Knowing that you never want to do something again, is wisdom. I never want to drink or do drugs again. And my low bottom is what allows me to work in this room and pass on what I learned to gentlemen like yourselves."

With a velvet hammer and silken chisel, his knowing words carefully chipped away at the pieces of broken stone sitting before him. Some of them were made of pure granite, rough, hard and impenetrable. Others were like brittle sandstone, they'd crumble if handled with a harsh touch. The gentle spirit deep within Clarence prayed these men could find love in a hopeless place. That they'd find something to live for, something to get sober for, something that stirred their sleeping souls. Though he loved his work, the pain he witnessed everyday overwhelmed him. Walking to the front of the room, he found a piece of chalk and started writing on the board. "Now my grand-daddy used to say "BOOZERS ARE LOSERS." He scribbled that on the chalkboard. "And he was right. He watched his own daddy drink himself to death."

Turning around to look into the sea of men, he wondered if anyone heard him at all. Some of them had vacant eyes, blank expressions. He figured them for the walking dead. Others, well it was hard to tell. "Now, I don't know if any of you noticed, but I stood up the whole time. I lost me the love of a good woman because I couldn't stop lying and cheating. I lost a home, 2 kids, my job and most of all my self-respect. I was a dirt bag, living on trash behind a building at 5th and Main Street. And at one time, before I fell prey to that demon rum, I was a naval officer. There was a time when I prided myself on giving a man 'My Word of Honor.' But alcohol and drugs eroded my word and I lost it all. Because the Big Book calls the dis-ease a 'subtle foe.' And even with all my military training, this is a battle I couldn't fight alone."

"Does anyone know what a 'subtle foe' is?" Clarence asked the room. Saul reached for the dictionary again. Clarence nodded giving Saul the okay to read.

"Subtle," Saul started. "Difficult to detect or analyze, barely perceptible, marked by having sharp discernment, keen, expert, crafty." Then Saul thumbed through the dictionary to find the word foe. "Foe: an enemy, especially in wartime, opponent, adversary."

"Thank you Saul," Clarence said as he looked at a few expectant faces. "So basically, addiction is a crafty mother-fucker who is coming to take you out. Is anyone else seeing the gravity of this enemy called addiction?"

But the room stayed quiet. Standing back, Clarence started to feel frustrated. No matter how much he wanted to press on, he had to pull back. Anything more would just smother them, and eventually burn them out. From what he could tell, this group was not even brave enough to talk or save themselves.

Generally speaking, 'dead men walking' were spiritually weak. Like a dry branch, their lifeless ways were withered and rigid. By serving only their own selfish natures, they turned into empty machines. Never mind the state of their heart. Without an incoming tide of genuine love, their inner essence was forcefully degraded, trying to survive in a world gone dark. Inwardly, either by Grace or tragedy, they had never experienced an act of surrender, a transformation which was a bridge of Light over the dark chasms. Their minds were closed to all wisdom. Those who could not be put straight, would have to break.

Only an Almighty Power could break through and create order out of chaos. Only pure love could forcefully straighten out something which a drunkard had distorted in his mind. While some in the room were arrogant and hard-hearted, others were just plain lazy. Like most addicts, they thought someone else would do the grunt work for them. Many were made cripples by the dis-ease, and couldn't accept a reality or authority higher than themselves.

For a long moment, Clarence stared out the open window, listening to the whisper of the wind-song, rustling through the leaves of the trees. His eyes rested on a patch of golden wild flowers growing along the hillsides. In a gray and white cloudy sky, he watched a tall army of evergreens swaying in the wind. The music of nature eased his troubled mind. Off in the distance, thunder rolled across the sky. A storm was brewing outside. But the motley crew in the room just sat in a deafening silence. Having hit that granite wall of indifference, Clarence made a humble prayer under his breath. Even he knew he was powerless over addiction, whether it was in him or someone else. But there was One who had all Power. As he made his soul-driven prayer, an invisible white fire rolled across the sky. Holy streams of Power searched for an open door, looking for a tiny spark, a patch of soil prepared for It. A ray of Light burst through the clouds while Clarence made the Call.

An overwhelming, uneasiness welled up in Daniels as the room sat there in the pressing silence. In his mind, vivid, scattered scenes replayed like a movie from his last drunk. The noisy bar, the half-naked women, the pelting rain, the blaring horn from the 18 Wheeler which almost ran him over, the wall of water that knocked him down, landing his withered body in the gutter. Hal's worried face flashed through his mind. Then hearing Leroy's voice in the shower as he started to come to. Skipping through these raw memories, he relived the shame of every painful moment.

On the wall, the clock ticked loudly as the second hand moved around the Roman numerals on the face of the clock. Within those endlessly long seconds, Daniels reviewed the last few years of his life; the drunken fights, the broken home, his time behind bars, homeless and bumming the rail, the attempted suicide, the endless nightmares. Overcome with shame and pained emotions, it was all more than he could do on his own. A tender sadness wove itself back into the memories of his childhood. Along the way, he'd lost something pure, something special. This thought left him with a feeling of deep inner emptiness.

Before Daniels made the choice to put himself into treatment, Miles had drilled one thought in his mind. In order for an addict/alcoholic to live free, a Higher Spirit had to counter the lower demon spirit called alcohol. In a series of letters, Dr. Carl Jung wrote this to Bill Wilson, one of the founders of AA; "Spiritus contra spiritum."

Listening to the clock tick off seconds on the wall, Daniels felt much like a drowning man. Summoning all his courage, he lunged for this lifeline Clarence kept on strumming like a worn out, tired banjo string. Something deep inside Daniels pushed him to be free. Almost a painful, inner longing urged him to awaken from this drug induced coma he'd been living in. He knew he had to want sobriety for himself. No one else could make that choice for him. Standing up, Daniels looked over at Clarence, who was deep in thought. "Sir," Daniels spoke, interrupting the deafening silence. Called out of his frustration, Clarence slowly looked over. A miracle happened.

"Yes soldier," Clarence gently responded as he met Daniels' tired eyes. From what Clarence could see, those eyes were burning with unshed tears. There was a lump the size of a baseball in his throat. But Clarence also saw a quiet confidence in those tear-filled eyes. In a moment of silent surrender, this shipwrecked soul, a veteran of foreign wars, was treading water to the peaceful shores of sobriety. It would take a lot of tenderness to heal those battle scars. But from what Clarence knew, tenderness was the best soil for an awakening.

"I want to live Sir," Daniels said out loud in a moment of unshakable faith. "I want to live."

CHAPTER SIX: A HERSHEY'S KISS

LOSER #86

He drinks, he smokes
'Hey how about another toke?'
Used to play guitar
But never went very far

No wife, but a kid
Be a parent? No never did
Not his, no time
'Hey! It's her responsibility, not mine!'

Poor me, can't you see
Bad luck, foul destiny
Tough breaks, where's the cake?
Pity me, for goodness sake

Poor Loser #86
Needs someone to be his fix
The right girl, a steady job
But he dresses like a slob

A diamond in the rough?
Or perhaps, just Billy Goat Gruff

"FOR HEAVEN'S SAKE, CINDY! JUST TAKE A BREATH! SHUT UP A MINUTE! WILL YA! I'M TRYING TO TALK HERE!" Rhoda yelled into the phone.

"Fine, finish your stupid story!" Cindy shot back. Her feelings were hurt by the abrupt shut down.

"So, I put the dinner rolls and butter down on the table," Rhoda kept talking. "And he looks up at me, and says "Ma'am, could you take the wrappers off the butter!" Can you believe it? A grown man! Dressed in a suit and tie, and he couldn't take the wrappers off the stupid butter!"

"So did you do it?" Cindy asked. "I would have told him where to shove his stupid butter wrappers! Like what, were his fingers broken?"

"No, I told him I wanted to meet his mother!" Rhoda shot back. "I wanted to find out who this decrepit woman was that turned her son into a complete mental cripple!"

"Boy, I hope you don't get fired!" Cindy snapped.

"FIRED! It's a freaking diner!" Rhoda squealed. "How do you get fired from a place that pays CRAP! The only way you make a dime, is by schmoozing some ass-wipe who can't take the golden wrappers off the freaking butter!"

Changing the subject, Cindy got brave enough to interrupt Rhoda's rant and ask a question. "So did that guy ever call you back?"

"You mean Loser #86?" Rhoda responded with a heavy sigh. "No, I never heard back from him. But he's got a kid. He doesn't pay child support or even see his daughter. I don't understand people like that. All he wanted to do was get high and get laid."

"What was his name?" Cindy asked.

"Ira, good old Ira," Rhoda hissed, still smarting from the short affair.

"You met him at that bar, didn't you?" Cindy asked.

"Yeah, going to look for a husband at the Cantina is like trying to find a diamond ring in a sewer," Rhoda admitted. "I don't know what I was thinking that night. All it takes is a few beers and I can't see straight." Taking a deep breath, Rhoda let out a deep sigh. "I want to blame it on Babs for taking me there on Valentine's Day."

"Yeah, she's nothing but trouble," Cindy agreed.

"But the night started out so fun. She brought that bag of Hershey's Kisses. I'll never forget her walking up to this guy, he was drop-dead gorgeous. The kind that would never give me a second glance. But she's got that mini skirt on and her long blonde hair blowing in the breeze," Rhoda's voice was full of envy. "Then she looks this guy deep in the eyes and asks if he'd like a kiss. Well the horny devil! He had that stupid look on his face, but he says yes! And then she hands him a Hershey's Kiss!"

"That's funny," Cindy laughed.

"I don't know where she comes up with this stuff! But that wasn't the end of it," Rhoda went on. "Then she wants me to do it, go up to a guy and ask him for a kiss….. But you know me, I look at a guy sideways and get all tongue tied, my stomach was all full of butterflies."

"So did you do it?" Cindy asked.

"Well, sure, how do you think I met Loser #86? Ira, oh, Ira! How could I be so dumb?" Rhoda lamented. "But I got a bigger problem."

"Yeah, what's that?" Cindy chimed in.

"I'm getting as big as a house! I can't stop eating," Rhoda admitted, feeling completely frustrated. "Between the french fries at work, and the Oreo cookie shakes and other crap, I can only fit into my sweat clothes!"

"Why don't you just throw it up?" Cindy threw in.

"THROW UP! You mean throw up my food? That is so GROSS! Disgusting!" Rhoda howled over the phone. "Where'd you come up with that?"

"Shit girl, don't you read the papers? All the movie stars do it! And so do the horse jockeys!" Cindy tried to side step the question. "Jane Fonda wrote a book about it. Didn't you ever hear of the vomitoriums they had in Rome or Greece? I can't remember which. But they had these huge feasts for days. People would gorge themselves until they had to throw up."

"Do you do that?" Rhoda demanded, as this horrible, disgusting idea traipsed through her mind.

"OH FINE! WHATEVER! Get fat then," Cindy side stepped the question.

"DO YOU THROW UP YOUR FOOD?!" Rhoda didn't let it drop.

"What do you care?" Cindy shot back. "The only reason you're asking is to feel superior to everyone else! When do you really give a shit about anybody else but yourself?!"

"What's that's supposed to mean?" Rhoda felt the sharp spear of

Cindy's words lance her heart.

"Look, I don't want to fight with you. I got to go," Cindy hung up the phone. Furiously, Rhoda redialed Cindy's number, ready to tell her off, when the call went straight to voice mail.

Without even thinking, Rhoda reached for a box of Mallomars cookies sitting on the counter. After she polished them off, she found the chocolate chip cookie dough ice cream in the freezer. Flopping down on the couch, she flipped on the television. Slowly she numbed her fury by excavating the chunks of cookie dough, out of the vanilla ice cream. Between the food and the television, she was fully mesmerized. In this trance-like state, she was completely unconscious of the amount of food she had shoveled down her throat.

When her spoon finally hit the bottom of the ice cream container, she snapped out of her food coma, for just a moment. She didn't plan on eating the whole half gallon. But watching an old John Wayne movie, she felt desperately alone. Nothing was going right. Tomorrow, she was supposed to start school at the local community college. Her plan was to study to become a para-legal. Maybe that way, she could finally get on the right side of the law.

Spears of loneliness stabbed her soul as she sat there in the semi-darkness of her living room. Intense anger sweltered in her mind like a muggy, hot August night. The truth was, she hated herself. Most days, she wished she'd never been born. What did she have to live for anyway? Jerks like Ira, who wanted to get laid after they took you out for fifty cent tacos on the second date? Inwardly, she knew she was nothing but a screw-up. Even her daughter didn't really know her anymore. As these vicious thoughts devoured her soul, their powerfully charged energy formed dense, dark clouds around her being. The longer she ruminated on her pitiful life, the larger and more powerful these thought-forms became. Soon they grew wings and took on scary forms.

About halfway through the movie, she felt sick to her stomach. Going in the bathroom, she stared in the mirror. She felt disgusted looking at her fat face and even fatter belly. Then, in a fit of fury, all her inner demons came unleashed. Their sharp, black talons carved through her mind, releasing a venom so evil, it ate her alive inside. "Well, you fat pig! You sure messed up this time," she said to herself in the mirror. "YOU'RE NOTHING BUT A SCREW-UP! A FREAKING LOSER!"

Then Cindy's words flew into her mind. Flipping open the toilet seat, she stuck her fingers down her throat and made herself gag. It was a

MIRACLE! All the ice cream came up, and a few chunks of the cookies. Then she did it again, and again and again, until she felt completely empty.

After she flushed the toilet and watched all the puke go down, a feeling of euphoria washed over her. After all the violent puking, her endorphins kicked in. She felt strangely high. It was a sick, but happy feeling. Even though she felt disgusted with herself, she felt better knowing that she got rid of it. Then on a crazy whim, she grabbed her car keys, and drove to the burger joint down the street.

When she pulled in the parking lot, there was a line of cars waiting in the drive-thru. With the engine idling, she felt anxious at what she was doing. But couldn't stop herself. After she ordered enough food for five people, she pulled up to the cashier window. Feeling embarrassed, she told a white lie to the cashier about having slumber party for her daughter. They wanted burgers to eat. Never mind that it was ten o'clock on a school night. She would die of embarrassment, if the cashier knew that she planned on eating all this food, only to throw it up. At the same time, it was a rush. Like getting two 'GET OUT OF JAIL FREE' cards. For the first time, she could eat whatever she wanted and get away with it. Or so she thought.

Just to be safe, she stopped by the mini-mart and picked up another half gallon of ice cream and schlepped all that food up to her studio apartment. All night, she sat in front of the television and excavated the chunks of Oreo cookies out of the cookies and cream ice cream. But it didn't make her feel better. With every bite, she felt guilt-ridden, which made her eat even more to drown out those harsh feelings. She couldn't stop binging. After hours of fussing with food, she made herself throw up. At the end of it all, she was exhausted and fell into a fitful sleep.

The next morning, she felt hung over from all the sugar. Staring in the bathroom mirror, she felt nothing but self-loathing. All the vomiting made the glands in her throat swollen. Her voice was raspy. On the counter was her bag of make-up. The dark bags under her eyes made her look ten years older. Her eyes were bloodshot from lack of sleep. In a desperate attempt to hide her shame, she piled on the concealer, make-up, powder and lipstick.

"*I HATE YOU!*" poured out from her criticizing eyes which stared back at her from the mirror. Furiously, she brushed her red curly hair back into a pony tail, put on her sweats and walked out the door. It was the first day of class. Her parole officer knew she was supposed to be there for retraining.

This morning, it seemed impossible to jump through every hoop to prove to herself that she could survive honestly in the world. Everything was piling up. Some things seemed to go from bad to worse. While she was incarcerated, she made her friends the legal temporary guardians of her daughter. Now, it wasn't so easy to get her daughter back. After she went to jail, Child Protective Services got involved.

Every morning, she felt the seething resentment at her shithead attorney stir inside her mind. He swore to her that he'd get her off. But, as luck would have it, she was convicted. The officers took her from the courthouse straight to jail. There was no time to take care of her daughter. Now she had supervised visitation, which all cost her money. After the jailhouse drama, the judge ordered supervised visits so Rhoda and her daughter could get reacquainted, since Rhoda was gone so long.

Driving off to class, Rhoda's mind was consumed with a deep-seated fear that her daughter would fall in love with her friends. Maybe she'd never get her back. It gnawed at her the whole time she was in jail. And now with all these obstacles, it seemed like the whole Universe was working against her. Everything seemed so hard.

After parking her car in the school parking lot, she grabbed her backpack and headed off to class. The last thing she needed was to show up late. In a fit of anxiety, she got there a few minutes early. Walking down the corridor to the classroom, she noticed a bulletin board next to the door. It only had one paper on it, with big bold letters.

DO YOU HAVE TROUBLE WITH FOOD?

OVEREATER'S ANONYMOUS.

12 NOON, MON, WED, FRI.

ROOM 222. BRING YOUR LUNCH.

"Bring your lunch," Rhoda whispered out loud to herself. "What the hell do they want with my lunch?" As it turned out, her classes met Monday, Wednesday and Friday. She had a long break from 11:30 am to 2 pm. Her last class got out at 3 pm. She had to admit, she had trouble with food. The time was right. But she'd eat before she got there. She didn't want anyone bothering with her lunch.

It was 12:05, when Rhoda finally found Room 222. It was in a row of bungalows next to the street. The back door was open, so she quietly snuck in. Inside the room, were a mix of people, all shapes and sizes. One woman must have weighed close to 300 pounds. There was a few skinny Mini's. But most people ranged in between. And sure enough, some of them brought their lunch. One woman was already speaking when Rhoda sat down in the back.

"Well, hi. My name is Billie Ray. I'm a grateful, recovering compulsive over-eater and bulimic. Basically that means, I'd eat everyone of you under the table, hit the bathroom and throw it up. Sometimes, I'd come back for more. After that, I'd starve for a few days so I could still fit into my skinny jeans," Billie Ray laughed. "I'd say my food was pretty crazy."

She picked up a carrot stick and crunched a few bites. "It got to the point where all I ever thought about was food. Whether I was going to eat it or not eat it. Then I'd just have those "fuck it days" where all I did was sit in front of the television and just binge and throw up."

Rhoda's ears pricked up when Billie Ray said that. It was like someone was reading her thoughts. She found herself settling into her seat, listening to what Billie Ray had to say.

"Now, I didn't always throw up my food. In fact, the thought never even occurred to me, until I was a senior in high school. Back then, I was just a little chubby. Maybe 15 or 20 pounds overweight. It wasn't tragic, but it was just enough to be annoying. So I'd starve for a few days. But now, that I think about it," Billie Ray waved her carrot stick in the air. "This guy John, who I'd known most of my life, he told me I'd be beautiful if I lost just 10 pounds! Can you imagine being just 10 pounds away from BEAUTIFUL? Well, needless to say, that got my motor running."

"Before the prom, my best friend Tammie wanted to get skinny to fit in this slinky dress she wanted to get. So we started jogging. Back then, I had this magic number. If I could just get down 110 pounds, I'd be beautiful and my prince charming would show up. But I have to admit, I was pretty faraway from being a princess."

"The problem was, me and Tammie worked in a service deli in the neighborhood grocery store. So all day, we'd be frying up chicken, serving it up with potato salad. And then there's always the rice pudding, which I couldn't stop eating." Billie Ray's eyes twinkled as she told her story. "It was next to impossible to lose weight when I was surrounded with food all day!"

Oh, Rhoda could relate to that. Working in a diner, with the

French fries and blue cheese dressing, made it impossible to lose weight.

"Right about that time," Billie Ray waved her carrot through the air. "Jane Fonda, this famous actress came out and said she'd had this problem with food. It was the first time I ever remembered someone talking about bulimia. She wrote a book and I found it at the library. In the book, she talked about these vomitoriums. People actually gorged themselves with food and threw it up."

Chills went up Rhoda's spine when she heard the word vomitoriums. Now she knew someone was reading her thoughts. Cindy just said the same thing to her the night before. Her arm was covered in goosebumps.

"So one night, Tammie and me were working the closing shift at the deli. Halfway through the shift, we had a thunderstorm that knocked out the electricity. I guess it blew a couple of transformers in the neighborhood and it was dark for miles. The store shut down for about an hour, while they tried to get the generator to work. Tammie and I were almost finished closing up the deli, when they reopened the store. We got hit with a mad rush. It was crazy." Billie Ray crunched on a piece of celery with peanut butter.

"Now, after we got hit with this rush, we were pretty far behind with all the closing stuff we had to do. It was after midnight when our manager came back to find out how much more time we needed. We told him about 45 minutes. So we get done and we're ready to go home. But the doors are all locked and we need the manager to let us out. We got on the PA and started calling him, but he didn't come down. Then we figured he was upstairs in the manager's office, putting the money away. So we go up there, and try to open the door. Well that's when it got really crazy."

"THE STORE ALARM GOES OFF!" Billie Ray laughed. "And we go racing down the stairs to the front desk, waiting for the police to show up. The dang thing is so loud, it's blasting my ears!" Billie Ray chuckled. "But ten minutes go by. AND NOTHING HAPPENS! NOBODY SHOWS UP!"

There were a few chuckles and laughs in the room. Rhoda, who'd never heard such a story, was sitting on the edge of her seat.

"So here we are. Me and my best friend trapped in a grocery store in the middle of the night. The Night Crew won't be there for a few more hours!" Billie Ray let out this huge sigh. "It was a compulsive over-eater's dream! And we ate everything! I'd say the strangest thing we ate, was honey buns with oysters on them. WE TOTALLY PIGGED OUT!" Billy

Ray crunched on a granola bar. "By the time we got done gorging ourselves, we both looked 9 months pregnant. Then it hit us like a ton of bricks. To get into our prom dresses, we'd have to starve for weeks to get rid of all these calories. At that moment, we were pretty deflated. Until I remembered the vomitoriums! So I looked at Tammie and said, "Some people just throw this stuff up!"

"Next thing I know, we're downing a couple diet Pepsi's to loosen all the food up in our bellies, swishing it all around. And then we go up to the bathroom, bend over the toilet and 'WA LA,' it all comes up! I can't tell you how excited we were! When the night crew finally got there, we'd eaten more than 3 thanksgivings dinners worth of food. But we weren't done. After that, we went to the all night coffee shop, had waffles and pancakes, with chocolate shakes. And threw that all up too. By the time we got home at 5 am, I was pretty beat."

"Now, I wish I could say that was the craziest it ever got," Billie Ray went on. "But after that night, my dis-ease really took over. For the next 3 years, I binged, threw up, starved, exercised, starved some more, and binged. Over and over again. It was humiliating. It got so bad, that when my boyfriend took me out for Italian food, I'd eat everything I could. Then, I'd leave early, just to get a gallon of ice cream to throw it all up. The poor guy spent all that money to take me out, just to have me cut the evening short to go home and puke."

"I felt so guilty about doing that to him, but I couldn't stop. Even when I wanted to, I couldn't stop. In college, I was still living with my parents. My mom knew something was up. I'd make these big feasts for breakfast, watch TV and then go take a long shower. Well, she'd stand at the door, listening to me puke. Then she'd start pounding on the door because she knew what I was doing. I just kept yelling at her, that I was in the shower. But she didn't go away. It was humiliating."

"One day on campus, I run into Kay Lee putting up her silly little sign on the bulletin board, and I asked her about it. She told me to come to an OA meeting and find out for myself. Well, that was a few years ago now. And I've been abstinent ever since. I took a 5 year candle on July 7. And you know what, I can still fit into my skinny jeans." Billie Ray's face beamed. "If you're new here today, and nothing I said made any sense to you, please come back to a few meetings before you make a decision on whether this will work for you or not. My best advice is to go to meetings, get a sponsor and work the 12 Steps. It's been the best remedy for my food problem and my life," Billie Ray finished. "Now let's open up the meeting for people to share."

When she first got there, Rhoda had no intention of staying for the whole meeting. But something inside compelled her to sit and listen. Some people were going through tough times. It was so easy to reach for something sweet to quiet their nerves. Yet, they didn't. They came to meetings instead. One woman, the 300 pounder, said she just finished her third step with her sponsor and had lost over 75 pounds already. A frail looking young woman, dressed in baggy sweats and a baseball cap, confessed that she weighed only 49 pounds. But she couldn't bring herself to eat. She was under the constant care of her doctor. Hearing this, Rhoda almost balked out loud. After the meeting ended, Rhoda picked up a couple pamphlets about the OA food plan. It was a simple diet consisting of 3 meals a day, nothing in between.

Billie Ray came up to Rhoda as she was looking at the pamphlets. "Hi, I'm Billie Ray. Is this your first meeting?"

"Yeah why? Does it show?" Rhoda asked nervously.

"Oh, it's not like that. I just wanted to know if you had any questions?" Billy Ray offered.

A little flustered, Rhoda just sighed. "I'm just having some trouble with my food. Last night, it really scared me. I did something I've never done before. Today, I just feel disgusted with myself."

"Yeah, I know the feeling," Billie Ray offered.

"I felt so out of control," Rhoda admitted. "It's been like that for a while. But last night was the topper."

"Well, they have OA meetings all over the city," Billie Ray said. "If you didn't relate to my story, there are other people you might relate to."

"Oh, I related alright!" Rhoda admitted sheepishly. "That's whats bothering me the most. I related a little too well to all the stories."

"Admitting we have a problem is the first step in recovery," Billie Ray confessed. "I know I was pretty sick when I got here. But, it's been a few years. I'm pretty good with my food, so long as I stay close to people in the program. It's easy to lose your abstinence, if you get too far away from the program."

"Well, I guess I got a question," Rhoda started. "What is the difference between a diet and this word 'abstinence' that you keep using?"

"For me, a diet is a temporary thing. Where abstinence is a way of life. It's a way of eating that is not destructive," Billie Ray offered. "It's suggested that we eat 3 meals a day, with nothing in between. But not everyone has the same kind of abstinence. It's more like a personalized food plan, that doesn't set you up to fail, like a diet does. Because abstinence isn't just about losing weight, though you will. It's about eating in a good way, that will keep your body, mind and spirit healthy."

"Hmm," Rhoda toned. "I see."

"Abstinence is a right relationship with food. See if this explanation helps. Most compulsive over-eaters get triggered by something emotional," Billie Ray began. "And we use food to numb out. The OA program and the 12 Steps help uncover and heal the emotional baggage we have, so we don't have to use food destructively."

Feeling overwhelmed with all her emotional baggage, Rhoda just sighed. "Yeah, well I got baggage."

"Look, here's a meeting directory. I'll write my phone number on the back. If I can help you out some more, just call. I don't bite," Billie Ray's laugh was infectious. Rhoda felt better just talking to her. "When I first started coming to OA, I went to a lot of meetings. It helped me to not be alone with food and the obsession to eat all the time."

"Obsession is the right word. I work in a diner," Rhoda admitted. "And I think about what I'm NOT going to eat all day. And then when I get home, I just blow it."

"Yeah," Billie Ray chuckled. "I found that a lot of compulsive over-eaters work in the food industry. It's our first love."

"Right now, I hate food," Rhoda admitted. "But maybe I hate myself because I can't control it."

"That's how it is," Billie Ray said. "That's why we got the Twelve Steps, borrowed from Alcoholics Anonymous. Doing those will straighten out the mind."

"You know," Rhoda started feeling a little uneasy. "I don't have many memories before the age of five."

"Sounds like you had a lot of trauma," Billie Ray suggested.

"Trauma," Rhoda scoffed. "If you call being raised in orphanages and foster homes trauma."

"Oh wow," Billie Ray empathized. "Well, my sponsor, Sylvia, gave me this tool to get down to the hard parts that are buried deep in our soul wound. It's called left hand/right hand writing."

"Never heard of it," Rhoda asserted. "And believe me, they put me with plenty of shrinks to help me find out what my problem was. Those bastards even hooked me up to electrodes to erase my bad memories."

"Wow, I'm so sorry. That sounds pretty rough," Billie Ray said.

"It was," Rhoda confessed. "I never knew if I was coming or going. You never have the feeling that you're home. So how does this writing thing work?"

"Well, all you do is start a conversation with you and your inner self," Billie Ray began. "First you ask a question with your dominant hand, and then you let your other hand answer it."

"What, like my right hand asks a question and my left hand answers it," Rhoda clarified. "How's that supposed to work?"

"Well, I don't know how it works. It just does," Billie Ray admitted as she pulled a piece of paper and pen out of her knapsack. "Look, I'll show you how I do it. And you can take this home and try it for yourself."

On the paper, with her right hand, Billie Ray wrote a question to her inner child. "Dear little one, tell me about Uncle?" Then she switched the pen in her left hand, and allowed it to write on the page.

Without editing the inner dialogue, the inner voice answered. "You mean the one I like?"

"No, the other one," Billie Ray wrote back.

"He scares me," the inner voice responded.

"Why does he scare you?" Billie Ray asked.

"Because he's mean," the inner voice replied.

"And that's how it works," Billie Ray stated as she handed the paper to Rhoda. "You'll see, that anything you ask your inner person, they will answer you. It's worked for me for years."

Rhoda was fascinated as she looked at the writing. "This is what you do to get to your buried memories?"

"It's one way," Billie Ray admitted. The room was completely cleared out of people as they talked about how to do this work. "But look, we got to close the room. If you'd like to go to coffee, we can finish this conversation there."

"Oh, I'd like that but I got a 2 o'clock class," Rhoda grabbed her purse and the meeting directory. "I'll probably come back."

"We're here to be helpful," Billie Ray smiled. "See you later."

CHAPTER SEVEN: SPIRIT FOLLOWS SPIRIT

MIDNIGHT WARRIOR

Looking around, I hear the sound
Of my heart beating through my chest
I whisper to Creator
"Don't let me wind up like the rest."

Over sirens blazing, I hear His still Voice
"My son," He gently whispers, "You have another choice."
A gunshot whistles passed my head
On the ground next to me, Carlos is dead.

Blood is oozing from his tattered chest
As he whispers his last labored breath
"I'm sorry mom..."
He says

Looking around, I hear the sound
Of my heart beating through my chest
I whisper to Creator
"Don't let me wind up like the rest."

Around the table, money flows
A white powder goes up my nose
Chillin' with my brothers from the hood
For only a moment, do I feel good

Angry spirits are stalking
As I go on the street, walking
Trouble comes, I'm on the run
My heart's gone numb, it's no more fun

Looking around, I hear the sound
Of my heart beating through my chest
I whisper to Creator
"Don't let me wind up like the rest."

Chilled to the bone, I'm all alone
One tear rolls down my cheek
It hits the ground, without a sound
I pray my soul to keep

Eyes are bleary, soul's gone weary
Death becomes my friend
Give me a light for my unholy pipe
I'm glad this is the end

Another toke, my spirit's gone broke
As the night steals away my soul
An Owl flies, my spirit cries
Longing to be whole

Through an open door, awaits a corridor
I find a place to rest
No more falling, Great Spirit Calling
Midnight warrior passed the test.

Morning light is so bright
Coming through panes of stained glass
Now I'm home, not alone
There is peace at last

Looking around, I hear the sound
Of my heart beating through my chest
I whisper to Creator
"Don't let me wind up like the rest."

Before the Inipi ceremony that night, Hal and Leroy headed out a few hours early. Up the winding canyon was a spot where some White Grandma Sage grew. Hal wanted to bring enough for everyone to have a sprig. Off a small side road stood a lone cedar tree. Nothing was as fragrant as fresh cedar for the Stone People, which gave a blessing to everyone inside the lodge.

Driving into the canyon a ways, Hal pulled in a dirt outlet alongside the road. It was a little hard to see in the brush and tall shrub oak trees, but there was a small trail he used to hike when he lived out here. Maybe a short quarter mile up the trail, was a small outcropping of rock where a stream ran in the spring. Now the creek bed was bone dry. But there in the midst of it, was an island of White Grandma Sage.

Pulling a pouch of tobacco out of his back pocket, Hal took a pinch and made an offering to the Spirit of the Sage. He thanked her for the blessing she'd bring the people that night at the lodge. And for all her healing and cleansing qualities. Then he pulled off a stalk and held it to his nose, letting the full musky aroma fill his in-breath.

"What is that?" Leroy asked as he came up the trail.

"This little buddy, is White Grandma Sage," Hal took another whiff of her musky fragrance. "It's what they use out West to smudge off with."

"It looks a lot different from the prairie sage we use back home," Leroy commented.

"Prairie Sage has long stalks," Hal commented. "But this grandmother grows in bushes. After I harvest some, her scent is all over my hands. I love that smell." Handing Leroy a grocery bag and some tobacco, he said "Here go fill this up. We'll bring one bag to the lodge and keep one for home."

Leroy picked off a leaf of sage and put it to his nose. It was a good, strong smell. Taking a pinch of tobacco, he moved further up the stream-bed and made his offering. One thing about working with Hal, Leroy learned so many things. Maybe it was because he was well traveled, but Hal had an appreciation of all cultures. From the looks of it, Los Angeles had every race of people walking its streets.

Only the sound of the wind rustling through the leaves of the oak trees pierced the stillness in this small canyon above the misty seashore. On the trail a little farther up, was a Mighty Oak Tree. Its waxy leaves reflected the golden rays of the sun, as the branches danced to and fro with the wind. Scurrying across the stream-bed, a chipmunk carried an acorn in its mouth. While high above, two hawks circled the late afternoon sky. The chaparral of the West was dry and dusty.

After they collected a couple bags of Sage, Hal and Leroy got back in the truck. A few miles ahead, along the roadside standing sentry, was one lone cedar tree. Pulling over to the side, Hal got out his clippers. With a pinch of tobacco, he made an offering to the Spirit of the Cedar tree. In gratitude, he thanked the cedar for the blessing it gave the people. Cedar crackled when it hit the glowing hot stones inside the Inipi. The smoke was a blessing to everyone.

After gathering a few small branches of cedar, Hal put them on the dashboard of the truck. "Hey, toss a couple stalks of that Sage up on the dash," Hal instructed Leroy. "There's nothing like the smell of Sage drying in the truck."

It didn't take long for Hal to get up the canyon to the gate where the lodge was being held. True to his word, Nate put a red flag on the gate. Sometimes up these dirt driveways, it was hard to tell one from the other. Putting up a marker made for less trouble. When Leroy got out to open the gate, two big German Shepherds started barking. Hearing all the fuss, Nate turned around and quickly called back the dogs.

Pulling ol' Betsy through the gate, Hal gently eased the truck off to the side. Amidst the rolling hillsides, the property was covered with great Oak trees. Off to the right on a piece of flat land, was the Sacred Fire place and the Inipi. With a big smile, Nate strode across the drive and extended his hand. "How are you my brother?"

"Fair to midland," Hal grabbed Nate's arm and gave him a bear hug. "It's been a while, Nate. It's been a while."

"Well, you don't look worse for wear," Nate replied. "What brings you back out to California?"

"Roy sent us to fetch a horse," Hal replied as Leroy walked up. "Leroy this is Nate. We've known each other a good while."

"Hey," Leroy said as they shook hands.

"You know Nate, Leroy did 3 tours over there in the Middle East," Hal offered.

"Oh yeah," Nate responded. "What branch of service?"

"Marines," Leroy offered as he surveyed this beautiful piece of land.

"Hmm...," Nate toned. "Maybe you're the one I've been waiting for."

"Maybe?" Leroy's eyebrows raised in question.

"See that guy over there with the crew cut?" Nate looked toward the fire place. Leroy nodded yes. "Brian just got back from doing two tours." Nate shook his head. "I don't know what happened to him over there. But he's been in some trouble. Maybe he'll talk to you."

Reaching through the truck window, Hal grabbed the branches of cedar off the dashboard, and handed them to Nate. "Here's some fresh cedar for the stones tonight."

"Hmm," Nate chuckled. "That's good you brought that, because I just ran out."

"Oh and that ain't all," Hal said. "Leroy grab that bag of sage out of the back. I thought you might like some to put around the stone pit."

"That's good," Nate said. "Just hand it over to the fire keeper. He can take care of that."

"So your kids here tonight?" Hal asked, looking around to see some familiar faces. He'd known Nate's kids since the early days when they were small.

A pained look came over Nate's face. "Oh, you don't know, do you?"

"Know what?" Hal looked surprised.

"I got divorced," Nate looked down. "She took the kids." A deflated look crossed his face.

"Oh man, I'm sorry. I guess we haven't talked in a while," Hal's voice was full of compassion. "I was sure the boys would be helping you out around here."

"Yeah, I thought so too. But sometimes the Red Road shakes loose whatever isn't bolted down. Ceremony wasn't her way, but it is mine," Nate admitted. "She told the kids I abandoned them for ceremony. And now they want no part of it."

"Oh, that must sting," Hal empathized. "I'm sorry Nate. You know, they might grow out of it. Which one do you suppose will carry on your altar when you're done?"

"It don't work like that," Nate shook his head. "Spirit follows Spirit, not blood."

With his bronze, strong arms, Nate picked up an ax and walked with Hal over to the wood pile. There was some wood that needed splitting before the lodge. He was a big man, with dark compassionate eyes. Raised on the reservation, he'd seen the rougher side of life. Like many, who were swayed by the whiskey demons, he'd spent a night or two locked up. But now, after years of sobriety and ceremony, he poured lodges at the local prisons and helped introduce Natives, who got lost in the system, back to their traditional ways.

Around the Sacred Fire place that night, many tribes were represented; Arapaho, Cheyenne, Apache, Chickasaw, Kiowa, Choctaw, Ojibway, Cherokee, Lakota, Dakota, Ho-chunk, Yaqui, Pueblo, and Algonquin. They all found their way to Nate's fire place through the work he did in an alcohol recovery center for American Indians. Centuries ago, some of these bands would never mix. Yet today, facing a bigger enemy, they came together. Here, they found a powerful solution for a spiritual malady which almost destroyed their way of life.

In the sprawling city of Los Angeles lived some 200,000 people of American Indian ancestry. This came about through a series of federal laws passed between the 1940's and the mid 1960's. In a 1940 Census, only about 8 % of Indians were living in cities. But that started to change in 1943, when the US Senate commissioned a survey of living conditions on the Indian reservations. Their survey found that these conditions were extremely poor; alcoholism, poverty, homelessness, unemployment upwards of 80% or more, diabetes, poor healthcare and malnutrition. These horrid conditions were mostly blamed on mismanagement by the Bureau of Indian Affairs (BIA).

Instead of addressing the poor, third world conditions and finding remedy to correct them, this survey lead Congress to believe that the tribes no longer needed federal protection. Indians would be better off if they were independent. Some senators were so in favor of this Indian termination, they likened it to the freeing of the slaves in the Confederate States of America.

In the mid 1940's the United States government issued an "Indian Termination Policy." This moved to sever the special relationship between the tribes and the federal government. At that time, the driving belief of Congress was that conditions for American Indians would improve if they became part of the melting pot and assimilated into mainstream society. The intention was to grant American Indians all the rights and privileges of citizenship, to end their status as wards of the United States and reduce their dependence on the federal government. The policy terminated the US government's recognition of sovereignty of tribes and any federal aid which came along with being a federally recognized tribe.

The House Concurrent Resolution 108 of 1953 announced the official termination of the Flathead, Menominee, Klamath, Pottawatomie and Turtle Mountain Chippewa, as well as all tribes in the states of California, New York, Florida and Texas. From 1953 to 1964, the government terminated recognition of a total of 109 tribes and bands as sovereign dependent nations. This policy ended federal support of healthcare, education programs, along with police and fire department which were available to Indians living on reservations.

Public Law 280, which passed in 1953, gave State governments power over Indian reservations. This power had previously belonged to the federal government. This was done to disrupt the relationship between the federal government and the Indian tribes. Neither the State governments nor the American Indians were happy with this agreement. Now the states had more responsibility, but no funding. And American Indians were subject to new state laws they didn't want.

To move this new policy along, the federal government started the "Urban Indian Relocation Program" in 1952. Here, the federal government enticed those living on the reservation to move to seven major cities, in hopes of getting job training and securing good work. But like most federal programs, there were big flaws.

In the cities of Denver, Chicago, Los Angeles, San Francisco, San Jose, St. Louis, Cincinnati, Cleveland and Dallas, the BIA set up relocation offices. BIA officials recruited "Relocatees" from reservations around the United States. The BIA's main duties were to help the new arrivals get settled into city life by providing them with temporary housing, job counseling and training programs. But not all the promises were kept. Not everyone found a job. Most lived in poor, skid-row neighborhoods. Some got in legal trouble for drinking in public. And many were just homesick for their families and familiar countryside.

While some Indians returned to the reservation, those who stayed in the city, found other Natives, usually members from other tribes. Here a new generation of Indians was created through inter-tribal marriages. The children of these inter-tribal marriages shared an identity of two or more tribes.

Largely forgotten today, this little known federal program created one of the largest migrations of American Indians in US history. Between 1950 and 1980, some 750,000 American Indians left the reservation and moved to the city. By the year 2000, 64% of American Indians lived in the city. This was a huge increase from the 8% in 1940. This massive social experiment still impacts the First Nations People today.

But for every action, there is an equal and opposite reaction. To combat the bludgeoning of their Spirit and the assault on their human rights, the psychological and physical abuses, the thoughtless violations of their sacred grounds, the endless despair of imposed poverty, along with the injustice Native people suffered at the hands of a heartless white government for centuries, a Red Power Movement began in the 1960s.

In cities, far away from home across the United States and Canada, brothers and sisters of the Red Nation banded together. Forming a powerful, inter-tribal alliance, they challenged the policies of neglect imposed on their People by the Congress of the 1940's. Through public protests, they made their voices heard and demanded change. Under the guidance of their holy men and spiritual leaders, the American Indian Movement became a voice for change and empowerment. It lead to a rebirth of the Old Ways and the dignity of their people.

But like every rebirth, it comes with sacrifice, pain and sometimes blood. When the Winds of Change blow strongly, either it stirs up a little dust or it can shake loose the rafters. Through marches across the Nation's capitol in Washington, ancient ceremonies, gatherings at sacred sites and a take over of government offices, the Red Power Movement drove a piercing awl through the deafened ear drum of white government. Sympathetic celebrities championed their cause, bringing it to the forefront of the media throughout the world.

By the end of the 1970's, the Red Power Movement had a few hard-won victories. Without the threat of going to jail, they could finally pray in their ancient ceremonies. Almost a century had passed since that sacred right had been taken from the First Nations People. And so now, many years later, around a Sacred Fire place in canyons of Malibu, they needn't fear harassment from police, because their right to pray was protected by federal law.

After splitting nearly a half cord of wood, Hal, Leroy and Nate walked up to the blazing Sacred Fire place. "You still got that table set up for making prayer ties?" Hal asked Nate.

"Yeah, it's over there, by the Oak tree," Nate pointed towards the tree. Under the canopy of a mighty Oak tree, was a small table with a couple of chairs. In a wooden box were cut pieces of blue cotton fabric, a pouch of tobacco and some string to make the prayer ties with.

"You make prayer ties before the lodge?" Leroy asked Nate.

"That's the way my Elders taught me. We made 32 blue prayer ties before we went in the lodge," Nate started. "It gets the mind out of the work-a-day world, and brings it into a prayer focus. When you're finished, you hang them in the ribs of the Inipi over your head. After the lodge, either give them to the fire or hand them to the fire keeper and he'll take care of it for you."

"Hmm," Leroy toned. "I like that. It sounds like a good way to settle into ceremony."

"Hey Brian," Nate interrupted. "Come here a minute! I want you to meet somebody."

But he was far away, locked in another world. With a dazed, thousand yard stare, Brian's eyes gazed intently into the flames. The tongues of the licking fire, blazing around the wood while it heated the stones, held him spell-bound. Whatever happened around him, his gaze never faltered, it never left the fire. Even when Nate called him, he barely shifted his eyes. With soft and gentle steps, Nate moved towards him, with Hal and Leroy in tow. Kneeling down beside Brian, Nate gently spoke. "Hey Brian, you in there? I got somebody I want you to meet."

Brian nodded but barely looked up. Having seen this before, Hal thought Brian was shell shocked. If enough shells rained down on a soldier in combat, leaving him without a means to fight back, he might lock himself away. Though Brian's outer man was physically there, the inner man was completely disassociated. A few big pieces had broken off inside. It'd take a while to gather them all up again. Nate sat down on one side of Brian, Hal and Leroy sat down on the other.

"Brian, this is Hal and Leroy," Nate started. "Leroy was over there too, in the Middle East, same as you. Maybe you two could get acquainted."

Hal stepped back when Brian kept staring into the fire. He motioned to Nate to follow him, "How long's he been like this?" Hal asked. "He reminds me of those guys that got 'shell shocked' after heavy days of artillery fire."

"Hard to say," Nate replied. "About a month ago, I found him walking down the wrong side of the highway in rush hour traffic. He was shit-faced drunk, out of his mind." Nate shook his head. "So I took him home. I have a granny flat in the back, where he sleeps."

"Does he have any family?" Hal asked.

Nate shook his head. "I knew him when he was a boy, and his mom. Back then, I adopted him like my own," Nate admitted. "But while he was overseas, she overdosed. He came back for her funeral. But from the minute I laid eyes on him, I could tell something was wrong. He wasn't the same guy that went over there."

"None of us were, Nate," Hal admitted. "There were times when I swung wide for days. One minute, I'd be suicidally depressed, looking for a tree to hang myself. The next, I was all fired up, looking for a good time. Then I finally crashed. I lost control quite a few times before I got sober."

"Yeah, I know," Nate confessed. "I didn't come back the same guy either. Everything had to be fireworks, you know. I needed that adrenaline just to feel alive."

"Yeah, well you were a paratrooper. It takes guts of steel to jump out of a perfectly good air plane. Remember back when I was living in that chicken coop?" Hal reminded Nate.

"I can't call that living, Hal. You didn't look much better than Brian back then," Nate added.

"Yeah, well it took a while to choose a life of purpose and meaning, over a life filled with excitement and heartache. But we made it, didn't we?" Hal wondered. "We've been through hell and back, but we're sober now. Maybe we should let Leroy talk to him for a little while. Sometimes those who've been there, know the way out."

"No truer words were ever spoken," Nate said. While Hal talked to Nate about starting up sweat lodges for veterans over at the VA, Leroy sat with Brian at the fire. For a long time, they just sat there, saying nothing. Going back in his mind, Leroy remembered how he felt after he got discharged from the military.

"Hey, I was thinking of making some of them prayer ties," Leroy spoke after a long silence. "You want me to bring them over here and we can put them together in front of the fire?"

His nod was so subtle, that Leroy almost missed it. Inside, Brian was just trying to hold on, before he lost it all together. In his mind, was a raging firestorm which never calmed down. Replaying again and again in his mind's eye, he saw the face of one Marine who was struck down by mortar fire. His screams never left Brian's mind. As a combat medic, he tried to do everything he could to save him, CPR and all the rest. But he failed. Right in his arms, the man died. Those half-closed eyes stared blankly at Brian the whole time, while he tried to bring the Marine back around. Now the memory of those half-closed eyes haunted him. He might not be in the war anymore, but the war was inside of him. He was afraid if he let a little of it out, the whole world would explode. Just like it did in the desert of hell.

"I'll be right back," Leroy said. Inside Hal's truck was an abalone shell, some dried sage and a pouch of tobacco. After Leroy got that, he found the table under the Oak tree, where there was a small wooden box with small squares of blue cotton fabric and some string. He counted out 64 pieces for him and Brian. Maybe doing something simple would snap Brian out of his trance.

Putting everything between them, Leroy sat back down. In the abalone shell, he put some sage and lit it on fire. It burned for a few moments before it went out, making a trail of smoke. First Leroy smudged the fabric and string over the sage smoke. Holding a pinch of tobacco, Leroy smudged it off before he made his prayer. Afterward, he put the tobacco in the blue square of cotton, folded the corners and tied it with a slipknot. He was about halfway through his prayers, when Brian looked at him and broke the long silence.

In a quiet voice, Brian asked. "You ever been to Wounded Knee?"

"We drove by a couple times, but we didn't stop," Leroy admitted. "I just saw it from the road."

"My mom took me there, before I enlisted. I saw the monument with the names of all the people and warriors who got murdered there," Brian recollected. "I ran my fingers over their names," he paused. "They killed a lot of our people. I think she wanted me to think about what I was signing up for, before I went in, you know."

"Yeah," Leroy responded. "I got a mother bear like that. So I know that feeling. Where's your mom now?"

Hearing that question was like someone threw hot coals right on his heart. Flashing through his mind's eye, he saw his mom's lifeless body laying in the casket. The sharpest details of that day were seared into his brain, leaving him with profound agony and sadness. Her eyes were permanently closed. Wearing her favorite dress, she lay there, with pink lipstick on. Feeling jabbed with an invisible red hot, sharp poker, Brian could barely catch his breath. To control it, he froze inside. The pain in his heart radiated throughout his body. It felt like he was on fire. His jaw was clenched tight. And for a moment, he was scared. Scared of the fury. Fighting it, he just had to stay quiet. NOT TALK, or he might let go. Leroy sensed something was wrong, but didn't know what to do. He looked over at Hal and Nate. Hal caught his eye.

But he couldn't contain it. All the rage welled up inside him with the force of a tidal wave. A hot fury flashed in his eyes. Brian looked over at Leroy. "She DIED!" Brian snarled in a whisper. "SHE DIED!" He said a little louder. "SHE DIED!" His eyes finally filled with tears. Like a volcano, he started to explode. But he fought it. He was holding on, holding on, holding on. For dear life, he was holding on.

"I'm sorry man! I'm so sorry!" Leroy said. But the dam burst. Brian's rage screamed out. Nate and Hal came running over to see what they could do. Coming up behind Brian, Nate wrapped his big arms around him. Brian struggled to get free. But Nate wouldn't let go. He'd seen Brian go off before. It got pretty ugly. It was still a couple hours before the lodge, so there were just a few people there.

"Come on, let's go walk it off!" Nate demanded.

"I don't want to walk it off! I want to kick the shit out of somebody!" Brian retorted, breaking free from Nate's big bear arms. It didn't make sense! None of it made sense. He couldn't get it right in his head. After all the men he patched up and saved overseas on the battlefield. As a combat medic, he rushed to get them on the chopper so they could get doctored up. He couldn't save his mom.

Not afraid of a fight, Leroy put his long hair in a ponytail and stepped up. "You wanna go? Let's go," Leroy challenged. He knew that dangerous fury well.

"I ain't got no beef with you man," Brian stepped back, feeling the heat of the fire.

"I don't got a beef with you either," Leroy admitted. "But if you don't blow that shit off, it'll eat you alive! SO YOU WANNA GO OR

NOT?"

Stepping in, Nate held his hands up. "You guys take it outside the flags. This is sacred ground and I'm not going to have that bullshit in here."

A flash of lightning burst from Leroy's eyes. "Come on dip-stick!" Leroy smiled as he challenged Brian, punching his arm. "I'll race you up that hill and if you still got anything left after that, I'll see if you can kick my ass."

Feeling the punch land on his left shoulder, the challenge was on. With all his fury, Brian came up behind Leroy pretty fast. So Leroy kicked into high gear, sprinting faster than an arrow flies. As they sped past the Mighty Oak tree, they flew up the hill like they were being chased by a pack of hungry, howling wolves. By the time they reached the top of the fire road, a foggy mist had crept up the mountainside from the ocean. Sucking in gasps of that salty mist, both of them were pretty winded. Bent over with his hands on his knees, Leroy was breathing heavy. On a small flat spot of Earth overlooking the fog-covered Pacific Ocean, they were surrounded by an outcropping of large boulders and scrub Oak trees. It was a great place for a duel.

"So you know any martial arts?" Leroy asked while he caught his breath.

"Tai Kwon Do," Brian offered, as he wiped the beads of sweat off his face.

"You any good?" Leroy came back.

"I could kick your sorry ass," Brian shot back.

"Okay, MOUTH! Show me what you got! Let's go!" Leroy challenged again. Squaring off, Brian tried to punk Leroy out with his meanest, angry-eyed glare. Not impressed with the goofy, screwed up devil-eyes, soul-staring, punk gangster expression, Leroy just started laughing, which infuriated Brian even more. Drawing all that fury out, Leroy lunged forward and lead with a taunting open-handed smack. For a split second, Brian felt the sting on his cheek as he sized up Leroy. Without a doubt, Brian knew he could take him.

"You fight like a girl," Brian snarled, his cutting words meant to tear flesh.

"What, you think you can take me? Come on Sissy-boy," Leroy teased, while he danced around the imaginary boxing ring, jeering and laughing.

With nostrils flaring, these two hot-blooded stallions took their fighting stance. Pumped full of adrenaline, their fiery eyes locked onto each other, gauging every move. Then, with a snap of a twig, all hell broke loose. Balled up fists sliced through the duel charged air. In a flurry of round kicks, thrown and blocked punches, clouds of dust gathered and small pebbles flew everywhere. Sweat poured down their copper-colored faces, while their fiery, earth-toned eyes flashed with fierce determination. Neither would back down. With all their might, they beat the crap out of each other until they heard Nate's truck come bouncing up the fire road with his horn blaring.

"You two dumb shits almost done here?" Nate hollered out the cab window. "I got a lodge to run in a half hour and I'm not gonna be wondering what the heck happened to you!"

Laughing, Leroy slapped Brian on the back. "You feeling a little better now?"

With a broad smile, Brian just cracked up. All his fury was spent on chasing Leroy up the hill. Trying to kick the shit out of him was just another way to blow off steam. Both of them piled in the back of the cab laughing their asses off. With dust flying, Nate made a U-turn and drove back down the hill.

CHAPTER EIGHT: WELCOME HOME

DAKOTA EDEN

Above the clouds, there is a place
Where the buffalo roam free
It is a Dakota Eden
Where my Spirit longs to be

Though my soul must wander
Through these earthly Plains
The heartfelt cries of yesterday
Are washed away by rain

The wars now have ended
As Love makes its way
Healing our broken minds
And hearts made of clay

So gather round you wanderers
And listen to my tale
How hearts melded together
And their Love pierced the Veil

With help of the Nature Spirits
Earth, fire, wind and rain
No more are we separate
For Great Spirit will forever reign

Love is our Arbor
Our shelter from the storm
Circle up your wounded hearts
Our Spirits are reborn

Do no harm, my loved ones
Bear your heart in mind
Let Love always watch over you
Until the end of time

    With a blanket draped over his shoulder, Leroy walked deliberately through the dense mist. He held his sacred pipe close to his heart. In all directions, golden waves of buffalo grass spread out before him. On the footpath, he passed under the archway which bore a small cross in the center of it. Alongside the walkway was the marker, a memorial with many names engraved upon the stone pillar. Standing in front of the memorial, Leroy read the names of his ancestors who perished there. More than a century ago, their bodies were cast into a common grave, after the Christian soldiers had massacred his people. They were dancing the Ghost Dance.

    Centuries of war, defeat and heartbreak left a very deep scar, a soul wound, as it were. For many, these battle wounds lay hidden deep inside. It left them with indescribable pain. In their hearts, there was an open, gaping hole which by itself, refused to heal. With every war, it was ripped open all over again. All this trauma left a dense spiritual fog in the consciousness of mankind. Its hatred and anger lay like a thick, heavy blanket shrouding the whole of Earth.

    In the firestorm of battlefields, where bloodshed was the greatest, many souls of warriors wandered lost. Other more deadly ghosts kept fighting. Having blood on their hands, burdened their spirit with a great debt. The weight of that load forced these spirits to be with those of their own kind. That is, until they yearned for peace and reached upwards to the Love of Creator. Until then, their souls would remain, wandering through the Shadow-lands.

    As Leroy walked to the outer edge of the small graveyard, a

bareback rider came galloping out of the mist. His powerful bronze arms held a spear in one hand and the reins of his spirit horse in the other. His long ebony hair flew behind him as he stopped his horse short in front of Leroy. With flaring nostrils, the spirit horse whinnied, its warm breath creating a cloud of steam in the mist. The young Brave's fiery, sharp eyes met Leroy's gaze. Raising his spear, he hollered at Leroy. "What are you doing here? Can't you see we are fighting a war?"

"I've come to bring you home, my brother," Leroy said. "Aren't you tired of fighting?"

To answer Leroy's question, the Warrior parted the mist with a wave of his hand. In that instant, Leroy saw the overwhelming horror of this spiritual storm. Blood-stained battlefields were the claimed and guarded territory ruled by the warlords of darkness and all their minions. With relentless hate, these fiendish henchmen held onto their demonic kingdom and the ragged human souls who died there. Betrayed by life, these wicked human spirits, boiling with evil, unloaded their poisonous venom on the dead and living alike.

In a flash of fireworks, Leroy saw the bold, cocky sinister forces which only spirit-eyes could see. Before him was a wild flurry of clashing swords and exploding, hate-laden cannon balls. Fire ripped through the air, destroying the war-torn countryside. Clouds of bloodthirsty, jeering demons beat their black wings through the smoke filled skies. Deafening war cries of maimed soldiers charged the atmosphere. Tearing through the air with leathery black wings, snarling ghouls battled viciously, striking at their enemies with blades of hell. All the while, the dark lords tallied their growing victories over human souls. With a roaring, spiteful laugh, one yellow-eyed demon warlord rode astride a screaming black missile, spewing evil and hate. Smokey black clouds were streaked through with trails of burning fire. Trapped by their own vengeance, some sagging, ragged soldiers had been fighting in the In-between for eons.

"But don't you see, all this war lays a heavy burden on our people," Leroy shouted over the din of battle to the young Brave. "They are choking on this poison and drowning from all the hatred and fighting. It fills our people with despair."

"But the soldiers keep coming! The soldiers keep coming!" the young Brave yelled. Over the killing fields, the souls of fallen soldiers from every war streamed in. It seemed endless.

Throwing his hands in the air, Leroy felt overwhelmed as he looked over at Hal. "This is going to be more than a one day ceremony!"

"Ya think!" Hal booming laughter echoed across the killing fields as the young Brave faded into the mist and was gone.

"YEOW! HISS! CRASH! BANG! BOOM!" Outside his window, something clattered to the ground. Rattled out of his sleep, Leroy heard the strangled yowl of two felines caterwauling. Slowly opening his eyes, he looked out the window to see what was making the noise. Under the strong light of the full moon, a flash of yellow fur streaked through the yard. Through the glass door, moonbeams streamed into his room, casting an eerie glow. It took a few minutes to settle into being awake. His dream still hung heavy in the air.

Getting out of bed, Leroy walked into the kitchen to get something to drink. As he opened the refrigerator door, the light inside flooded through the kitchen. In the door was a gallon of orange juice, fresh squeezed, from a farm down the road. After Leroy poured himself a glass, he went to sit out on the back porch swing. Gazing out over the sparkling ocean, the moon lit up the foamy white crest of the waves. The crashing sound of long breakers filled his ears.

In his mind, he kept going back to the dream. The pieces of his life began to make sense. For years, he wondered why things happened the way they did. Now the puzzle pieces were falling into place. There was a greater purpose to all of this. One that he was just beginning to understand.

But he would have missed it all, if Hal and Kyle didn't show up years ago and pulled him out of his alcoholic stupor. Pulling a quilt over his shoulders, he began to understand the Grand Weaver of the blanket of Life. How each happening, each person was a sacred piece of yarn woven into the intricate pattern of every life.

As he finished his orange juice, the ocean beckoned to him. Something in his Spirit felt compelled to take a run. Dawn would be here soon. And this morning, he could run like the wind. It only took a few minutes to throw on his sweats and running shoes. Not wanting to wake Hal up, he crept quietly through the house and went out the side gate by the garage.

Thick like pea soup, a heavy mist hung over the shoreline. There was no sound, save his footfalls and the thunder of the crashing surf. The scent of citrus blossoms and jasmine floated through the morning mist. Within moments he found his rhythm as he trekked down the the winding road towards the beach. When he hit the sand, Leroy took off his shoes.

Small clouds of steam formed each time he exhaled. Unlike the hard asphalt, the cool sand gave way to his feet. It felt good as he raced down to the water.

Before he met Hal, Leroy was one of the greatest scoffers of anything spiritual. He thought it was just a crutch people used to get through everyday life. But now, after years of sobriety and ceremony, he saw Spirit everywhere. Even last night, when he sat around the fire with Brian, he saw how Spirit worked to break the spell which the trauma of war had cast over him. No, he'd witnessed too many miracles, where Spirit touched ground, to think otherwise. The more pure his inner life became, the easier it was to see Spirit in all things. Though a shred of his pride would hate to admit it, Leroy had become a spiritual man.

The bubbling sea foam ebbed across the shoreline as the waves went back out to sea. Under his pounding footfalls, he felt the small sand crabs burrow into the wet sand. They left small bubbles where the Sandpipers quickly followed to get some breakfast.

In this world of fire and ice, life must be experienced to draw out the jewels of wisdom and find a meaningful purpose. Sitting with Brian, Leroy found compassion for a brother trying to heal his inner war wounds. Because he had lived through that same agony himself. To own it, he had to live it. At that moment, he felt great appreciation for Hal, who came along at just the right time, and compelled him change his life.

In small demonstrations of compassion, the Great Weaver made Himself known. It took courage to lift up the downtrodden; to alligator wrestle with them in their greatest time of need. But this is what a man of courage was for. Courage came from the heart. It had little to do with great intellect, big money or increasing power. It required true grit and elbow grease to do acts of kindness which inspired and empowered others.

Of course, having free will coupled with clouded minds, not everyone would get it. For water always sought its own level. A man had to be willing to reach upwards before a change could come. But even then, a true healer of the soul didn't need to tear a man down in order to doctor him. First he began by looking for the half-asleep good qualities in a person and nudged them gently awake. Afterward, he used true spiritual principles, such as love and tolerance to build up their lagging spirit. With gentle prodding, a change of wrong desires would slowly come about. The doctoring transformed these wrong desires through a spiritual understanding. A pure mind is strong because it knows the truth.

Thinking about the dream, Leroy knew he was being called to a Higher Branch of Service. As he raced to the cliffs, he stopped to climb on the rocks at the end of the beach. Standing there staring out at the thundering surf, he raised his hands to the sky and called out. "Great Spirit, what would You have me do? I AM but one man. How can I change all this?"

The roaring surf pounded and pounded relentlessly on the walls of the cliff. Clattering stones tumbled against each other as each wave shifted them back out to sea. It was a raucous, natural melody coupled with the whistling wind coming around the cliff. Finally, sitting back on a jetty of rock, Leroy looked out at the enormous ocean. Then out, from under the surf, appeared the head of a small young blue whale. Its head bobbed up and down in the waves. For a moment, Leroy felt awe, looking at one of Nature's greatest creatures. It was a moment out of time, surreal, timeless.

Slowly, the sand dried on the bottom of his feet. Brushing off the grains of sand from between his toes, a thought occurred to him. As he rolled a grain of sand between his fingers, he realized these small grains of sand had once come from the cliff. Everyday the waves pounded the rock, making one stone grind against another. However many lifetimes it took, the ocean never stopped sending waves to grind the stone into sand. The waves just kept coming.

All he had to do was make a start. Creator would send in new recruits to keep the mission going. "Thank you Great Spirit and my Lady of the Ocean. You've showed me what I need to do."

With that, his stomach started to growl. Over the hillsides in the East, the rising sun slowly burned a hole through the mist. At the foot of the cliffs, wild flowers bloomed along a narrow foot path going up the hill. Racing back to the spot where he left his shoes, Leroy spotted an old surfer van. Along the side panel was an old, cracked painted mural, probably something out of the 1960's. Leroy heard there were camps of old hippies living in the hillsides out West. But at the very top of the mural was a small cross over a broad archway. Underneath it read, "REMEMBER, GREAT LOVE AND GREAT ACHIEVEMENTS INVOLVE GREAT RISK."

"Ah," Leroy toned. "That's what You wanted me to see."

Behind the open back doors of the van, stood a long haired, bearded fellow pulling on his wet suit. "You talking to me?" the old fellow asked.

"Oh, I didn't know anyone was there," Leroy laughed. "I was just reading your sign. I think I was meant to see that today."

"Oh, ya mean my old surfer's creed," the old man smiled. "My ex-wife used to think I was crazy going out into a 15 foot swell. One day, she told me if I died out there and made her a single mom, she'd come out in the water and kill me again!"

"Yeah, I can see where that be risky," Leroy chuckled.

"But you'd have to be out there to experience the Great Love," he smiled pointing out at the water. "When a man conquers his fear, he gets to know what 'great achievement' is."

"I'd say you're right about that," Leroy said as he dusted off his feet and put on his running shoes. After a short run up the winding road, his peaceful morning was disrupted by the cacophony of leaf-blowers, lawn mowers and helicopters reporting the morning car crashes, clattering overhead. The smell of gasoline and street dust assaulted his sinuses. Pulling trash cans into the air with a mechanical arm, a noisy garbage truck rumbled down the neighborhood streets. Off in the distance, he heard the morning rush of traffic, coupled with blaring sirens screaming down the highway. When he walked in the door, Leroy found Hal sitting in the kitchen drinking his morning brew.

"Well, you're up pretty early," Hal said as Leroy sat down at the table.

"Yeah, I had this powerful dream. Then I heard the cats making the worst noise," Leroy offered.

"Yeah, those darn yowling cats. Sometimes you got to throw a shoe at them to get them to shut up and move along," Hal said. "So what was your dream?"

Leroy poured himself a cup of coffee. "I think I was at Wounded Knee," he started. "I had my Cannupa in my hand, when this rider, a warrior, came riding out of the mist."

"You were at the Knee?" Hal pondered. Rays of the morning sun streamed into the kitchen windows, lighting up the room.

"Yeah, and I was there to do some kind of ceremony to help the Spirits go home," Leroy surmised.

"That'd be a heck of a ceremony. I suspect it'd take some real fire power to get all that darkness moved out of there," Hal added.

"Well, you were there, you were in the dream with me," Leroy came back. "The Brave kept saying 'The soldiers...'"

"Keep coming," Hal finished his sentence. "The Soldiers keep coming." Hal looked at Leroy in disbelief. "I don't know what to say, Leroy. I've heard about this before, people having the same dream. But I never had it happen to me." Hal scratched the top of his head, like he was trying to remember more of the dream. "What do you think this means?"

"Heck if I know," Leroy started. "But I think we're supposed to go to Wounded Knee."

"I think you might be right," Hal admitted. "I might need to square this away with some of the Elders. I don't want to ruffle any feathers. But this seems like an important mission to me."

"Maybe it was just a dream," Leroy started doubting.

"That weren't no dream, Leroy. Spirit showed you and me what's got to be done, and we don't have the right to question it. All you can decide now, is if you are IN OR OUT," Hal stated firmly.

"Of course I'm in," Leroy affirmed. "I has holding my pipe in my hands when that Brave came riding out of the mist and talked to me. How could I not be in?"

"Just checking," Hal confessed as he got up to refill his morning coffee. "I've seen people back out of their visions before, and they suffered for it. I'm not sure how to pull this off, but I got a feeling someone does. So we'll just see what we got to do to get her done."

"I saw my first hippie down at the beach this morning," Leroy chuckled. "He had this mural painted on the side of his van. It said: "Remember, Great love and Great Achievement involve Great Risk."

"Kinda a crusty looking old saw-tooth?" Hal asked as Leroy nodded his head. "That must have been old Harry," Hal chuckled. "He was always talking about the Dalai Lama or something zen like that. For years he'd try to get me out there on one of his long boards. But I told him, Indians don't swim!"

"Well you don't," Leroy laughed. "But I swim and I'm Indian."

"Yeah, I remember how well you did in the water," Hal poked at Leroy. "But listen up, I'm thinking of going into town and getting breakfast. There's a diner I haven't been to in a while and the cook there makes a mean chile relleno omelet."

"That sounds good to me, I'm pretty hungry," Leroy offered. It didn't take them long to get showered up and get on the road.

****

Standing at the counter, Rhoda was eying the coconut custard pie sitting inside the glass door of the display refrigerator. All this gnawing temptation made her a slave to her stomach. Now, her food was completely out of control. Without a second thought, she could slide a whole slice of pie down her throat. Once she started her feeding frenzy, she became a ravenous shark, gobbling up everything in sight. Just looking at the pie, the battle for control was already starting.

For the last few months, every night after work, she had a food orgy at her studio apartment. One dismal, endless night, she went out in the rain dressed in only her housecoat and slippers, to buy another pint of ice cream and a box of donuts. No matter how many times she willed herself to stop eating voraciously, it didn't work. Working in a restaurant made it very hard to stick to her diet. Most of the time, she'd start binging right after her lunch break. It didn't stop until she demolished a pint of ice cream and then threw the whole mess up. None of her pants fit her anymore. Even though she went to a few of those Over-eater Anonymous meetings, she didn't really feel like the program was working for her.

Opening the door of the diner, Hal was in a talking mood. "Look Leroy, we got to give them the best of what we got or somebody's going to die. When people start messing with the 12 Steps, they slide down a slippery slope. Most of them end up dead! I've met drunks who prayed on their knees every night to a porcelain god, but couldn't humble themselves before their own Creator. Sobriety is the only gift I know of, where you got to make sacrifices in order to save your own life. Humble means teachable, Leroy. There ain't no other way. Most of these yahoos want the gift of sobriety but they don't wanna do the work!"

When she heard the word "sobriety" Rhoda's ears pricked up. Her OA sponsor, Billie Ray suggested going to AA meetings to listen to them talk about sobriety. "Sit anywhere you like gentlemen," Rhoda called out to Hal and Leroy as she grabbed a couple menus. Her tight stretch polyester pants made her feel like an overstuffed sausage. With her thighs rubbing together, she waddled over to their table. "How you two doing today? Can I get you some coffee and orange juice," Rhoda suggested.

"Make me one of those Arnold Palmer concoctions, you know the lemonade mixed with ice tea," Hal said. "I already drank a half a pot of coffee this morning."

"Make that two," Leroy added, as he looked at all the pictures of movie stars hanging all over the wall. Most of them were signed. At the tables in the center of the diner, were a couple guys with cowboy hats on. They were talking about doing stunts on a movie set. At the counter, sat an old actor who played Moses on the Big Screen, drinking a glass of chardonnay and reading a thick book. A relation of the late folk singer Woody Guthrie sat at the counter, reading the morning paper.

"Is Rudy still working back in the kitchen?" Hal asked. "He knows the omelet I'm thinking of."

"Rudy's off today, but Izzy's back in the kitchen. Honestly, Izzy makes a better omelet than Rudy," Rhoda confessed. "Rudy always overcooks them."

"Yeah, Rudy makes me a mean chile relleno omelet," Hal said. "It's been a few years since I've been here."

"Don't you worry. Izzy can cook you up an omelet that will make your mouth water," Rhoda asserted. "We don't have that one on the menu anymore, but I know he can make it up. It might take a couple of extra minutes to get the ingredients together."

"Take your time," Hal said. "But bring me a side of them multi-grain blueberry pancakes instead of toast."

Rhoda turned towards Leroy. "Do you know what you're having already?"

"I'll have what he's having. It sounds really good," Leroy sat back and relaxed.

"Now, do you want the hot salsa that Oscar makes just for the cooks in the back? It'll burn a hole in your stomach, just by looking at it. Or do you want the mild one we get from the jar?" The old regulars, who knew the special menus, were more likely got get the house salsa than the store-bought.

"You mean Oscar's still making that red salsa with all the seeds in it," Hal chuckled. "You could burn a hole through a steel pipe with that flaming sauce."

"Yes he does, and he just made up a fresh batch this morning," Rhoda smiled.

"Well, bring me some of that. But ask Izzy if they have some of that Salsa Verde to go with the eggs. I'm not sure I can stomach Oscar's fire breathing dragon salsa all over my omelet. I won't be able to taste anything for a week," Hal laughed.

"Sure thing, I saw Oscar making his Salsa Verde earlier," Rhoda said before she walked off to put in the order and get their drinks.

"So what do you think about Brian?" Leroy finally asked.

"Well, Leroy," Hal started. "A man can't mount two horses at the same time. It's one or the other, recovery or death. I've seen his kind before. He's so twisted up inside from what he saw over there, on top of his mom's suicide."

"Was it suicide?" Leroy asked confused. "I thought she just O.Ded."

"I don't see much difference between the two," Hal answered. "If an addict puts too much dope in the needle, and shoots up, well, the results are the same."

"Yeah, it's sad," Leroy empathized. "I can just imagine how much pain he's in."

"Well, I've been there," Hal confessed. "I held Arlene's dead body in my arms after she mixed sleeping pills with booze. I carried that guilt with me for a long time. But with drunks and addicts, it's either ruin or redemption. Surrender is a BITCH, Leroy. You don't got too many other choices."

Sauntering in from the outside patio, came one of the morning regulars, Moe from Chicago. Though his given name was Maurice, everyone called him Moe. From his rougher days, he had one lazy eye that wandered when he looked at you. Before the diner opened, he pulled up in his ivory Cadillac and coveted the patio table closest to the hotel pool. That way, he and his cronies could watch the girls go swimming. Grabbing the pot of coffee, Moe waved it at Rhoda. "I'll get my own coffee, Rhoda. Since it looks like you're busy," he chided. He loved giving her a hard time. Being mostly retired from the Mafia, Moe moved out West for the California sunshine.

"Oh, stop bothering me," Rhoda shot back as she waved Moe off. Standing at the computer terminal, Rhoda was in earshot of everything Leroy and Hal were talking about. She hung onto every word, as if they were talking to her. After putting in their order, she went back in the kitchen and told Izzy about the two salsas Hal wanted. Not wanting to miss much of the conversation, she quickly got the two Arnold Palmers together and brought them back out to the table.

"You know Leroy, if Brian is one of us, he's got to decide that for himself. The only thing we can't give him is the willingness to recover. That he's got to pray up all on his own. If a man wants help, he's got to reach up to Creator and ask. Not the other way around," Hal surmised. "Creator don't come chasing after drunks. He only steps in when asked."

"'Here you go gentlemen," Rhoda said as she put the Arnold Palmers on the table. "I talked to the cook about the omelets and it's all good to go."

"Well, thank you ma'am," Hal said as he took a sip of his drink. "Ah, that's good."

On a whim, Rhoda leaned in real close to the table and whispered. "I couldn't help but overhearing, but are you friends of Bill W.?"

A knowing smile spread across Hal's face. "Yes ma'am, we are, that is I am. I can't speak for Leroy over here." Leroy just chuckled and nodded his head.

"Well, ya see," Rhoda kept whispering. "My sponsor had me start going to AA meetings. But I got problems with food. So I'm not sure I'm doing the right thing, ya know."

"Well," Hal started in his most soft spoken voice. "Sometimes you got to change your playgrounds and your playmates, if you want something else. I'd have a devil of a time getting sober working in a brewery, but I know a man who did. How's a person supposed to get clean when they're surrounded by temptation?"

"Oh, I see what you mean," the lights went on in Rhoda's eyes. "You think working in a diner is too tempting?"

"Well, only you can answer that question, ma'am," Hal responded kindly. "I'd be staring at those pies all day long, if I had to work here."

"Oh, those damn pies!" Rhoda finally admitted. "I can't go a day without finding the broken piece and eating it all up. The other day, I smashed a piece to bits just so I could eat it."

"That's what I mean. You're surrounded by temptation," Hal whispered. "See, to get rid of a weed, you gotta pull it out by its roots. Otherwise it grows back. When you got a weakness, it's like a weed. It's got to be done away with altogether. Otherwise, it gets deadly. First it numbs your heart. Then it messes with your mind and last, it destroys your body."

"You know something, you're absolutely right," Rhoda stood up. "I didn't want to face it before, because I thought I was just being weak. But I am weak around this food."

"It says in the Big Book, we had to concede to our innermost selves that we were alcoholics, being that that was the first step in recovery. I don't think it's much different with food," Hal added.

"Hmm," Rhoda toned. "I'm so glad you came in here today. You helped me see something I wasn't willing to look at. I didn't want to admit that I was powerless over food. I mean it's just food. It just lays there, doing nothing. How can I be powerless over something that's dead?"

"Does it talk to you? Call to you?" Hal asked knowing the answer.

"You bet it does," Rhoda admitted. "It gets me up in the middle of the night. I stand there with the refrigerator door wide open and I don't remember how I got there."

"Then it's not dead," Hal replied. "That's a powerful temptation when it gets you out of bed."

"You can say that again," Rhoda shook her head. "Nighttime is the worst. Sometimes I'm afraid to lay down and go to sleep. These awful memories pop into my mind and keep me awake."

"Fear is one of the deadliest emotions we got," Hal agreed. "It steals away our peace."

"Hmm," Rhoda pondered. For years in jail, she had good reasons to be afraid, because bad things kept happening. But now, all that was behind her. Yet, those lurking memories still crowded into her mind. "So what do you do when you can't sleep and you got these terrible images going through your head?"

"Well, I like to sleep with a light on myself," Hal admitted. "But reading seems to work for me. But if I got something I gotta get off my chest, I do a spot check inventory and put it out on paper. That way it's not rattling around in my brain anymore."

Just then Izzy rang the bell in the kitchen window, letting Rhoda know her order was up. "I'll be right back with your food, gentlemen."

Leroy just sat back and smiled. Wherever they went, Hal just had a way about him. People felt safe to tell him their most embarrassing stuff.

"What?" Hal jested. "I was just carrying the message." Leroy laughed.

That afternoon, when Rhoda was done with her shift, she stood outside Clark's office, mustering up her courage. Riddled with anxiety, she paced outside the office door, while he was on the phone with the vendors. Clark and his wife owned the diner for the last 20 years. But Rhoda made up her mind, she wasn't going to let food rule her life anymore. When she heard him hang up the phone, she knocked on the door.

"Hey Rhoda, how was the day today?" Clark asked, leaning against his paper cluttered desk.

"It was alright," she stammered a little, wringing her apron in her hands. "I got something to say and I'd like you to let me finish before you interrupt me."

"Okay, what is it?" Clark agreed.

"I gotta quit the restaurant, Clark. And it's not because you or anybody did anything wrong," Rhoda started. "I just can't work here anymore."

"But we really like you Rhoda..." Clark responded, his brow furled at this news. "You're good with the customers, and a hard worker. I'd hate to replace you, when it takes so long to train a new person. What's the problem?"

Getting all flustered, Rhoda just blurted it out. "I got to quit Clark! No offense to you or your wife, but I just can't work here anymore!"

"But I don't want to let you go," Clark got adamant. "It's too hard to find someone that people like. Even when you get uppity with them, they still like you."

"Yeah," Rhoda was almost in tears. Every nerve in her body was on fire. She felt herself get hot as the words burst out of her mouth. "But you don't understand, Clark. I eat a whole pieces of coconut custard pie without chewing and throw it all up in the bathroom. I can't stop eating and it's killing me. I'm sorry Clark. I didn't want to say this, but I got to leave this place today!"

Clark took a deep breath. "I'm sorry Rhoda. You're right, I didn't understand. It'll take a few days to get your paycheck together and I'll mail it to you. You got all your hours on the time card, right?"

"Yeah, it's all there," Rhoda sniffled. "I'm sorry too. I really liked working for you and your wife. I'll see you later, okay?"

"Sure thing," Clark replied as he watched Rhoda walk out the restaurant door.

Running to her car, hot tears streamed down her face. A firestorm erupted in her mind as all her inner demons came unleashed. Fumbling with her keys, her hands shook madly as she tried to unlock the car door. Streaks of black mascara mixed with her tears. Black circles formed under her eyes. Inside the car, she looked in the mirror. Her eyes, black like a raccoon's mask, were filled with self-loathing. *"You stupid idiot!"* her insides screamed. *"Why'd you have to go an tell Clark what a sick loser you are! STUPID! STUPID! STUPID!"*

Rhoda felt entirely humiliated confessing her deep, dark secret to her boss. Why didn't he just let her go? Why did he have to ask so many questions? Without even knowing how she got there, she found herself in a burger joint drive-through. Visions of chocolate shakes, brownies, eclairs, ice cream, danced through her head. Powerless to stop herself, she order all the foods she swore she'd never eat again. This was it! Her last binge, she promised herself.

Hours after throwing it all up, she finally called her sponsor and told her the big events of the day. Her sponsor told her to pray about it and that she'd meet her at an OA meeting in the morning. Rhoda scoffed like she always did. God, what God? But she remembered what Hal had said about willingness being the only thing he couldn't give that poor kid who lost his mother. Rhoda knew that emptiness only too well herself.

So that night she found a different attitude, a willingness she didn't know she had. In front of her bed, she humbly got on her knees. "God please help me. I'll do anything to get this devil monkey off my back. I quit the diner, so I wouldn't be tempted every day. But I can't do this alone. I need help."

The next morning Rhoda woke up with a food hangover, feeling a little shaky. Looking in the mirror, she dreaded going to an OA meeting. But she made herself go anyway. Billie Ray told her that she only had to go to meetings until she wanted to. Rhoda laughed. Like what, did Billie Ray think she was stupid?

Getting there a few minutes early, Rhoda sat in the parking lot, staring at that stupid, faded pink door that had OA in black bold letters written on it. It'd been over 6 months since she went to her first OA meeting. In that time, she'd string a few days together without binging and throwing up, but she could never control her food for very long.

Another car pulled up. It was the secretary of the meeting, Stella. Rhoda waved as they made eye contact.

By Rhoda's standards, Stella was alright. Rhoda watched her get out of the car and start to open the meeting hall door, when she turned around. Then to her horror, Stella walked up to Rhoda's car. Rhoda rolled down the window.

"Hi Rhoda, you're here early," Stella said. "How'd you like to lead the meeting this morning?"

Scared to tell the truth, Rhoda almost declined. "Me?" Rhoda asked, making a mental note to NEVER come early to a meeting again. "Are you sure you want to ask me to lead a meeting?"

"Well, sometimes the best way to own your seat is to tell your story," Stella smiled, like she knew a secret. "It's just a 10 minute share, and then you take hands. It's pretty easy."

"But I don't have a whole day yet," Rhoda tried to weasel out of it.

"Oh," Stella started. "If I waited until everybody had a perfect abstinence, we'd never have a program. All you got to do is tell the truth."

There was a quiet surrender in Rhoda's eyes. Something told her she was ready. "Okay, I'll do it. But..."

"Great," Stella said, looking relieved. "Look, in AA, those guys put the plug in the jug and never have to take another drop of alcohol as long as they live. They don't need it to live. But for us, here in OA, we got to take the tiger out of the cage three times a day and play nice with it. It's progress not perfection."

Slowly the parking lot filled with cars. All the familiar faces were there. Each one took their seat while the coffee brewed on the back table. Nervously, Rhoda took her seat next to Stella and flipped through the notebook with the meeting format. This was the first time she'd lead a meeting. The butterflies in her stomach were doing somersaults while the clock signaled it was time for the meeting to start.

Glancing around the room, Rhoda felt calm as she looked into all the loving eyes in the room. Sylvia, Billie Ray, Fanita, Giselle, Phyllis, Lisa, Shirley and Marty all smiled as she introduced herself as a compulsive over-eater and bulimic. For 20 minutes, Rhoda sat in the front of the room and told them her whole story. There wasn't a dry eye in the whole place. After the meeting ended, people came up and hugged her. They thanked her for her honest share because most everyone had felt the same way she had at one time or another. For the first time she felt truly accepted. All the love in the room wash over her, she was finally free.

"Welcome home," Stella whispered in Rhoda's ear, giving her a great big hug.

CHAPTER NINE: A POWERFUL PRAYER

Silent giant Redwood trees
The wind rustles through their leaves
The raven sounds his echoing caw
I stop for a moment to feel the awe

The silent forest is filled with sound
Yet there are no others like me around
My footfalls crackle with each step
As my troubles of life, I soon forget

As the natural sounds soothe my soul
The peace returns that the city once stole
Within me awakens the Holy of the Holy
Great Spirit brings forth, oh such glory

The winter of my soul turns to spring
In this glory of wonder do I sing
Hear the Voice, please hear my plea
Now, with open eyes, do I see

Barreling down the highway in the wee hours before dawn, Hal's old beater truck lead the way of a small caravan of cars. Above them, twinkling stars blanketed the big sky as their headlights cut through the dark. Word traveled fast on the Red Road Highway about Leroy and Hal's vision. That by itself, didn't surprise Hal none. But that morning, seeing the long line of cars parked on the side of the road by the ceremony site, put a big lump in his throat.

"Would you look at that Ben! Three of those cars are from California! That one's from Florida and there's a few from Oregon," Hal was beside himself.

"I suspect there's more than 70 cars here this morning," said Ben looking around as they drove through the dawn's early mist. It was still a good couple hours before sun-up. From across the way, Ben saw the glowing golden flames from the Sacred Fire reaching towards the sky.

As Hal pulled the truck into the make-shift parking lot set up for elders and helpers, there was a mini-van with New York license plates which read "Disabled Veteran WW2." Holding onto a walker, an elderly man, wearing his Dress Blues covered with medals, slowly ambled across the parking lot towards the fire. Right next to the mini-van, was a truck. Its license plate read: NAVAJO CODE TALKER.

"Oh man," Hal choked back the emotion. "I had no idea. Did you know the Navajo Code Talkers outsmarted the Japs in World War 2?"

"I heard about that," Leroy piped up from the back. "The Japs couldn't break the code of the Navajo language."

"That's how we beat them," Hal started. "But I don't think they let that secret out until the 1960's. So most of those Navajo warriors never got recognized until much later."

Dressed in camouflage fatigues, walked a younger soldier with two prosthetic legs. Seeing the man's face, Leroy thought he recognized him. "Stop the truck HAL!" Leroy shouted from the back seat. "I think that's Turtle from my unit!" With his sacred pipe slung over his shoulder, Leroy barreled out of the truck. Thunderstruck, Hal and Ben watched as Leroy ran up to the soldier and threw his arms around him.

"Now that about does it for me, Ben," Hal whispered as a lone tear ran down his face. Finding a place to park, Hal and Ben got out of the truck. There were people milling around everywhere.

"There must be over a hundred people here," Hal admitted as he looked around the ceremonial grounds.

"There are even more souls than that," Ben gathered as Tat-tey, the Wind, made whirlwinds around the fireplace. In the midst of all these strangers was a unity, a oneness of Spirit. In this humble Native cathedral, love was the true inhabitant.

Traveling from far and wide, mothers and fathers, sisters and brothers, aunties and uncles, grandmas and grandpas, all came together. Each had lost a loved one on the battlefield. In a basket on the earthen altar by the Inipi, was a pile of tobacco pouches. Each tobacco pouch was an offering for this prayer being made, for those who'd lost their lives in battle.

Before this day came, there were many Talking Circles where Leroy and Hal sat with Elders and Medicine Men to discuss the mutual vision they had. It's powerful enough when one man has a vision. But when two men share a dream, the Powers of Heaven and Earth join forces, conspiring to bring it together.

Since the West is the direction where the Sun sets, drawing the day to a close. It was decided that they'd build a West Facing Inipi to help those stuck in the In-between to cross over through the West Gate. Many Elders didn't lose sight of the fact that Hal and Leroy were on Chumash land when they had this shared vision. The Chumash are the guardians of the West Gate of Turtle Island.

Behind Hal and Ben, walked Frank, Ernie, Jed and Kyle. They parked about a quarter mile down the road behind the row of cars. "Would you look at all these people," Jed said out loud.

"Yeah, it's something, ain't it?" Hal started. "Hey, I got a pile of stones in the back of my truck we brought out from California. Can you help me get them over to the fireplace?"

"Sure thing," Ernie replied as they all pitched in to get the stones piled up. Looking around at all these people, Hal knew they'd have to pour more than one lodge. So after a few minutes of counsel with the fire-keepers, they all agreed to add more stones and wood to the fire, after the first lodge.

Quietly on the wings of the morning, across the sprawling grassland, the songs of Nature filled the air. Morning birds twittered while a chorus of crickets chirped. For miles, headlights cut through the darkness as more and more cars showed up. Among them was a truck with California license plates. Driving most of the night, Nate and Brian pulled into the parking lot, loaded with wood and supplies. In front of the Inipi, Hal scanned the gathering of people and started to make an announcement about the ceremony. Hearing Hal's booming voice cut through the morning fog, Nate stepped up beside him, holding a big bag of fresh cut cedar for the stones.

"Ah, hell Nate. You made it," Hal was overcome with emotion. "From what I understand, there's more cars coming."

"Well, when you told me about the dream, Leroy said it was going to be more than a ONE DAY CEREMONY!" Nate smiled.

"Yeah, I guess you're right about that," Hal said. "I just never organized anything this big before."

"Well, you got help. Me and Brian will stay as long as you need us to," Nate offered. "I'm hoping he can spend some more time with Leroy. They seemed to understand each other."

"Yeah, well if you call kicking the crap out of each other, understanding," Hal chuckled. "Then I guess you're right. They both went through hell over there in the desert."

Finding his way through the mist, Brian stood by the memorial. He ran his hand over the names of those who were massacred on this ground over a hundred years ago. On the Wind, he could hear his mom's laughter peel across the prairie. "I'm here, mom," Brian swallowed hard. "I know now why you brought me to this place. I understand how hard you were fighting your own demons just to stay alive. But every battle ends the same, don't it? People die."

Fighting back the tears, Brian sat down on the ground. "I'm trying to hold on mom. Nate won't let me out of his sight. We drove all night, just to get here, mom. He had me pick a ton of cedar before we came. And we even brought some stones for the lodge. When I get in the Inipi, mom, I'm going to say a prayer for you. I don't want you to get stuck because you lost the fight. I love you mom." With that, the most sacred water of life flowed from his eyes and ran down his cheeks. A few moments later, Leroy came up behind him and tapped Brian on the shoulder.

"Hey, I saw Nate and he said you came with him," Leroy started. "I'm glad you made it. I want you to sit next to me, when we go in the lodge."

"Yeah, sure thing," Brian said wiping his eyes. "My mom brought me here, to this place. I can feel her, ya know. She comes to talk to me when I'm dreaming."

"That's cuz she loves you man," Leroy put his hand on Brian's shoulder. "We're gonna get ready to go in soon."

Standing in front of the fire, Hal wondered how he was going to pull this off. More and more carloads of people drove up. "AHO MITAKUYE OYASIN!" he hollered across the fire to get everyone's attention. "I AM SO GLAD TO SEE EVERYONE," Hal began. "THIS CEREMONY STARTED OUT IN A DREAM, A VISION, THAT ME AND LEROY HAD ON THE WEST COAST. IT'S TAKEN A LOT OF TALKING CIRCLES AND MANY DAYS OF PREPARATION TO GET THIS PRAYER GOING. SO IF YOU WANT TO SWEAT WITH US IN THE INIPI THIS MORNING, PLEASE GO GET READY. I REALIZE THERE ARE A LOT

OF US HERE, BUT I WANT EVERYONE WHO WANTS TO PRAY INSIDE THE INIPI TO GET IN. WE'LL PROBABLY BE RUNNING LODGES BACK TO BACK ALL DAY. SO DON'T WORRY IF YOU DON'T GET IN THE FIRST ONE. LIKE LEROY SAID IN THE DREAM, THIS AIN'T GONNA BE A ONE DAY CEREMONY!" Hal chuckled. "NOW WE'LL BE LOADING OUR CANNUPAS HERE SHORTLY, SO IF YOU HAVEN'T OFFERED SOME TOBACCO TO THE FIRE, NOW WOULD BE A GOOD TIME TO DO THAT!"

"NOW THIS IS A SIMPLE PRAYER," Hal continued. "MANY OF US HAVE LOST A LOVED ONE ON THE BATTLEFIELD. SOME OF US HAVE LOST LOVED ONES TO THE DEMONS IN THE BOTTLE OR SOME UNHOLY PIPE. THIS PRAYER IS SIMPLE. IT'S FOR A HEALING FOR THOSE ON THE OTHERSIDE AND FOR THOSE OF US WHO WERE LEFT BEHIND. THE SIMPLER WE KEEP OUR PRAYER, THE STRONGER IT WILL BE. SO I'M ASKING THAT ALL OF US GO DEEP INTO OUR HEARTS AND PRAY FOR A HEALING FOR OURSELVES, OUR LOVED ONES AND ALL OF HUMANITY. WE'LL BE CALLING ON THE HIGHER POWERS TO CLEAR UP ALL THIS SOUL TRAUMA. IT LEAVES A HEAVY BLANKET OF SORROW ON EARTH AND ALL THE PEOPLE. YOU CAN IMAGINE AFTER CENTURIES OF WAR, HOW THICK THAT BLANKET OF SORROW MUST BE."

There was stillness that fell over the prairie as Hal spoke to the people. Though he never fancied himself a public speaker, his booming voice reached everyone. As the people called their departed loved ones to mind, their souls began to gather nearby in the Spirit World. A line of people began to form to offer a pinch of tobacco to the fire. With that pinch, they held their departed loved ones in their heart and tossed the tobacco into the fire.

"AFTER I'M DONE TALKING, WE'LL LOAD OUR SACRED PIPES AND GET READY TO GO IN. I THANK YOU ALL FROM THE BOTTOM OF MY HEART FOR COMING TO SUPPORT ME AND LEROY WITH THIS PRAYER. SEEING YOU ALL, REALLY TOUCHES MY HEART. AHO MITAKUYE OYASIN!"

Looking around for Ben, Hal finally found him talking with some of the Elders. "Hey Ben, you gonna come in the lodge this morning?" Hal asked.

"I think my work is outside by the West Gate," Ben replied. "I think I'd be more useful there." Sam, Ben's grandson, was standing close by and heard his grandpa's intentions. Listening carefully, Sam considered what his grandpa was explaining.

"Hmm," Hal toned. "I hadn't thought of that."

"Well, I got a suggestion," Ben offered. "Let the people introduce themselves inside the lodge and say the name of the loved one they are praying for. That way, when their Spirit comes through the lodge, I'll be standing by the West Gate ready to guide them home."

"Ben, I don't know what I'd do without you. You've always got my back," Hal said thankfully.

"Just trying to be useful," Ben replied. The glow of the Sacred Fire reflected in his eye glasses. "There's one other thing you might what to keep in mind."

"What's that?" Hal questioned, knowing Ben only gives out information as needed.

"Well, there are souls stuck in the Shadows who've never been prayed for," Ben started. "People damned them to hell because they committed horrible crimes. After they were executed, most people forgot about them. So you might want to call on the Spirit of Forgiveness and the Rescuers. They'll come get these souls out of the Shadows. As much as I don't like what they did, they are our brothers and sisters. The weight of their heavy load puts a pressure on the living."

"Because their Spirits are stuck," Hal conceded.

"Exactly," Ben agreed. "See, all of them had a chance to get out, Hal. Creator never meant to leave his children behind. But when the Light appeared, they were afraid to go into it. They thought they'd be punished for their wrong-doing. So instead, their souls stayed with what they knew. Either around the people they loved or what was familiar, like their hometowns. But their dark energy polluted everything. It's not just battlefields that they're stuck in. Many of them died in prison."

"So in a way, you're saying that they had a hand in what happened to them," Hal understood.

"We all create our own hell," Ben summed it up. "It's the grand blanket of Life. We are all part of the weave. Some of us just weave in darker colors. Those souls stuck in the In-between, their sadness and anger affects everybody. Healing the sadness is just part of it. We have to get to the root of the problem, if the world stands a chance at changing."

"Man, this is a big job," Hal admitted feeling somewhat overwhelmed.

"It's all right," Ben chuckled. "You got enough heart to handle it.

Creator sent the right men for the job."

"I'm glad you think so Ben," Hal softened. "I guess me and Leroy better get saddled up. I got a feeling it's going to be a helluva ride."

Darkness is the absence of Light. Just like sin, a mistake, a wrong committed against another, comes from a lack of love. In the lowest reaches of the Spirit World are the Shadow Lands. These are the dismal hells of the spirit and mind. In this sea of shipwrecked souls, are those who lived loveless lives, were driven by selfish desires and went down the wrong path. After their bodies died, the heaviness of guilt pulled their souls down to these dreary places. Because they feared their fate, some refused to go into the Light upon physical death. And so they became earthbound.

Those who fiercely denied the existence of Great Spirit, the Almighty, created an endless ache in their souls. To numb that spiritual void, they soothed themselves with sweet sins. When their bodies finally gave out, they found themselves drawn to the same hatreds, cruelties and lusts of their lower nature, which pulled them down in their physical life.

It was the loveless, barren qualities of their inner-man which drew them to these dark dungeons. In the Shadow Lands, a man's high social status never mattered. If inwardly, he was driven by lust for power, greed and temptation, he'd find his station among others who match his inner world. It didn't matter if he was a King or criminal. In the Spirit World, his soul is measured by its spiritual gravity, the weight of its debt. Money and worldly power acquired in physical life are meaningless on the Otherside.

Even in the Shadow Lands, the Creator's laws are still in effect. The debt a man created in his physical life, must get repaid. Many souls wait in long lines to be born again, in order to clear away the wreckage they made in lives past. If a man created harm to another, there were two ways which the debt was cleared through Universal laws. First, through making amends, that debt must be forgiven by the one who was harmed. Otherwise, Life had to repay the culprit in kind. What they sow, they must reap. What matters is a man's intentions, his thought-life. For his thoughts draw to him other like-minded souls.

In the world of fire and ice, fear is one of the darkest and most powerful emotions. It casts a long shadow over those who live unholy lives. It has to be fought and conquered before peace and growth can come. In the deepest swamp, the hardest ones to reach are souls who gave up on Life. Whether self-reliant or rebellious, they never sought the

Master Within to guide them. Since their minds were closed, they didn't listen to the Inner Voice or obey a Higher Will. Perhaps in their misery, they drew dark spirits to them, making matters worse. Their fear of endless grief and pain consumed them. So in a moment of utter despair, they took their own lives.

After committing suicide, they were drawn down to the Shadow Lands. Once there, they found themselves covered in a hard shell of desperate sorrow. This cocoon of iron chains was so thick, it was almost impossible to reach them. Only a pure, determined love had the needed power to cut through the chains which bound them. Loving prayers from the living are healing waters for these lost souls.

Fortunately, these hells were never meant to last forever. Every soul must eventually rise. To be eternally damned meant a soul chose to separate from the Light of Truth and didn't grow spiritually. Either out of ignorance or stubbornness, they refused to aligned themselves with Creator's Will. They always put their own will first. By doing that, they paralyzed themselves and couldn't rise above what their own earthbound intellect and self-will permitted.

The everlasting inferno, eternal damnation, stemmed only from the warped imaginations of man. Many lost souls wandered a long time in the darkness. To escape from the lower regions, a soul had to get weary of his plight. He had to see where his beliefs and convictions were faulty. No soul is ever left without comfort, unless he wills it that way. For any soul who longs to reach upward, to resist his lower nature, there is always help from the Higher Beings.

Kneeling before the earthen altar, Hal and Leroy got ready to load their sacred pipes. The blazing hot fire cast a warm glow on everyone around the Sacred Fireplace. A hush fell across the prairie as Ernie started singing the Pipe Loading Song. With each pinch of Chan-shasha, Hal made a conscious prayer for all those loved ones and the forgotten ones on the Other-side. Both he and Leroy had lost men in battle. Seeing all the people lined up around the fire, made him well aware that many people carried the same pain.

The first two Cannupas on the altar that morning belonged to Hal and Leroy. But before the days end, many more sacred pipes would be loaded and smoked. When Ernie finished singing the Pipe Loading Song, Hal and Leroy placed their sacred pipes on the altar. Afterward, they all shook hands.

"OKAY EVERYBODY! GET READY! IT'S TIME TO GO IN!" Hal's

voice boomed over the prairie.

Thank goodness those who'd built the Inipi had a feeling a lot of people would come. So they built it a bit larger than normal. It easily fit two rows of people. Pouring the water this morning, Hal was the first to crawl inside. Leroy would set the stones. Outside the Inipi door, Ernie stood with an abalone shell of smoldering sage. He smudged everyone off before they went inside the lodge. Knowing a few of the veterans and sun dancers, Hal called in the front row first. Then the people filed in one by one, behind them. This morning the lodge would be packed in, cheek to cheek.

Once all the people got settled in, Hal asked the fire keeper for his Cannupa. As the first seven stones came in, Leroy placed these glowing Ancestors in the stone cradle at the center of the Inipi. With his sacred pipe, Hal touched each one. Afterward, Nate put a pinch of cedar on each glowing stone, it snapped and crackled with a trail of cedar smoke going up. Once all the stones had come in, Hal handed out his Cannupa and called for the Water of Life, Mni Wichoni.

As Leroy and Hal passed the bucket of water over the glowing stones, a splash of water spilt over the lip of the bucket. The stones crackled and popped as a searing steam filled the lodge. Setting the bucket of water between them, Hal poured a few ladles of water on the stones. Hot steam shot up and billowed throughout the lodge. Then he called to the fire-keeper and asked him to close the door. Once the door was shut, it was nearly dark inside the lodge. The glow of those blessed Ancestors illuminated the faces around the circle.

"For those of you I've never met, my name is Hal. My doorman, who set the stones, is Leroy. We've both sun danced a number of years, and been schooled by our Elders in the Old Ways. While we were out West, Leroy had a dream, a vision, that he was standing right over yonder, by the edge of that small graveyard. He was holding his Cannupa, when a Spirit came riding out of the mist on a horse. This Spirit showed him that the battlefield is still active to this day. Over a century ago, our ancestors were massacred here. Like the good warrior he is, Leroy knew he was there to be of service. But it'd take more than one day to do this work. At first, I didn't remember the dream. Until he told me I was there, and then I saw it all. This morning, I humbly sit behind this bucket. I know it's going to take all of us to get this job done." Searing hot steam shot up from the stones as Hal poured another dipper of water on the glowing hot Ancestors.

"Now, we're not here to be comfortable," Hal started. "If we wanted to do that, we could be home, sitting in our easy chair reading the funnies. So when it gets hot, just put your face down to Mother Earth. She'll take care of you. Since we came here to pray, make sure you put your whole heart into it. With the job ahead of us, we don't have room for half-baked, mediocre prayers. I was talking to my buddy Ben outside the lodge a few minutes ago. From what I gather, it's not hard for a soul to get stuck in the In-between."

Hal paused a moment to gather his thoughts. "You see, the souls of drunks might hang out at the speakeasy, gulping down the alcohol fumes with the breathing drinkers at the bar. Another spirit might be some black-hearted baby killer, executed by the law, damned to hell and forgotten about. Or he might be a brave warrior, blasted out of his body, who keeps fighting for his people on the Other-side, but gets stuck on the battlefield. Either way, these Spirits got held down by the gravity of their wrong-doings or earthly desires."

"The problem is," Hal went on. "This darkness puts a heavy weight on us. It poisons us breathing folks and makes us sick. For one reason or another, they chose to miss the bus and stayed where they lived in their earthly life." Throwing another dipper of water on the Grandfathers, they hissed and spit, gurgled and bubbled as searing heat filled the lodge.

"From the counsel that Ben gave me before the lodge, we'll call on Great Spirit, Wakan Tanka, Tunkashila, and ask Creator to send down His Rescuers and the Spirit of Forgiveness to help our brothers and sisters get home. Now I want you to go deep in your heart and ask for a healing for yourself, your loved ones and the whole of humanity."

"But," Hal paused, feeling compelled to address the worst of it. "Even more important, is a cleaning out of the bitter-root of this war madness. See, when we pray, we're telling Creator that we are part of the whole. But when we go to war, we separate ourselves from others. So which is it? Are we part of the whole or separate from the many? We can't be both."

"From the little I know about life, one thing is certain. When we commit a wrong or an injustice against someone else, either we pay now or we pay later with interest. We can right that wrong by making amends. If we're forgiven by the person we harmed, the debt is cleared up. But if, in our pride or arrogance, we don't make amends, well Life has no choice but to serve us up the very same pile of crap we dealt out. But this time, we get it back in spades. That way, we know what it was for. I think that's why some of the most miserable people live the longest, so they got time to clean up the mess they made."

"To get this prayer started, we'll go around the circle and introduce ourselves and mention the loved ones we're praying for. Keep this prayer simple. We're asking for our loved ones to be helped on their way home. Go ahead Leroy."

Looking around at the faces lit up by the glowing stones, Leroy took a deep breath. It had been a long travel to get to this moment. "Morning, I'm Leroy. I'm thankful to be sitting here with everyone. The first Spirit I'm praying for is that brave warrior who came riding out of the mist that morning when I was standing by the graveyard in my dream. I don't know his name, but we know each other. And all the other souls who I saw on that Spirit battlefield, caught in the In-between. I ask Creator to bless them all with healing. I've been in combat. Seeing all that blood twists a man's mind. So I back up Hal's prayer to heal the war madness here on Earth. Aho Mitakuye Oyasin."

Standing sentry at the West Gate, Ben heard the thunder of galloping hooves coming out of the early morning mist. Gifted with Spiritual Sight, Ben saw this powerful Brave, with his ebony hair flowing behind him, caught by the wind. *"Ah,"* Ben thought. *This is the Brave who Leroy prayed about."* Sitting astride a great warhorse, his powerful bronze arms held a spear decorated with many eagle feathers in one hand and the reins in the other. Behind him trudged a large band of battle-torn and war-weary souls. Hearing the Call, they were drawn to the pure flame of the Sacred Fire. Following closely behind the Brave, the souls of young children huddled close to their mothers.

Trudging through the muck behind them, were the souls of soldiers dressed in tattered blue uniforms. Others were dressed gray uniforms. These soldiers came from both sides of the Mason-Dixon Line, the border between free states and slaves states. Having fought in one of the bloodiest wars on American soil, their souls were worn out and longed for rest. This morning, they heard the Call of their loved ones calling them home.

A short 30 years before the massacre at Wounded Knee, the United States split in half over the evils of slavery. In the South, tobacco and cotton fields were taxing and depleting the soil. Needing fresh soil and slave labor, southern plantation owners wanted to expand slavery to the new states. But the North was slowly abolishing slavery and declaring themselves free states. As Abraham Lincoln was elected president in 1860, many southern states declared that they would secede from the Union. And so the War between the States began.

In this murderous battle, brother battled against brother. More than 700,000 soldiers lost their lives. Many of them were buried right where they fell on the killing fields. Blood stained the soil. Soldiers who were captured, ended up in wretched prisons. Often they were tortured and left to starve. Many rotted away in this living grave through disease, vermin and starvation. All this horror left a deep scar on the souls of the people. This trauma took life times to clear up. After the end of the Civil War, it wasn't possible to find all those fallen troops.

Without a proper burial, many souls stayed where they died. Funerals were meant to be a crossing-over ceremony to guide the soul into the Land Beyond. It was never meant to be a festival of grief, which is a powerful emotion that ties the newly departed to the living.

With his old Indian blanket draped over his shoulders, Ben held his sacred pipe close to his heart. He stood alongside his grandson Sam, at the West Gate in welcome. To be cleansed of their inner darkness, this long procession of souls stopped to bathe in the pure flames of the Sacred Fire. With its divine Power, it purified their Spirit before they entered the Portal of Light. Never having witnessed this before, Ben and Sam stood silent in the glowing firelight, holding their sacred pipes to their chest. It was an honor to watch these Spirits bathe in the Sacred Fire. Letting out a whinny, the nostrils of the warhorse flared as the Brave approached the Sacred Fire on horseback. Clothed in buckskin, the Brave looked into Ben's compassionate eyes, as he slid off his steed.

"Welcome Home, my Brother," Ben said to the young Brave as a doorway of Light opened behind him. Alongside the Spirits of his Ancestors, in that golden doorway, the young Brave saw the Great Ones who came to welcome them Home. To know the meaning of Home, a soul had to wander through all of Creation. Leading his trusted steed by the reins, the Brave walked into the flames of the Sacred Fire, guiding his horse behind him. For a long moment, they bathed in the holy flames, melting away a century's worth of dross they had collected in their life time. Before he walked through the golden doorway, the Brave turned to Ben and Sam. With piercing eyes, he met Ben's gaze and whispered a song of thanksgiving. As each soul crossed over into the Light, there was great homecoming celebration on the Other-side.

Inside the lodge, Hal felt a tingle go up his spine. Through the blankets covering the Inipi, Hal heard Ben's voice welcoming the Spirits home. *"It's working,"* he thought to himself as he threw dipper after dipper of water on the piping hot Grandfathers. Gurgling, spitting and hissing, blasts of steam rose from the stone pit filling the Inipi with searing heat.

Sitting in the back row, Hannah peered at the glowing stones between Brian's elbow and top of Leroy's knees. Being the daughter of a World War Two veteran, she knew the aftermath of war very well. Her father didn't get sober until shortly before he died. But all the years before his judge ordered sobriety were riddled with violence and drunken bouts of madness. For him, the war never ended.

Praying quietly to herself, Hannah placed the palms of her hands on the gritty, blood-stained Earth. Growing up gifted with spiritual sight, she was no stranger to Angels and demons or the spiritual warfare brought on by hate. In a silent whisper, she called on the Higher Powers to clear all battlefields of evil, where the forces of darkness reigned in terror. "Great Spirit, Grandfather, Mighty I AM Presence," she began. "Bless and heal all our loved ones who were lost on the battlefield. Let Your purifying Love clear away the hatred which poisons our souls," Hannah whispered. "Send Your holy Warriors to remove the hordes of hell, now and forevermore."

With his eyes held transfixed to the Sacred Fire, Ben prayed silently for all the souls lost in the In-between. More and more human spirits continued to march through and bathe the golden flames. Off in the distance, Sam spotted something he'd never seen before at a ceremony. "Grandpa, would you look at that! What do you think it is?"

Along the perimeter of the ceremonial site, stood a glowing, thick row of heavenly Warriors, shoulder to shoulder. Their shimmering swords caught the light of the Sacred Fire as their formidable presence made a stronghold which the dark forces could not penetrate. Beyond them on the battlefield, lay the demonic kingdom where the fighting still raged as swords clashed and sparks flew.

Inside the Inipi, the power of the heart-felt prayers began to build. The more powerful the prayers, the more holiness and glory charged through the heavens. All this Sacred Fire Love sent a shock wave which shook the skies.

With his spirit-eyes turned skyward, Ben looked just in time to see a thousand, tiny points of Light descending from every direction. "Oh Sam, never in my life have I witnessed this," his quiet voice declared. "Somebody inside must be praying to clear the battlefield." Struck silent, Sam watched this fierce, spiritual firestorm in awe.

With brilliant wings that scattered white fire in all directions, a holy Warrior whose Being shone like lightning, landed a stone's throw away from where Sam and Ben stood praying. His sparkling eyes approved of the prayers as his glowing sword of blue flame hung at his side. His Being shimmered with living Light as he walked along the path with all the souls of ragged soldiers passing through the Sacred Fire. With a powerful Love streaming from His eyes, He guided and welcomed them all home.

Stomping the ground outside the perimeter of Light, an immense hulk of a spirit, a devil monkey with large black talons and burning yellow eyes, hissed and shouted toward this holy Warrior. "Micah, You'll never get away with this! This battlefield is MINE!"

Across the ceremonial grounds, more shimmering wings rolled like thunder as these heavenly Warriors landed near the Sacred Fireplace. Taking this threat in stride, Micah smiled at the gnarled, glowering beast. "And yet, the saints keep praying."

Burning with the heat of battle, the talons of this towering demon warlord grabbed his sizzling sword and cut through the air. Sparks flew, with its eyes afire with wrath, it screamed. "We were INVITED HERE!" he roared, spewing out streams of hate. "This is OUR territory!"

"Aw," the heavenly Warrior toned. "It seems that the invitation has been rescinded. We've been invited here now."

"Not without a fight, Micah!" the humongous devil monkey roared. "THIS IS WAR!"

"Grandpa, what does he mean they were invited?" Sam whispered to Ben, watching this whole scene unfold.

"War, they were invited by war," Ben whispered back, not taking his spirit eyes off the scene brewing before him. "When a person feels hate, it invites them in. Anything that poisons the body or the mind, invites the beast in. Great sinners and great saints are cut from the same clothe, Sam. Where they end up depends on what road they choose to take." Feeling compelled by an inner Voice, more of the bystanders who stood around the Sacred Fire, started praying.

"WE WILL CRUSH YOU! AND YOUR SAINTS!" hissed the snarling demon warlord, his cutting angry words were dripping with fear. A dark fire brewed in his fierce yellow eyes, festering with hostility and spite. His blade of hell slashed through the air, burning with an angry fire. Outside the perimeter of Light, angry blades of hell flashed as the demonic devil monkeys jeered, taunting the Warriors of Light.

Two of the arriving heavenly Warriors gently lit upon the top of the Inipi, holding their swords of Light in their powerful glowing arms.

Unfurling their brilliant wings of Light, they created an impenetrable shield atop the dome of the Inipi. Inside the lodge, Hannah grabbed two handfuls of the once blood-stained Earth. A passion welled up inside her heart as a prayer whispered from her lips. "Heal these battlefields with YOUR PURIFYING LOVE!" she prayed, her spirit was awash with the Presence of Love. "Heal these battlefields with Your Purifying LOVE! Heal these battlefields with Your Purifying LOVE! Right NOW! This instant and forever!"

"The perimeter is secure, Captain," came Dakotah, one of the heavenly Warriors.

"Good," Micah approved. "Now shield the Saints from this hissing venom, so none of it poisons their prayers." With glowing wings of Light spread across the Inipi, a circle of heavenly Warriors protected those inside the lodge. The impassioned, heart-felt prayers charged the Heavenly Host with love, increasing the Powers of Light.

As the calls to the Higher Powers went out, strong winds of change blew across the prairie, blasting loose the crawling black cloud of iniquity which had hung over that land for centuries. On roaring wings of fire, descending in brilliant streaks of light, the Warriors of the Higher Realms began to strike at demons from the sky. Across the field of battle, the Lords of White Lightning thrust down their crackling lightning bolts to purify the ground as the flaming blue swords of heaven clashed with the angry blades of hell. In the fire of battle, many foul spirits were driven off the killing fields. In groups, they were gathered into a holding place where they could cause no more harm.

Inside the lodge, the pelting heat was melting away the heartache. After another dipper of water, Hal called to Brian to start his prayer. "Go ahead, Brian."

"Hi, I'm Brian. I want to pray for my mom, Cara May. She died last year from a drug overdose when I was overseas. I just made it back in time for her funeral. It's hard to believe she's really gone, you know. I feel her around me all the time," Brian's voiced cracked as he held back his deep hurt and anguish. "Before I enlisted in the Service, she brought me here to this place, to Wounded Knee. I think she wanted me to understand how battles really end. A lot of people died here. So I pray Creator sends His Rescuers to bring them Home."

Locked away in the caverns of the blackest night, Cara May's soul was blanketed in a web of dark thoughts. Chains of loneliness and sorrow bound her mind. Like a cocoon, the threads of every dark thought wove itself around her. Being so wrapped up, it was nearly impossible to see anything else. In her earthly life, she struggled with a painful unwillingness to believe that there was an Almighty God who created this miserable world.

Now, she was stuck in the ghettos of the lower world. Small hovels were strewn all around her. It was a shanty town of spiritually bankrupt souls, the wasted genius of humankind. Here, they thrashed around, wailing in their self-inflicted sorrow. The poisoned seeds they planted in their earthly lives created this dire harvest of bad fortune. Many had been forgotten. Some were never prayed for. Trapped in a world of hellish thoughts, they were unable to see anything else. Someone had to help them, because they could no longer help themselves.

It's not that she wanted to die that day. Somewhere along the way, she was set adrift on the dark seas of hopelessness and despair. Cara May just wanted the pain to stop. Filling the needle with poison was her way out. She just wanted oblivion. But killing herself off, she broke one of Creator's Cosmic Laws. In her weakness, she deprived her soul of the chance to work out its needs and fulfill the purpose of her life. This self-destruction created greater wreckage. Now she was stuck in the same darkness that she tried to escape from.

In her mind, she heard her mom screaming, "Cara May! If you don't change your wicked ways, you're gonna catch hell for what you do!" A wry smile crept across her lips, when she realized her mom was right. She could never please that woman. "*At least I proved her right,*" Cara May thought to herself. "*I'm trapped in my own hell.*"

Years before, Cara May closed down her heart to protect herself against the pain. Incapable of feeling pain, she couldn't feel anything else either. Her heart was dead, long before her body died. The drugs, alcohol, men and running away were all temporary distractions. They were a band-aid on a gaping wound that wouldn't heal. The root of the pain ran deep. She felt cut off from life.

It started when she was growing up. Most of her life, Cara May felt orphaned by alcoholism, unloved and unlovable. As a little girl, she stood between her fighting parents and tried to get them to stop. But they were caught up in the madness of alcoholism. All the craziness left deep invisible scars. Then out of the blue, her mom found Jesus and stopped drinking. That's when her dad gave up and left. But still the madness continued. It just took a different form. Shaking her Bible in Cara May's face, her mother dragged her off to church. All the way there, her mother hollered. In her threatening rants, her mother swore Cara would be damned to hell if she didn't find Almighty God and give up her wretched ways.

At one point, nothing made sense. So, at the age of 18, the "Relocation agent" on the rez found her hanging around the corner store. He convinced her that getting off the rez would be a way out. He gave her a one-way bus ticket to the West Coast, to the city of Lost Angels. There she met other American Indians who lived in the ghettos of downtown Los Angeles.

Alone and far from home, it didn't take long for life to spiral out of control. With no real direction, her mind and heart were scattered to the Four Winds. Unsure of where to turn, she followed the path of least resistance. With no real skills, she worked at a stupid factory job for minimum wage. The dismal conditions finally crushed her spirit. Even after working a 40 hour week, she barely made enough to make ends meet. Without real guidance, she didn't have any direction.

Oblivion seemed like the only way out of the pain. Under the influence of drugs and alcohol, her spiritual slumber grew deeper and deeper. One day, with a needle in her arm, she asked herself, "*If this was life, why was I ever born?*"

In the city of Lost Angels, it didn't take long for her to cross paths with the long arm of American justice. Being caught for drunk driving, she went to jail and ended up in drug court. That's where she met Nate. He was a Native American drug and alcohol counselor who tried hard to help her out.

Praying hard for his mom, a strong, bright Ray of Love streamed from Brian's heart. Like a powerful flood light, it traveled to where she was, locked in her sorrow. This strong Ray of Love guided the Rescuers through that troubled shanty town, so they could find her deep in the shadows of the underworld.

"Then, in county jail," Brian went on. "A few years ago, my Uncle Bacon was murdered. They never found out who did it. But somebody knows. So I'm asking Creator that the truth comes out, so this can get settled." While Brian prayed, his Uncle Bacon's Spirit hovered over the stone pit in the middle of the lodge. With a Buddha grin on his face, Uncle Bacon sat cross legged, looking into his nephew's eyes. Not believing what he was seeing, Brian wiped the sweat dripping down his forehead from his eyes.

"I pray for a healing for all the men and women who died in prison. I pray their souls get rescued from that miserable place. In the military, I was a combat medic, and I seen a lot of blood. I seen a lot of dead people. Their blood stained the Earth. I know they got blasted out of their bodies. Most nights they come into my dreams. So for all the people stuck in the battlefield in that desert of hell. I ask Tunkashila to forgive them and bring them home. Aho Mitakuye Oyasin."

Knowing the brutality of the killing fields himself, Hal tossed a dipper of water on the stones. "Okay, who's next?" Hal asked.

"Your mom was a pistol, Brian, when I met her," Nate started. "My name is Nate. I met Cara May about 15 years ago, when she got in trouble for driving drunk. I worked in rehab, helping out with Drug Court at the time. I'll never forget that face she made when she got ordered to rehab. She didn't want to spend anymore time in jail. The first time she sat in my office for counseling, she rolled her eyes at me and said "Please don't talk to me about JESUS! My mama told me enough about Him already. If there is a God, I never seen Him and I don't want to know about any God who'd make a world like this!"

"I never met a woman so hard-headed. I saw her a couple times a week for counseling. We had to make sure she fulfilled the conditions of court, went to AA meetings, got a sponsor and worked the 12 Steps. But she kept telling me she wasn't like those crazy people in AA. All she needed to do was settle down, find a good man and get married. So I told her to write down everything she wanted in a man. Go all out and hold nothing back," Nate laughed. "What he looked like, what kind of money he made, how educated he'd be. Oh, it covered every area," Nate laughed again. "Then the next week, after she wrote it down, I had her read it to me. It was a wish list. After she read it, she looked at me and said "Okay? Now what?" That's when I told her to become everything on that list, and he'd find her." Nate chuckled. "Well, she threw me a nasty look, crumbled that list up and threw it in the trash. I fished it out and kept it in her file."

"We knew each other a long time," Nate sighed. "She'd sober up for a while, but it never stuck. There was something about Step Two that she couldn't swallow. I think it was that "Christian God" her mother shoved down her throat. So I told her about Pte San Win, White Buffalo Calf Woman. I don't know what it was. Maybe because Pte San Win was a woman, but Cara May sat in the lodge and prayed to her. I taught her this song. And if it's alright with you Hal, I'd like to sing it for her," Nate asked.

"I remember Cara May," Hal said. "Yeah, go ahead, Nate. Here, I'll pass you the drum." Reaching behind him, Hal passed the drum to

Leroy and it found its way to Nate.

A well of emotion came up in his throat as Nate pounded on the drum a couple of times. "I never gave up on you Cara May," he started as his eyes filled tears. "I never gave up on you. You know this song, sweet girl. I'm gonna sing it for you and pray that Creator sends his Spirit Helpers to come find you. I love you Cara May," Nate pounded on the drum a few more times. In a strong voice, he started singing.

"Winyan Wakan ki Cannupa yuha u wey..." Nate's voice boomed through the lodge. Sitting next to him, Brian sang along, with other voices in the lodge. "Taninyan yuza yo hey..." Streams of Love flowed from their hearts. Their heartfelt prayers reached through the ethers to where Cara May lay cocooned in her sorrow. "Winyan Wakan u wey... Taninyan, taninyan yuza yo hey..."

While the drum pounded in time with the heartbeat of Mother Earth, the sweet song found its way. With soul-driven prayers, their streams of Love reached Cara May. Something deep stirred inside her. The slow burning Love of Creator, the spark of the divine which lived inside her, slowly awakened her shut down heart. At first she thought the Light was a part of her nightmare and she felt afraid.

"Pte San Win ki Cannupa yuha u wey..." Nate continued singing. Mixed with steam and heat, strong loving voices filled the lodge. "Taninyan yuza yo hey... Pte San Win u wey... Taninyan, taninyan yuza yo hey..."

Then a miracle happened. Through the hard shell of her cocoon, she could hear it! She could hear their voices. Like a gentle rain, streams of Light washed over her. While Hal splashed a few more dippers on the stones, the steam carried their prayers up to Creator. With all their love, Nate and the others kept singing.

To descend down into the Shadow Lands, the Rescuers had to 'tone down' their Light. Otherwise vibrating at such a high level, they would be invisible to the lost souls trapped there. Without her permission, it was impossible for the Rescuers to pierce Cara May's cocoon, until she was desperate enough to change. It took a slow inner maturing, a longing for Light and a never-ending cry for help, before the Rescuers could step in. Waiting for a sign, the Rescuers stood ready to help Cara May out of the Shadows. It had to be her choice to leave there. With her free will, she had to reach upwards to the Love of the Most High which was always waiting. Until then, she'd remain paralyzed and lost. Only the Living Power of the Creator could help her.

The Rescuers are special teams of advanced souls who work within the Laws of Truth. Having lived selfless lives, they willingly traveled down through the Shadow Lands to help lost souls. Before temptation and the fall of man, human spirits lived in Paradise. Back then, these rescue teams were completely unnecessary. Human spirits worked alongside the Great Ones. No one was lost. So there was no need of them. Just as there is no need of forgiveness in Heaven. For in the Higher Realms, souls live by the Laws of Divine Love.

But once the Game of Duality, Light versus Dark, started on Earth, so much had changed. Many human spirits were snared by weakness through the Principle of Temptation. Gradually they descended from the Upper Realms into creations of their own hate. From this spiritual poison, a dense fog gathered which formed a Veil between the Higher Realms and Earth. Now, mankind could no longer see the Great Ones. Through man's own choice, he'd fallen from Grace.

This Game of Duality, the great experiment of mankind, was a compromise between the High Holy, Divine Consciousness and a desire to experience a world of fire and ice. It began with a challenge, a wager between Light and Dark.

It takes a great Adversary to make a Master. The pursuit of knowledge, along with spiritual mastery were the goal of each human spirit who embodied on Mother Earth. The stakes were high. With every challenge they faced, human spirits chose between the two opposing principles, Light or dark, Love or fear. Either they climbed to their greatest spiritual heights and gained their Victory. Or if they failed on the Path of Life, their inner light diminished through wrong-doing and they plunged to a spiritual death.

Spiritual death, otherwise called 'Second Death,' in itself, is a complete undoing. It is a disintegration of the soul's personality which is gained through living many lifetimes. After the spiritual personality is undone, what's left is the original spark of the Divine which it was created with. Then this spiritual seed begins its journey to mastery once again.

According to the Will of the Most High, the only way this cycle would be considered complete, was when each human spirit fulfilled all its teachings. Learning the lessons of Wisdom and Truth was the goal. Once it gained mastery, a human spirit achieved its spiritual freedom. Then, it would make its journey upwards, back to the Spiritual Realm where it originated. No matter how far they had fallen, all human spirits must eventually rise and gain their Victory.

The Challengers were a team of Great Beings from the Higher Realms who descended on Earth to take on the role of Adversary. Through temptation, their goal was to destroy everything weak. Relentlessly, they worked to that end. The mighty Wolf actually came to mind the sheep.

Working outside the Law of Love, the Great Trickster misused his spiritual powers and introduced the Principle of Temptation. Knowing that each soul is judged by its inner light, He peppered the thoughts of human spirits with seeds of hatred, ambition, jealousy, doubt and fear.

These corrosive seeds confused the human spirits. By choosing the wrong path, they strayed from the True Path of Spiritual Growth and Mastery. As the dense Veil grew, human spirits felt separated from the Source of All Life. This illusion of separation inflicted a painful wound upon humanity. It revealed itself as an inner ache, a loneliness which never healed.

Using sinister tools, the Tempter pitted one brother against another. Instead of looking toward the Creator to be their source and supply, the Trickster swayed them with worldly power and possessions. This distracted them from their soul's longing, their Natural Inheritance. Love and cooperation was replaced with fear and self-reliance.

Here, the Adversary set traps to test the strength and faith of human spirits. If the Tempter couldn't bring down a man by his weakness, he used a man's love against him. Those who wavered, who were not strong in themselves, often stumbled and fell into the Tempter's snares. Many were lost and descended to their worst nightmares. There are many hells within Hell.

As life on Earth evolved, accounts had to balance and all old debts must be settled. Wrong choices and a guilty conscious weighed the human spirit down. Good choices lifted up the spirit. To reckon the wrongdoing created in each lifetime, human spirits became subject to cycle of birth, death and rebirth.

Upon physical death, human spirits entered a station where their souls were cleansed. Here, they were judged on their inner life, not their worldly possessions. No outside judgment was necessary. They all found fault in themselves. And besides, what condemnation could be harsher then their own? Their entire life literally flashed before their eyes. They not only relived their own experiences, but also those whom they'd harmed or loved. Every horrifying experience left a very deep scar in the soul of man. Many traumas took a few lifetimes to clear away. In each lifetime, they vowed that they would do better.

Some souls who deviated to the Darkness, were drawn down to depths which they could not find their way back from. Their wrongdoings slowly diminished their inner light. They lost sight of the normal course of their spiritual growth. Having pushed themselves away from the Light, they were separated from every opportunity to grow and mature as a soul. Paralyzed by false beliefs and fear, they were lost and never championed their Victory.

As they spiraled downward, the weight of their wrongdoing made their souls dense and heavy. Without help, they alone couldn't rise up from this dungeon. Eventually, their souls were drawn into a disintegration, where they suffered a spiritual death. Their unsavory personality, which took lifetimes to create, was completely dissolved down to the original spiritual seed. Like a rejected stone, their personality was ground down to dust. Their life stream was erased from the Book of Life.

But others, who stayed alert and allowed themselves to be spiritually guided, were protected from the Prince of Darkness. To make the Adversary powerless, all mankind needed was to make an effort to recognize and follow Creator's Laws. The power of making good choices put a protective circle around them, which was capable of crushing the evil pressing to get in.

These souls, who strove for Light, faced many challenges to advance their growth. As they grew stronger, they blossomed powerfully and were uplifted towards spiritual heights. With each victory, they conquered the Darkness and gained spiritual mastery. By overcoming weakness, human spirits aligned themselves with the Will of Creator, staying within the Laws of Love. Understanding the Natural Laws, they worked in harmony with them. As human spirits strove after Divine Love, they were immediately invulnerable to every temptation.

Through the fires of the battlefield between Light and Dark, emerged two classes of people. Those who survived the trials by fire through faith, Victory and triumph, became like fine steel. And those who lost their inner light, lived in misery and became lost. It was easy to tell one from the other.

Human spirits who achieved their Victory, Spiritual Freedom, became the Great Ones. Their Love served mankind for many centuries. With Joy, they aligned themselves with the Laws of Creation. Every Master went through the tests, trials and struggles which faced all mankind.

But after one Master, the Blessed Quan Yin took her stand with Life and won her Victory, she discovered that her loved one was snared by the Dark. Here, the blessed Quan Yin declared that she would not enter Heaven until there were no more souls lost in the Shadows.

It was only through great Love, that Quan Yin stayed to help her loved one from the terrors and distress created by wrong-doing. And so it was, other Great Ones stayed behind to rescue their loved ones from the depths of the Shadows. All their efforts to help these lost souls brought them even greater strength.

Deep inside, a disgust rose up inside Cara May's tormented mind. Her entire life, she'd been drenched in sorrow. Down to her core, she felt unloved and unwanted. Her cravings for oblivion finally brought her to here, this dismal, dank place where the sun never shined. She wanted out. Nate kept telling her, "Before you get better Cara May, you gotta be sick and tired of being sick and tired." His voice seemed to break through this hard shell of self-pity she was wrapped up in. Something shook inside her, demanding her to wake up!

The drum kept pounding, as Nate's voice boomed out the last verse of the song. It echoed across the prairie, across the ethers and deep into the Spirit World. "WE LOVE YOU CARA MAY!" Nate hollered at the glowing Grandfathers, hoping she could hear him. "WE LOVE YOU CARA MAY!" Streams of Light flowed from their hearts as the drum stopped beating. Their Love burst through the darkest night. It found her in the shadows. Cara May was bathed in a loving glow.

"What's all this light?" she finally asked as her hand swept away the web of dark thoughts she was surrounded by. Like writhing severed snakes, the chains which bound her became loose. When she opened her eyes, she saw the Rescuers standing there.

Tenderness was the best soil for an awakening. For even in the most corrupt heart, there's a chord which vibrates to kindness and a sense of justice. It knows when it's been dealt with rightly. With beaming smiles, They looked into her weary eyes. "You are loved," They said with their eyes radiating pure Light. In an instant, the dark cocoon around her shattered, falling away in a million tiny pieces. A monstrous weight was lifted from her body.

"You mean all that time I was wrong?" she asked Them, as she sat there in her hovel.

"You just couldn't see it," They responded. "You were locked away in a cocoon of wrong beliefs. Not only that Cara May, but for 56 years you lived in chronic alcoholism. It's easy to go down hill living in that hard reality. Being around those demons will drag anyone down."

Hearing the truth, Cara May shook her head. "Nate told me I couldn't battle it by myself, but I didn't believe him. I thought I was stronger than those people who went to meetings. I didn't want to be like them. They were always talking about God doing this and that for them. I thought they were lying. And I didn't believe in Him."

"It's almost impossible to fight the Wolf by yourself, Cara May," the Rescuer said gently. "We go out in teams, because the shadows are so strong. Its influence might get into our minds too."

"But what about God?" she demanded as she glanced around this valley blanketed in endless night. "Why would He make this ugly place?"

"Oh, that's such a long story," the Rescuer replied. "Would you like me to tell you about it as we walk out of this place? You do want to get cleaned up and go Home, right?"

The dank, curdled air was cold. A clammy chill shivered down her spine. Looking around at the ghetto of the underworld, her ragged clothes and dark surroundings, Cara May sighed. With tears streaming down her face, she finally surrendered. "Yes, I want to get cleaned up and go Home."

Dark, boiling clouds hung over them as they walked through the slums of the Shadow Lands. So many others were locked in an iron cocoon of chains, marinating in their own sorrows. Their hollow eyes stared listlessly into space. Still others wailed in a grief so deep, no one could reach them.

"What happens to them?" Cara May asked looking at the lost souls in the underworld.

"Well, that's why there is Us," the Rescuer began. "We come down here, from the Higher Realms to coax them out of their slumber. Some of them are so shut in on themselves, they are hard to reach. But we don't give up. It's much easier, when those who loved them in their earthly lives, pray for them. Because Love is powerful enough to penetrate the hard shell of sorrow they've wrapped themselves in."

"But I still don't understand," she said while they pressed on through the Valley of the Shadow of Death. "Why would God make this place?"

"You mean Hell?" the Rescuer asked as they walked the a long, thorny path out of the Shadows.

"Is this Hell? It must be," she concluded, looking around at all the terrible suffering.

"Sadly, Hell exists," the Rescuer started. "But it was never a Divine institution. Mankind created this out of their own choices. Man alone supplied Hell with all the strength it needed to exist, because he chose a wrong path. Even when he was warned, in his stubbornness, he still clung to the wrong way. Though Earth belongs to the Realm of Darkness, it is the last planet that can be saved. It's one of the furthest outposts."

In a way that only a true physician of the soul could work, the Rescuer didn't tear Cara May down. Employing tenderness, he recognized the sleeping good qualities within her troubled soul. With gentle nudges, he'd awakened them and then, built upon them. Working with true principles, this loving way transformed her wrong desires through a spiritual understanding.

In a gentle voice, the Rescuer began to speak of the "Game Of Life" and how this all began. "You see, Cara May, eons ago human spirits lived in Paradise and worked beside Angels. They learned how to use the 'Living Power', which is neutral and rests in Creation for all human spirits to use. With this treasure, they could become 'lords in Creation' in the World of Matter."

"You mean lords of destruction," Cara May added. "Have you been to Earth lately and seen all the bombs and weapons they use?"

"Well, whatever the Dark encompasses, will eventually disintegrate. Have you ever heard of the Seven Deadly Sins?" the Rescuer asked.

"That sounds really familiar," Cara May responded. "I think Nate said something about them in a group he ran for alcoholics. He said they were in the 6th Step of the Twelve and Twelve. Something about lust, pride..."

"Wrath, greed, envy, sloth, gluttony," the Rescuer filled in. "They are actually Spirits. Sin is actually a demon lurking, trying to gain entry through the door of your heart or mind. Temptation is the tool they use."

"So they whisper to you," Cara May started to understand.

"Yes, they do," the Rescuer agreed.

"And then you do something stupid," Cara May caught on fast.

"Like the Spirit of Despair who whispered to you the day you decided to fill the needle full of poison," the Rescuer explained. "Mankind has been infested with these unfriendlies since the dawn of time. But mankind chose to follow them, rather than the dictates of their heart."

"I made a stupid mistake that day," Cara May admitted.

"You listened to the whisperings of an unfriendly Spirit, who came to test your faith," the Rescuer gently explained. "Since you had no protection or effective defense against him, you believed those whispers to be true. But you were never worthless, Cara May. And even though you never believed in the Almighty, the Creator, He has loved you still."

"I never felt it," Cara May admitted. "Even when my mom dragged me to church, I never felt it."

"The Spirit of Love resides in the one true church," said the Rescuer. "Sadly, even Christ's message was twisted and distorted by those who wanted to have power over the masses. You see, all this wild confusion was created by human beings who misused the Divine Power. This Power was lent to them to create."

"Or destroy," Cara May added.

"Yes, given the power of choice between good and evil. By Itself, this Living Power is neutral," the Rescuer continued. "It doesn't distinguish between good and evil. It only responds to the nature of a man's choice. Human spirits are the stewards of this creative Power. They are responsible for every choice they make."

"Yeah," Cara May started to comprehend. "It seems to me, they were like stupid kids who played with fire and burned the whole house down."

"True... But Cara May, mankind was never given dominion over the Earth to abuse and destroy Her or the other kingdoms which reside here," the Rescuer started. "All kingdoms evolving on Earth, whether man knows of them or not, have the right to live and share the planet, no matter what form they take. The Spirit of Earth herself is a sovereign Being. She has her own Divine Powers. The minerals and gems are Her energy systems. The crystals are her arteries and the mighty trees which men cut down, are her lungs. The oil that bubbles up from the ground, is her very blood. But some of those souls that you saw in the lower regions, had a strong inner craving for power. While they lived, they trashed the Earth Mother and her many kingdoms, to fill their pockets with gold. Yet, they forgot one thing."

"Oh, what's that?" asked Cara May.

"That ultimately, all those destructive energies would return back to them," the Rescuer began. "You see, when mankind's energy gets imbalanced, where there's more dark than Light, it creates a vortex in Earth's energy grids. All this whirling, destructive human energy results in what man calls a 'natural disaster.' But, that's only a half-truth. What's really happening is, all their destructive energy is coming back to them. You can be sure of one thing. The seeds mankind plant in life, the prayers that they make, all creates the harvest they will reap, right down to the weather. And they will get it all back, good or not, even if it takes many life times."

"So why if God is all powerful, doesn't He take care of these idiots who are destroying everything?" Cara May questioned.

"If the Higher Powers did it all for you, how would you ever learn and become a Master of Divine Expression?" the Rescuer asked to stir her thinking. "Your soul has a purpose, a divine mission, if you will. For the soul to soar upwards and mature, it must experience Life, one step at a time. Which means, a person has to be awake and live in the present moment. Once a person surrenders their human personality or ego to the Will of the Most High, they become more refined. After this transformation takes place, they start walking their true spiritual path."

"Hmm," Cara May started to receive this information. It reminded her of what Nate was trying to do with all the addicts and alcoholics he worked with. He kept telling her, she had to surrender, but she didn't want to hear it. Now she was beginning to understand why.

"You see, mankind was given two gifts, which separate him from the other kingdoms residing on Earth. Intelligence was to guide mankind through his earthly journey, but it would always be bound to time and space. Intuition was mankind's connection to Spirit, which would make him a co-creator on Earth. This Spiritual connection would help mankind bring forward all the good things. This is how it was meant to be," the Rescuer sighed. "That is, until man fell from Grace."

"You mean when Eve tempted Adam with an apple," Cara May chimed in.

"The First Couple were well aware of Creator's Laws," the Rescuer added. "But they were snared by the subtle persuasions of the Light Bearer, who came to play the Adversary. Using temptation, the Light Bearer set a snare to test the strength of the human couple. But when they wavered from the Divine Will, and gave into temptation, they were cast out of Paradise and thrust onto a road of destruction."

"Are you talking about the Devil?" Cara May asked. She'd heard that word growing up so many times, she felt like she knew Him personally.

"Some people call Him that. He's actually a Great Angel, who descended, came down from the Divine Realms to bring polarity, Light and Dark, to the World of Matter," the Rescuer explained as they traveled through the Land of the Fallen, where the most hopeless characters dwelled.

"See, once man fell from Grace and continued to do harm, a great Darkness began to settle over the Earth. This shadow, a spiritual fog, as it were, obstructed the view between the Spiritual realms and human world. The more harm mankind did, the denser the Veil became between Spirit and man. Until one day, man could no longer see the Angels he once use to work beside," the Rescuer explained.

"But why didn't God stop them?" Cara May queried, because where she was didn't look like Paradise.

"Oh, He did, many times," the Rescuer explained. "Do you remember Noah and the Great Flood?"

Cara May's mind flashed back to a time when Nate brought out his Sacred Pipe. He explained that the pipe stone was red because it was made from the blood of the Ancestors who were drown in the Great Flood. That's why it was a sacred stone. "Not much," Cara May admitted. "Just some story Nate told me about why Pipe Stone was red. He said it was the blood of the people who drown in a Great Flood."

"Well," the Rescuer began. "At times, the Almighty washed away people swayed by evil from the Earth. But the threads of temptation remained."

"Because of the Tempter," Cara May added.

"Exactly. Mankind chose temptation and the Creator gave them Free Will. To put it simply, human spirits gave up eternal Peace and Harmony to have material things and a craving for knowledge and power," the Rescuer replied.

Seeing the puzzled look on her face, he made his explanation simpler. "Okay, the Adversary had two basic strategies to test the strength of a soul's faith. Either, They used temptation and snared you by your weaknesses. Or, if you didn't fall for that, They would use what you loved against you. It's true, the Light Bearer set the traps. But man jumped in with both feet!"

A light started to go on in her mind, as she saw all this laid out in front of her. "Why would they do that? Didn't they know how much it would cost them?"

"Obviously not. You see, the Tempter's messengers are very crafty. To get human spirits off their true course, the Deceivers simply misplaced the sign posts or turned them around completely. Sometimes They threw them away all together," the Rescuer explained.

"That reminds me of the witch in the Wizard of Oz," Cara May remembered. "She did all kinds of things so Dorothy didn't get to Oz."

"Yes, like that," the Rescuer agreed. "With all the flying monkeys, her witches brew to make them fall asleep. Those are the traps laid out to expose their weaknesses."

"But they had the good witch, Glinda," Cara May recalled. "She undid the sleeping potion, so Dorothy could get to Oz."

Finally, a fairytale proved to be their common ground. The Rescuer felt relieved. "Yes, you're right. The Adversary desperately tries to prevent mankind from ever waking up. Do you remember when Adam was put into a deep sleep and woman was created from his rib?"

"I think so. It's been a long time," Cara May admitted.

"Well, no where in that Holy Book did it say that Adam ever woke up," the Rescuer suggested.

When they got to the Land of the Twilight, Cara May noticed a rosy glow shining over the horizon. Behind a long fence, were throngs of people pressing themselves against it. Holding their Holy Book in their hands, they ranted and raved, demanding that their Savior come and take them to the Promise Land.

"Who are all these people?" Cara May finally asked as they walked through this shadowy valley. The light was so dim, she could barely make out the outline of the rolling hills, the green meadow and the tall bushes.

"They are caught in system of wrong beliefs," the Rescuer offered.

"Wrong beliefs?" Cara May questioned, thinking that the Holy Book must be true.

"Well, let me explain it this way," the Rescuer began. "They thought they knew the Word of the Almighty, but didn't live according to the Word."

"So you're saying they were hypocrites, going to church on Sunday and sinning the rest of the week," Cara May was familiar with those people.

"That's true for some, but others used that Holy Book like a weapon. They created fear in the hearts of others, rather than teaching the healing Word of Truth, which Christ meant it to be. You see, the healing power of the True Word remained dead within them. Had they used it correctly, they would have called it to life within themselves. You hear all the prayers they're saying, right?"

"Yeah, it sounds like what I learned in church," Cara May added.

"Most of them are just repeated words," the Rescuer began. "Things they learned by rote memory. These rote prayers aren't genuine. They have no heart, no life force to give them power."

"Like a car without gas," Cara May whispered as these teachings started to make sense.

"Yes, or a light without electricity," the Rescuer agreed. "Many souls lived their earthly lives according to a fixed dogma, which they wore around their neck like a yoke. They were slaves without any will of their own. Since they weren't allowed to think for themselves, it suppressed their own individual development. And this is the tragedy. It destroyed the possibility for their souls to ascend, to make the journey upward, back to the Source of Light."

"You see, Cara May, if there is no heart in a prayer, they are only empty words. A lukewarm prayer doesn't have the power it needs to bear fruit. It's the power of the Heart which gives the prayer its wings. The passion, the feeling, a prayer is said with, brings the necessary power for a prayer to do its work. Only say the words which vibrate in your soul," the Rescuer concluded. "Those are the ones which will receive a blessing."

"Oh," Cara May toned getting some understanding.

"Then you have others who only pray to get themselves out of trouble," the Rescuer added.

"You mean like Jail House Prayers," Cara May laughed having made a few of those herself.

"Exactly. The problem is, they never stopped to ask the Almighty if the choice they made was according to His Will," the Rescuer explained. "You see, every decision has a consequence. Had they opened themselves up to the small, still Voice which spoke the Truth, their lives might have turned out differently."

"Nate always said 'Go with your gut, Cara May. It won't let you down.'" Now Cara May understood what he was trying to say.

"That's right," the Rescuer agreed. "It's usually out of ignorance or self will that people go against the Laws of Creation. Then they wonder why their lives, or even after-lives, turned out so badly. The direction of a person's destiny is always determined by themselves alone," He continued to explain. "It depends on what they wish and desire."

"Like my mother?" Cara May asked. "She'd hold that Holy Book in her hand and tell me if I didn't change my wicked ways, I was going straight to Hell." Those words were like poisoned arrows, which pierced her young heart.

"Yes, I know your mother," the Rescuer responded. "She's over there somewhere, listening to a famous TV minister who made millions of dollars 'preaching the Word of God.' But he never personally aligned his life with the Creator's Laws or healed one soul. He didn't live according to what was True or Pure."

"That sounds like her," Cara May said out loud. "I used to ask her, if he was a messenger of God, why is he living in a ten million dollar house?"

"Well, you see, it's not that these people were bad, but their hearts were blocked. The mind, which is lifeless and cold, took over. Out of their mouths spewed meaningless, but cunning, nothings. The Word of Truth was meant to be a healing agent, not a tool to do harm," the Rescuer explained.

A resentment welled up in Cara May that blocked her from a God of her own understanding for many years. "My mother punished me with that Holy Book," she admitted. "After she got a hold of Jesus, I was nothing but a low life sinner."

"I understand Cara May," the Rescuer said compassionately. "But many were false shepherds, who used the Holy Writ to invoke fear in people. Out of ignorance, people fell prey to these spiritual highwaymen who gave them glittery tinsel rather than shiny pure gold. Their knowledge was false. They exploited the Living Word for their own selfish purposes. Instead of uplifting the downtrodden, they threatened them with eternal damnation. Rather than use that Divine Power to heal the sick, they basically twisted the Truth to assert their own power. But without the Living Power of Creator, their words had no life of their own."

"Birds of a feather, flock together," Cara May recited a childhood rhyme.

"Yes, that's right. Even here in the lower realms of the Spirit World, that is true. But those who lead their flock astray, nothing can help them until they lead every one of their misguided sheep back onto the True Path," the Rescuer explained.

"That's going to be a lot of people," Cara May sighed as she looked into the crowds of human spirits trapped in the Land of the Twilight.

"They had a part in it," the Rescuer went on. "Those who strayed from the Truth and were seduced by false promises, never benefited from it. Instead, they suffered for allowing themselves to be so easily influenced by wrong opinions. They never investigated these beliefs. They didn't think for themselves. Sunday morning, they flipped on the television and allowed themselves to be swayed. Now, they're handcuffed to false beliefs out of fear. Truly, there are none so blind as those who refuse to See."

Sadly for the Rescuers, human spirits who, out of their conceited beliefs, thought that they knew everything better while they lived on Earth, were the hardest souls to reach. How differently these 'faithful believers' imagined their Home-Coming to be. They thought they'd be welcomed joyfully and treated with respect. But they never allowed the Word of Love and Truth to become active within themselves. Most just prattled trivial nonsense while living on Earth.

"So how did they all get here?" Cara May asked, astounded that so many were trapped in the Twilight.

"Well here, every man is judged by his inner life," the Rescuer started. "Not by the outer, which is how it is in man's earthly life. A lot of people lived what I call 'gray lives.' They just followed orders and made up good reasons to do bad things."

"I know that one," Cara May admitted. "You work all week, just to party on the weekends."

"And if you got a moment, you gave God one hour on Sunday," the Rescuer chuckled.

"Well, only if I wasn't hungover from Saturday night," Cara May admitted.

"Sadly, most people are lagging behind in their spiritual development," the Rescuer admitted. "Especially if they didn't have any high goals for eternity. They just rushed through their earthly lives enslaved by human desires. Most of those here, never thought about improving their inner life."

"Wait... you mean people who had millions of dollars, kings, queens, presidents, those people could be down here?" Cara May asked, a little confused.

"If they caused others great misery, their inner Light was most likely dim. Then yes. They'd be drawn down to the lowest realms, where the most selfish and violent human spirits go. Mistakes bring pain," He explained.

"You can say that again," Cara May chimed in.

"Just look at their lives, Cara May. How did they live? Just because a person dies, transitions from his earthly body to his soul, doesn't mean his personality changes. So many here, just craved importance rather than being of true service. They wouldn't summon up the strength to conquer their lower natures. So, they were held earthbound. Bogged down by their vanity, stupidity, their conceit and narrow-mindedness. That being said, they didn't fulfill their true purpose," the Rescuer conceded. "If they were mean-spirited, miserable people, they will be with others who are the same as them."

A light went on in her head, as she finally understood Divine Justice. "So if you're mean, you go to the same place as other mean people?"

"And if you're are kind, you go to the place where the kind people go," the Rescuer agreed. "It's all a matter of spiritual gravity."

"Spiritual gravity? What's that?" she asked.

"It's a measurement of how much light a person carries within themselves. Those who are kind, carry more light than those who are mean. Then there are the Higher Realms, where those who selflessly serve Creator and others go," the Rescuer replied with a simple answer.

"So," Cara May started with a moment of reflection. "I got here because..."

"You got here because you took your life. Even though you didn't really want to. You put the poison in the needle, knowing that it was too much. So you made a wrong choice. And in your sadness and despair, you ended up with other souls, much the same as you. All locked away in the dark reaches of your own mind," the Rescuer offered without judgment.

"How did I get out?" she finally asked after a long silence.

"Love," the Rescuer smiled. "Your son Brian, along with Nate prayed very hard for you. They sang a song that you loved. All the people sent their love to you. Love is a bright light, a shining star which allowed Us to find you in this dark place."

The whole thing hit her so hard, she started to sob. "You know," she started. "Nate used to go to these AA meetings called "KYHOOYA." He said it stood for 'Keep Your Head Out Of Your Ass.' He'd poke me in the ribs and laugh so hard, saying 'Kih WHO YA! Cara May! Kih WHO YA!' Then he'd hand me a tissue and say, 'Once you pull your head out of your ass, Cara May, you can wipe the shit out your eyes with this tissue! Trust me, you'll have a whole better view and it doesn't stink so bad.' Sometimes he bugged me so much, I wanted to kill him. But he told me, he'd never give up on me. Looks like now, he never did."

"They love you Cara May," the Rescuer confided. "You just didn't know it. The dis-ease created a uneasiness inside your soul. Like a worm, it bored a hole into your mind and brought a state of unrest. This disquiet happens to be the most dangerous enemy for the soul. It's responsible for the breakdown in the soul's natural defenses. This is how the evil gets in. Eventually it caused the whole system to collapse."

"I know the song they sang for me," she started to shake her head. "Nate taught it to me, when I went with him to the Inipi. He said I had to give back. And since I had a good voice, I could sing in the lodge. I felt the words coming into my mind, just before I stood up. I saw all that light around me and wondered what it was. I feel so stupid now for what I did. I let so many people down. People who loved me, and I couldn't see it."

"You'll get another chance," the Rescuer empathized. "There is no such thing as eternal damnation, unless you want to stay in the dark. But given the choice, most people don't."

"I can't see why they would. It seems so futile down here, to be stuck like that," Cara May responded.

Along the Twilight borderline, was a long fence which held the throngs of people inside. Each board in the fence was a wrong belief that held them back. Pushing against the fence, the mob's cries for salvation grew even louder. Many called to their Savior, demanding to be taken to the holy lands. But their tormented minds bound them to what they had created in their earthly lives. Mankind can only ascend upwards by living the Truth, by adapting to the Laws of Creation.

"What about Jesus?" she finally asked, hearing all these people lament and pray. "Wasn't He supposed to take away the sins of the world?"

"Hmm," the Rescuer toned, knowing all the controversy around the Son of God. "Christ's birth was a gift from the Father to his Creation. But they were too blind to see it. He is the Bringer of Divine Truth, a powerful Way Shower. His whole mission was to guide people back to the Truth."

"Then what happened?" Cara May asked as they got closer and closer to the fence, where throngs of people shouted to their Creator demanding salvation.

"When He lived on the Earth, the people were not ready for such a powerful Teacher, a Prophet and the Light," the Rescuer responded. "They couldn't see the powerful Spirit which He is. For Spirit alone is Life. As far as taking away the sins of the world," the Rescuer continued. "Each soul is judged by their own inner Light. No one, except the Creator, can take away another man's sins. Each person has to atone for their mistakes themselves, and make right the wrongs they committed in their earthly lives."

"But the preacher said," Cara May shook her head. "That Christ died for our sins."

"Christ overcame death. By his ascension, he showed that death was not real. Christ, an innocent man, was betrayed and murdered," the Rescuer explained. "He committed no crime, but was crucified on a Roman cross over 2000 years ago. You see, Cara May, a person's beliefs may not be the Word of Truth. But even here, they find their own kind, according to how they lived and believed in life."

"Murdered?" that word hung in the air, as Cara May processed all the things she was told growing up. "I remember that the Roman soldiers made him a crown of thorns and one stabbed Jesus in the side."

"The Roman empire was a brutal sort of people," the Rescuer sighed. "To be crucified was a brutal way to die."

"Not only that, but they fed the Christians to the lions!" Cara May remembered from her history lesson. "Why did God allow Christ to be murdered?"

"The Adversary lay in wait for him," the Rescuer went on. "Don't you remember how Herod killed all the babies? The Darkness was so convinced that Christ's Light would reveal Them, that It persuaded the leaders of that time to murder anyone who might be Christ."

"Wow, that's rough," Cara May said, finally seeing how big this Game of Duality really was.

"It would be if the damage was permanent," the Rescuer offered.

"Even when the Adversary himself offered Christ the whole world, if Christ would come over to his side, Christ never wavered. He remained true to His inner nature, which was Love."

"So that's what it means to be Christ-like?" Cara May asked.

"I believe so," the Rescuer said.

"So what about forgiveness? If Christ didn't die for our sins, I guess all those Hail Marys and Our Fathers I said after confession, didn't mean anything. Or take away the stupid stuff I did that week?" Cara May asked a little puzzled.

Looking at her perplexed face, the Rescuer chuckled. "Well, did you say those prayers from your heart?"

"No, not really. The priest just said I had to do 25 Hail Marys and forty-five Our Fathers as penance," Cara May admitted.

"Well, if you didn't mean it, they were just empty words," the Rescuer admitted. "A priest can't absolve anyone of their sins, Cara May. He doesn't have the authority to do that. Only Creator can wipe a man's personal debt clean."

"So why did they tell me to say all those prayers?" Cara May questioned.

"Some ritual the Church put together, I suppose," the Rescuer said. "Much of Christ's message was distorted over time. Some used It to gain personal power, rather than align themselves with the Power of the Divine."

"Some part of me always knew those prayers didn't mean anything," Cara May finally put together. In life, she railed against the idea of God because her blind eyes saw no evidence of Him.

As they approached the long fence, the Rescuers walked right through it. For a moment, Cara May hesitated. She thought about her mother being trapped in this place and wanted to help her. Reading Cara May's thoughts, the Rescuer held out his hand to Cara May. "When you are ready and healed yourself, you will have the needed power to help out in the Shadows. But first, we need to get you rested and healed. Are you ready to come with Us?"

Looking around at all these people, she shivered. This is the torment she grew up in. There was no way she'd stay in there now. Just listening to their harsh words while they ranted and raved, made her feel incredibly tired. In that instant, a great, unquenchable longing for Love and Truth filled her soul. Without a doubt, she knew nothing that Earth life offered or what lay in these lower realms, could satisfy it.

In a moment of deep contemplation, she realized that all she'd thought before, were mistaken ideas. Suddenly, her face was overcome with an expression of peace and calm. Her eyes lost that troubled, anxious look and started to shine more brightly. Letting out a huge sigh of relief, her heart filled with the purest hope. It helped her to raise her foot in the right direction. Without a further thought, she grabbed the Rescuer's extended hand and passed through the fence.

Gradually, their surroundings grew lighter and lighter as they continued to walk. The gray, dark reaches of the Shadows faded away, as they entered a beautiful, wild flowered meadow, surrounded by towering, snow-capped mountains, great evergreen forests and winding crystal blue streams. That's when she heard the whinny of her grandpa's favorite horse, the one she learned to ride on as a child. Moments later, it came galloping up to greet her. Squealing in child-like glee, Cara May rushed over to put her arms around that trusted steed.

"Is my grandpa here?" Cara May asked stroking the horse's face, looking around at the beautiful countryside.

"Yes," the Rescuer answered. "You'll see him later. Right now, let's go over to the Home, where you can rest and get cleaned up."

The pelting steam filled his nose, as Nate handed Hal back the drum. Tears streamed down his face as he thought of Cara May. Losing her to the dis-ease of addiction left a great hole in his heart. He'd seen so many get taken out by drugs and alcohol over the years. But it never got easier to lose the ones you loved. Over the glowing stones, Nate could see Brian's head hung down low. Nate loved him like he was his own son. This time, he'd make sure that Brian knew he always had a place with him.

"Is everybody okay?" Hal asked as he placed the buffalo horn back in the bucket. Murmurs and whispers of 'Yeah' came back from around the lodge. "Okay, then who's next?"

"Hi, I'm Nancy. I'm a long time friend of Hal's and Nate. When we heard Hal was putting on this ceremony, I told my Half-side that we had to take a road trip. So we followed Nate and Brian all the way from California. I wouldn't have missed this for the world. When I was a little girl, they drafted my dad into the US Army and sent him to Korea. He went missing and never came back. I had uncles that went to Viet Nam and a nephew that went to Afghanistan. After they got an honorable discharge, they started drinking hard. They weren't ever the same men, that went into battle as came out."

"A few years ago, my uncle died from cirrhosis of the liver. We don't know what happened to my nephew. He went missing about a year ago. Nobody's seen him since. I found out you can be 'Missing in Action' even after you get back to the States. I'm asking Creator to bring back my nephew. It's killing my baby sister to not know where he is. And I ask for a healing for all those men and women who served their country and never came back. Like Brian said, I ask Creator to send His Rescuers to bring them all Home. Aho Mitakuye Oyasin." Pouring a small dipper of water on the Grandfathers, Hal waited for the next person to share their prayers.

Meanwhile across the demon-infested battlefield, wild fireworks exploded across the cloudy skies. Micah, captain of the heavenly Warriors, shot through the sky like a flaming comet, while the hulking warlord and his minions gave chase. Twisting and turning over the checkerboard farmland, Micah rocketed through the heavens. Speckled with barns and pastures filled with cows chewing their cud, this spiritual warfare blasted though the thunderheads.

In Micah's wake, the trail of sparkling fire washed over the smoky skies with purifying light. As the passionate prayers inside the Inipi grew stronger, their power charged through the Heavens, bringing more Light to this troubled place. In a burst of brilliant wings, more and more heavenly Warriors charged through the killing fields, wielding their flaming swords against the powers of night. With suicidal abandon, the demonic warlords screeched their deafening war cries and flung themselves into the dogfight. Wailing cries amongst the shadows pierced the air, as the dark cloud was swept away by heavenly forces.

"My name is Andre' and my great, great, grand-daddy was born a slave," his strong, smooth southern drawl began. "His name was Otis and his grandparents came over to here on slave ships from Africa. They were beaten and shackled, but they prayed to their African Gods for mercy. Them white folk was afraid of those African prayers. They called them black magic. Mostly, because it sent the evils done to the people back to these white slave owners, like a boomerang. They was afraid they'd reap what they had sown." His deep, penetrating voice flowed like molasses through the lodge.

"Now, my great, great grand-daddy was a big, strong man. Most of the time, those slave owners used him like he was a stud-horse, like a stallion. He was forced to sire childrens just for their size. But he never got a chance to love them, or hold them to his-self. He was just property to the white man, to be bought and sold like chattel, to be used and then thrown away. When the Civil War broke out, Otis escaped and headed north to join the Army. He fought against the South, putting an end to slavery forever. But that didn't change the hate," Andre' stopped for a second to catch his breath.

"After the war, Otis found his-self a Choctaw woman who knew about medicines. She doctored his torn up body and ministered to his soul. With her medicine ways, she healed his soul sickness. By and by, they had themselves a little girl. He finally got to hold his child to his heart and protect her like she was his own. It's their blood that runs through my veins today. It their ancestral drum that beats in my heart. My prayer is to heal the hatred that is making our people sick."

"More people of color fill the prisons, than anybody else. Prisons, which only make a profit if they are full of our people. So many are lost to drugs and alcohol. The city streets are filled with gangs. Our young ones don't have sober parents, or parents at all. I don't know where it started, but I'm asking Creator to send the Great Ones to heal the cause of all this hatred and hurt our people have suffered. The suffering won't stop, until we end the hate. I thank you for bringing the people together to make this prayer happen for our loved ones. Aho Mitakuye Oyasin." Throwing another dipper of water, Hal waited until the next one started to speak. The prayers were powerful this morning. So many people had lost their loved ones to war and hatred. It overwhelmed him at times.

Listening to the sound of the people's voices, Leroy took a deep breath, feeling the steam of Hal's last dipper of water surround him. Going into silent prayer, Leroy closed his eyes, hearing the gurgling stones singing their water song. After a moment, the Brave, the warrior from the battlefield, appeared in front of him. "Come on! Let's go," the Brave commanded. Without a thought, Leroy's Spirit followed the Brave to where a great white stallion stood waiting. Clutching the horse's mane, the Brave pulled himself onto the horse, and held his hand out to Leroy. Leroy grabbed the Brave's powerful arm and flung himself over the rear flank of the horse. With his heels, the young Brave kicked the white steed in its flanks. Galloping faster than an arrow flies, this brilliant white steed bolted across the prairie grasslands. As his heart pumped full of adrenaline, Leroy held on for dear life while this great steed outran the wind. Thundering hooves beat the Earth like a powerful drum, pushing ever faster, when Leroy saw ahead of them. They racing straight for a cliff.

As they neared the cliff's edge, the Brave gave one last strong kick to the horse's flank, pressing it to full speed. At the edge of the cliff, the powerful hind legs of this great white stallion pushed off the ground with the force of a rocket, bursting into the sky. In that instant, near the top of the horse's front shoulder, the white stallion grew brilliant wings. Looking down, Leroy watched the Earth pull away. With its great wings beating against the wind, the stallion, now turned Pegasus, flew higher and higher. Crossing through the towering thunderheads, Leroy and the Brave came upon a Gathering of Spirits.

With his powerful bronze shoulders thrust back, the Brave strutted deliberately through the crowd of Spirits and came up behind one man, a Chief wearing a full headdress. Leroy kept pace close behind. As the Chief turned around, the Brave swept his arm in Leroy's direction. As Leroy stepped forward, he recognized the Chief. It was Sitting Bull, the Dakota Chief from Standing Rock. Gazing into Leroy's eyes, the Chief spoke. His words echoed through Leroy's being. "Thank you, my son," Sitting Bull said.

With that, Leroy felt himself thrust back into his body. The pelting steam from the glowing Grandfathers was beating on him. "Thank you my son," Leroy whispered out loud, trying to take in the immense meaning of those words. Ever since Hal brought him into his first lodge, he had a feeling that these Old Ways were his own. But now, he could see it all in a much larger way.

"You say something Leroy," Hal questioned as he poured more water on the stones.

"No, it's okay. I'll tell you later," Leroy replied not wanting to lose this sacred moment.

"All righty then," Hal went on. "Now, before we open the door. I got a few people I want to make prayers for. You know, one of my mentors told me 'There's no pancake too thin, it ain't got two sides.' Just like our stories. He counseled me that 'there's always my side, your side and the truth.' His name was Alan. He was, by far, one of the most crotchety old timers in AA I'd ever met. And he had 28 years sober before he died from organ failure from Hep C. It was a sad set of consequences he had to suffer because he shot dope after he came home from Viet Nam. Now Alan had this on going feud with a Korean war veteran named Lenny. They're both gone now. But I got to sing Alan a few songs the night he passed. So I ask Creator to bless up all those veterans who suffered from PTSD after they came back for their military service."

"Now, the day after Christmas back in Makato, in 1862, the United States Government strung up 38 Dakota Warriors. It was the biggest execution in the US history. One of them warriors that got strung up that day, was a great uncle of mine. At that time, they'd been rounding up Indians and putting us in these concentration camps they called reservations. All the while, the BIA was stealing the provisions and money promised our Dakota relatives in trade for millions of acres of our land. With them thieving BIA people selling off our provisions, our people were starving. So a hunting party went out to get some food. One of them got caught stealing some eggs and they killed 5 white people. That's how the Dakota war got started. It ended with the imprisonment of 300 Dakota warriors, outta which they hung 38, who were my ancestors. From what I understand, Ol' Abe Lincoln pardoned one of the braves meant to be hung that day. I can't imagine what that Brave must of felt like knowing he was number 39, and got to go free."

"These United States of America had rough beginnings. In the four hundred years of Indian wars with the Europeans coming over here, there's been blood on both sides. From what I read, those white folk got exiled from their homeland by their own King. He sent his undesirables across the Great Water to fend for themselves. Now, they tried to make it over here. The problem is, those land grabbers have been trying to exterminate our people ever since. Today, I ask for a healing for all those lost during the Indian wars, whichever side they were on. See, when I ask for healing for the enemies of my people, the truth can come out. Healing brings truth. From what I gather, us breathing folks are only free when ALL OF US ARE FREE! I ask Creator to send his Rescuers to bring them all home. I'm honored to sit behind this bucket and help with this prayer. That being said, let's open the door," Hal finished his prayer and dumped the rest of the water on the stones.

With great enthusiasm, all the people called "AHO MITAKUYE OYASIN!"

Clouds of steam billowed out the flap as the fire-keeper opened the door. "Give us a back door," Hal called out as he passed out the water bucket. Hanging low in the Southern sky, were two stars nestled into the deep azure backdrop. A rosy glow came into the lodge from the fireplace in these last minutes before dawn.

Stepping away from the parade of homecoming spirits streaming through the West Gate, Ben peeked his head in the door. "It looks like 30 more people showed up Hal, the cars keep coming."

"Well, I'll be," Hal replied not sure what his next move would be.

"I guess we'll be running lodges back to back until we get everybody in."

"We're already talking about building an East facing lodge," Ben said. "From the looks of it, we got people coming from all over Creation."

"What?" Hal chuckled. "Did somebody send a telegram?"

"Aho Mitakuye Oyasin," a young voice said from the back row.

"Yeah," Hal responded, as he wiped the sweat off his brow with a towel.

"Somebody posted it on Facebook," the young voice said. "This morning it already had 10,000 Likes."

Not knowing much about social media, except that it was a way for people to communicate en masse, Hal just laughed. "Well, what exactly did they say?"

"They said it was A Prayer for Veterans from every war," the young voice replied.

"Well, when Spirit moves, it don't waste much time. I guess we better get cracking," Hal replied. "Fire-keeper! Bring us seven more stones!"

Then Ben leaned into the lodge door, quietly whispering to his friend sitting behind the bucket. "From the looks of it Hal, you got a lot of Angels, holy Warriors, around you."

"From the power in all these prayers," Hal thought. *"There better be."* With compassionate eyes, Hal looked at Ben. "That's good to know, old buddy. That's good to know."

And so it went. By the time Hal and Leroy finished the first sunrise lodge, small tent cities were being constructed all around the land. A make-shift kitchen was already in the works. With many hands, a council teepee was put up in nothing flat. Normally ceremony was an undertaking by invitation only, when a person made a request for a prayer. But it seemed the whole world needed this prayer.

In the long part of the afternoon, Hal went back to his truck to fetch his phone. There was a missed call from Roy on it. So Hal called him back. As the phone rang, Hal took a gander at everything that came together on this big day. It overwhelmed him.

"This is Roy," Roy answered.

"Yeah, Roy, I saw you called and I wanted to get back to you before things got too big out here," Hal started.

"How's it going so far?" Roy asked, while Emma stood in the doorway listening in.

"Well, we had maybe a hundred people here when we pulled up at dawn, and more keep coming," Hal replied.

"Wow, a hundred people? Word must of got out, huh?" Roy replied. Emma motioned her dad to put the call on speaker, so she could listen in.

"Yeah, somebody in the lodge said it got posted on Facebook, of all places. Said it was a prayer for veterans of every war," Hal went on. "We got tent cities coming together and a make-shift kitchen, to boot."

"You need anything?" Roy asked, knowing from experience how these things went.

"Well, if the wood holds up, we'll be able to keep the lodges going," Hal said. "So far, I think we got enough propane to keep the camp stoves going. But who knows. I never thought it'd get this big."

"Well, listen, I got enough wood chopped out back. I can bring a pile of it in the trailer. If you think you need it," Roy offered.

"Hmm," Hal said. "That'd be great and you can stay for a lodge."

With pleading eyes, Emma looked at her dad and shook her yellow-curled head up and down. Roy smiled and put his hand on the top of her head. "Well, it looks like me and the Little Miss will make it out there as soon as we can," Roy chuckled. It wasn't long after Hal started working for Roy again, that he brought them to their first Inipi ceremony. Emma, Roy's little half-pint, took to ceremony like a fish to water.

So the next morning, at dawn's first light, when Roy pulled up towing a trailer packed to the gills with wood and supplies, Ben wasn't the least bit surprised. Out of the corner of his eye, he'd been watching Emma for quite a while now. Ever since she started coming to ceremony, he knew there was something special about her.

From the first time she sat in the Inipi with Hal, Ben, Leroy, her dad and some of the other mainstays, Emma felt like she'd come home. Listening as Ben spoke in his ancestral language, it sounded distantly familiar. After the lodge, she'd sit with Ben and he'd teach her many of the songs which were sung in the Inipi. Having a strong voice, she loved singing.

As he saw the men unloading the wood from the trailer, Ben went over to lend a hand. "Good morning Ben," Emma called across the wood pile.

"Morning Emma," Ben smiled. "I got word you were coming."

"Did the Wind tell you again," Emma joked knowing Ben's relationship with Tah-tay.

"Naw, she's been telling me other things," Ben went along. "Hal broke the news to me late last night. It's good that you're here."

Emma came over and gave the old man a hug. Her bright, smiling green eyes melted the crusty hard shell around his heart which comes from living alone too long. "You know something Ben?" Emma asked in a whisper.

"No, what?" Ben replied.

"I think you're the only one I can tell this too," she leaned in speaking softly. Ben braced himself for something foreboding.

"What happened?" Ben finally asked.

"Well, last night... no early this morning," Emma started. "I had this dream that a man passed me a hawk feather."

Ben smiled. "You know Emma, there's something I've suspected about you all along."

"What's that?" Emma asked, cocking her blonde curls to the side.

"Well, I don't know how to break it to you Emma," Ben looked down, saying this in the most serious tone. "But I think you're more Indian than you know."

Relieved to hear that, Emma chucked.

Looking into her eagle eyes framed by her high cheek bones, Ben smiled. "You're what I'd call a White Indian.

Emma laughed and gave the old man a squeeze. "You might be right," she said. "I feel right at home around all this ceremony."

"Well, I think it was meant to be that Hal found you and your family at WalMart. You needed to come live out on the prairie and remember who you are," Ben finished. "Now, we'd better get this wood stacked up. It's gonna be another busy day around the fireplace."

A couple days after they constructed the East facing lodge, a veteran sun dancer from Montana offered to pour a South facing lodge. Being from a Turtle Clan, he heard about the ceremony and wanted to offer his help. That night the people gathered in the Council Teepee to discuss this new lodge and other things that had come up. It was a council of Many Nations.

"Aho Mitakuye Oyasin. It seems to me," Hal started standing up in front of the people. "That when Leroy had that vision, he knew it'd be more than a one day ceremony. I want to say, I'm grateful for everyone being here, making those deep heartfelt prayers and pitching in around the fire place. I can tell by the number of people that keep showing up, two lodges might not be enough. So I'm willing to have our Sun Dance Brother from the Turtle Clan build a South Facing lodge, and take care of that prayer, if he wants to."

With her white, handmade shawl wrapped around her shoulders, wearing a ceremonial ribbon dress, an Elder Grandmother turned sharply to Hal the moment he paused. "Are you willing to be here until every prayer is made?"

"How could I let Creator down, when He's given me so much already? I got my work, like everybody else. But I believe this is important," Hal asserted.

Keeping everyone warm, a gentle, crackling fire blazed in the center of the teepee. It cast a warm glow on all the faces watching. Off to the side stood Raymond, his eyes, the color of soft Earth, gazed into the fire. Since he was a young child, he'd walked a medicine path. Quietly he shook his turtle shell rattle as he prayed, offering some cedar to the counsel fire. Quite a few decades ago, he was born in middle of a thunderstorm. At the moment of his birth, rays of sunlight burst through the kitchen window of his grandmother's cabin, lighting up the whole room. His mother named him Raymond, after the rays of sun which blessed him the moment he came into the world.

Of course, as a teenager, his relationship with the Thunders grew. After he turned thirteen, his grandmother found him outside in a wintery blizzard. Seeing him surrounded by white snow, she heard his voice talking behind the house. As she opened the backdoor, a crashing thunderbolt jolted her body off the back steps. Thunder snow shook the heavens as white lightning crackled through the snow-white blustery sky. From then on, she named him "White Thunder," Wakinyan Ska.

As his gaze melded with the fire, he could see with the eyes of his soul. In his mind's eye, he saw a large Medicine Wheel. On it, the Red Road of Man ran from East to West. It was the road, wherein many streams of destiny, traveled from early days of birth to the final days of decay. Having built the East and West facing lodges, the ceremony represented this path from man's sunrise to his sunset.

But the Blue Road of Spirit, which runs from South to North, would stop at the Sacred Fireplace, if there was only a South Facing Lodge without a North facing lodge to balance it. In order to build a South facing lodge, they'd also have to build a North facing lodge. Then the Red Road of Man and the Blue Road of Spirit would come together at the Sacred Fire Place. He could see that this is what Spirit was asking them to do. Standing up, he motioned to be heard.

"This is no small prayer for healing that's being asked to be born," Raymond started as he drew a large Medicine Wheel on the ground with a stick. "The crossing-over of Spirits lost in the Shadows, is only the beginning. There are other things we need to consider too."

"Right now, as I speak the very lungs of Maka Ina, our Redwood forests, the guardians of the West, are being destroyed." Raymond's jaw set tight, when he said this. "So loggers and developers can line their pockets with money. These thoughtless men would destroy one of Earth's most precious treasures for the sake of few dollars. We breathe clean air because of these great forests all over the Earth. Our very being is deeply interconnected with the plant kingdom, which makes the oxygen. The Spirit of the Redwood Trees are the wise giants who have cradled and nurtured the people on Earth from the very beginning. They are the historians, connecting us with the our ancestors, our roots and our past lives."

"Years ago, my sun dance brother, Ohiya, ran a four year Sun Dance, out there in the West, to stop the cutting down of virgin forests. After the first year of the dance, that ruthless logging company went bankrupt. By the time Ohiya finished that dance, a new logging company bought out the old one. In a humble manner, they told the people they would respect the Old Standing Ones, the record keepers, who are the Guardians of the West."

"It's almost every day, I read about some oil spill," Raymond went on. "This oil is the blood of Mother Earth. These careless fools are draining her blood to make money. Their minds are possessed by greed. And so they create wars over this black gold, which stains the Earth with our blood. It mutilates Her children. And so her Spirit cries."

As the power of his words filled the air, looming thunderheads began to gather in the East. "But what troubles me the most," his voice grew somber. "Are those crazy ones, who brutalize the innocent, those who have no voice, the four-leggeds. From what I see, it will take all of us together, with our Ancestors in the Spirit World, to heal this planet from human destruction. But our Brothers on the other-side can only match our efforts. We have to be willing to do as much as they do."

To draw down the needed purity and love to heal this great planet, took a person with the required humility. The self-importance of the ego must be stripped away, to allow the Power of the Most High to flow through. Merely having the ability to run a ceremony was not enough. The conduit had to be clean. For the needed Power to flow through and anchor down, here on Earth, the will of man must meld with the Will of the Most High. All selfish desires had to be put aside. For they only paralyzed his abilities to soar. Oftentimes, a man who had those abilities, but lacked the required humility, went through a series of humblings. These bone-crushing experiences chipped away at the impurity of a man's being. This humbling process was, at times, excruciatingly painful. After a man left behind all that was unnecessary or wrong, it effectively made him ready to serve Creator in the Highest capacity.

"If you look at the Medicine Wheel," With a stick Raymond began drawing on the ground, a large circle with a cross in the center, representing the Medicine Wheel. "The Red Road of Man goes from East to West. We have that represented right now, with our East and West facing lodges. But to build a South facing lodge, the Blue Road of Spirit, which runs from south to north, would stop right in the middle of the fire place. This would not be balanced."

Over the distant hillsides in the East, brewed a tempest of Love and purification. Large, towering, dark-bellied thunderheads gathered together over the killing fields. The air began to shake as the heavenly wings of the Thunderbird beat against the sky. With their lightning bolts in hand, the holy Warriors known as the Fire Elementals, coursed through the heavens. As they rode on the wings of the Thunders, their Lightning Bolts crashed into every hot spot of this spiritual battle. Spinning, twisting and whirling, the Spirit of the Wind danced in sacred circles, shaking loose the spiritual filth from across the golden prairie. All the spirits of Nature came to the aide of Mother Earth, to help her in this momentous time.

Invisible to man's naked eyes, the Nature Spirits, known as Elementals, were the builders and administrators to all of Creation. This included the seas, the mountains, the rivers, the forests, the meadows and the countryside. As well as the soil, the rocks and the plants.

For centuries, the Nature Spirits suffered greatly at the destructive hand of man. Gnomes, fairies and elves struggled to survive, while keeping balance and harmony on Earth. But now, they were supplied with a Source of Living Power coming to Earth, by the Will of the Creator. Earth was to be made clean of all the destructive agents. All harm caused by human spirits would roll back on the originators and a Great Harvest would follow.

"What's being shown to me," Raymond continued as he drew circles over the four directions on the Medicine Wheel with his stick. "Is we need to complete this circle. Then the Power will come together, here at the crossroads, where the Red Road and Blue Road meet." Dancing across the killing fields, the roar of the Thunders answered in bold voices. Rods of white lightning flashed across the sky.

"See, when the Blue Road of Spirit comes together with the Red Road of Man," Raymond went on. "Healing and rebirth will come to Earth. From East to West, the Red Road of Man travels across our Great Mother. This is our journey from the sunrise of our birth, to the sunset of our decay. It's our life cycle."

"Going from South to North, flows the Blue Road of Spirit," Raymond drew the crossroads with his stick on the ground. "It will bring the Ancestors together with the people of Earth. To honor our brother from Montana with a South facing lodge, we must complete the circle with a North facing Inipi. Then the Red Road of Man will come together with the Blue Road of Spirit."

"All the people must be allowed to welcome their ancestors home, if we are to clear away the heavy blanket of sorrow which has come through centuries of war. Then the people will become Free and cooperation will come to the many nations of people who live on Maka Ina. This is what Spirit has shown me," Raymond concluded. "And so I believe, it must be."

The moments of deep silence were jarring around the circle in the Council Teepee as his words touched ground and sunk in. Overhead, great clashes of rumbling thunder rolled across the cloud covered sky. Standing at the head of the council, Hal waited for a moment before speaking to see if anyone else wanted to be recognized.

"You know," Hal started as he gazed into the flames of the Council Fire. "Talking about Ohiya made me think about a Sun Dance that happened in Cannon Ball, North Dakota in 1937 on the Standing Rock Reservation. Ohiya showed me an article which was written up in the Sioux Pioneer. Over a 1000 people came to that dance, from all over Montana, Wyoming and the Dakotas. That day, there was a photographer named Ivan Dmitri, from New York , who came to watch the Indians dance for rain. He took a whole bunch of pictures. From what I understand, that write up made it to the Saturday Evening Post."

As Hal was talking, Emma remembered an envelope which she had left in the truck. While Hal and Leroy were on the road, she called up the Archives Department of the Saturday Evening Post. A few days ago, the article came in the mail. Nudging her dad for the keys to the truck, she raced to the truck to get it. The manila envelope was sitting on the dash, where she left it.

"When me and Leroy were out in California, we watched this show on Climate Change, what they call global warming. They showed all the floods, the storms, the earthquakes, fires, tornadoes and hurricanes that have been happening on Mother Earth," Hal started. "Even the Chief of the Inuit People of Alaska weighed in, because the polar ice cap is melting and they're losing their hunting ground. What registered for me was, this isn't climate change, Mother Earth is plum pissed off. And she's got good cause. What Ray talked about, with this being a bigger prayer than we realize, made me think. We got an opportunity to really draw down the Love of Creation to heal Maka Ina. I agree with the idea of having balance in the Sacred Hoop. We've been out of balance for a long time." All throughout the Council Teepee, people whispered amongst themselves, as they realized the importance of what they were undertaking. Nudging Hal, Emma handed him the manila envelop. "What's this?" he whispered in her ear.

"Open it," she whispered back. Hal glanced into the envelope and saw the rich pictures of the 1937 Sun Dance, taken many decades ago. Gently he pulled the article out.

"Where'd you get this?" Hal whispered. Emma pointed to the top of the article, where it said "Saturday Evening Post." Hal's heart smiled, his face beamed from ear to ear. On a small table in the teepee, he laid it out.

"Well folks," Hal started. "Looks like my girl Emma here, ordered a copy of that article from the Saturday Evening Post, about that 1937 Sun Dance in Cannon Ball. I'm going to lay it out here on the table, if you want to take a gander at it. It says right here that 1000 people showed up for those few days. What that tells me, is we can take care of this prayer, and it don't matter how many people show up."

Stepping up, Ben asked to be recognized. "I can see what Ray was talking about lighting up four lodges. That would draw tremendous

Power down from the Creator. I asked my grandson Sam what he thought, and we both agreed it'd be a good idea. So I'd like to offer putting up a North facing lodge, and me and Sam will take care of it." Murmurs shot through the people inside the teepee. Another hand went up in the back of the teepee, as Jon, a Comanche from Oklahoma, stepped forward and asked to be recognized.

"My great, great grandfather had a lot to do with starting the Native American Church," Jon started. "When I heard that y'all were going to run this ceremony for veterans, I wanted to come up and offer putting up a teepee. That Paiute fella, Wovoka, who had the vision about the Ghost Dance, well the people who were killed here, were dancing the Ghost Dance when they got shot down. From what I recollect, that's the first time that Grandpa Peyote found its way to the North. But I'm offering to run a Teepee Ceremony to honor up the Ancestors who were dancing with the medicine when those Christian soldiers shot them down." More stirring whispers came from the people, as they realized how many were willing to step up to see this prayer come together. In Ben's mind, he could see the condor from the South circling the Sacred Fire Place with the eagle of the North.

Standing across from Hal, the Elder Woman stood up again to speak. "I can see how many are offering their time and heart to this prayer. It's very moving to my heart. But how long will this prayer last?"

At that moment, a clash of thunder rocked the Teepee. Hal stood in front of everyone, feeling somewhat overwhelmed. "Well...," Hal started as he looked out into the sea of faces. "From what I'm guessing right now, we'll pray this up until all our thunder is plum wore out."

Standing off towards the south-east part of the circle were 3 Men of the Cloth. Though their white collars were concealed by a jacket or a scarf, they had listened intently to this whole procession. Armored with exorcism salt and the Manuel for Minor Exorcisms, Father Rob stepped bravely forward into the center of the circle, asking to be recognized. His salt and pepper curly hair framed his furled forehead as he started to speak. "My name is Father Rob," he bravely said out loud. "And I heard about this prayer ceremony from a woman I performed a few exorcisms on a while back."

There were murmurs in the crowd of people inside. An Elder woman stepped forward and cut him off. "It's because of your kind that our people here got murdered! There's a lot of spilt blood on the hands of the Church!"

Hal stepped forward to calm things down. "Now let the man speak. We can't go accusing him of the murders that were committed here a life time ago. This is a prayer for veterans and their families. Everyone has a right to pray. State your business, Father Rob," Hal finished.

"Well, I understand that the Church and Columbus had a lot to do with the annihilation of many tribes across the Americas," Father Rob began as the murmurs in the crowd agreed. "I haven't killed anyone myself, but I've lost loved ones who fought in foreign wars. I came with two of my fellow brothers and we wanted to help with the deliverance and blessing of this land."

"How can you make amends for the family I lost a hundred years ago?" the Elder woman asked. "My ancestors were gunned down on this land by Christian soldiers. I know about the Roman empire, how they brutalized the people from all over Europe and the Middle East. Their Church did the same thing, starting holy wars all over to have an empire."

Father Rob sighed a deep sigh. "You know, years ago, I was an ignorant man, even an arrogant priest. I believed that the Roman Catholic Church was the one true church, that is until I met Molly. She needed an exorcism because she'd been attacked for 10 years by some witches from South America. Even though she was baptized as a baby, she left the Church at 14 and didn't come back for 40 years. When she told me she prayed with Indians in a sweat lodge, I told her that Indians prayed to spirits that were not of God. She told me flat out that wasn't true. In the Inipi, they only prayed to the Creator." There were many whispers among the people as he spoke.

"Now, by the time she met me, she'd paid thousands of dollars to psychics and Santeros, to help her with this spiritual warfare," Father Rob continued. The first time I sat down with her, I performed an exorcism. Her mind was completely clear, but it only lasted a week before the demon came back. When I went to bless her house, the peace lasted 24 hours before all hell broke loose. I had to get a team together to pray for her. But in that time, I learned some things about myself and about the ceremony that she was so loyal to. So when she told me about this ceremony to bless up this land and help with the spirits, I had to come see for myself. I may not be able to make up for all the loss suffered by misguided murderers. Christ never killed anyone. But I'd like to help out with this prayer and begin the forgiveness that needs to happen between us all."

Hal stepped forward and looked into the sea of faces. "Well, I've listened to all of us speak and I think that this is going to be a very powerful prayer. It's true that many bad things happened here, but I believe that Great Spirit is bringing this all together so we can peace among us. Does anyone else have anything else to say?"

No one else stepped forward. And so it was decided that the axis, the line representing the Blue Road of Spirit would have not only a North and South-facing lodge, but a teepee placed just south of the Inipi. That way, all those who prayed with Grandpa Peyote could honor up their Ancestors as well. Father Rob and his two Padres would do a deliverance and blessing on the land and for anyone else who wanted it. And the people kept coming.

After the Council Meeting came to an end, Leroy found Emma in the crowd of people. They grabbed a towel and took a long walk along the bluffs, above the Ceremony site. A sea of people flowed through the sacred piece of land forming a whole community. As the word spread, they came together from all over, to share in the vision that Leroy and Hal had. As he looked back to see all the bustling people, Leroy put it all together and felt overcome with gratitude.

Beaming with a smile from ear to ear, Leroy felt lightheaded while they walked along a deer trail up the small hillside. Overhead, large, brooding, dark gray storm clouds blanketed the sky. In answer to their prayers, the Fiery Elements coursed above the killing fields in a tempest of Love. Unseen to Emma and Leroy's eyes, Micah, the holy Warrior and Dakotah, with his holy shield, walked along beside them. Though the black cloud of doom had been pierced through with many arrows of Light, Micah wanted his main saints secured from the black talons of deception and darkness which still crawled beneath the soil of this blood-stained land.

Spiritual shock waves rumbled through the air as a bolt of Light ripped through the sky. Rods of White Lightning, the Thunder's electric force, continued to sweep away all that was unholy. From the sweat lodges below, Leroy and Emma could hear the pounding drum along with the voices singing those ancient medicine songs, calling to the Higher Powers. As the music floated across the sprawling grasslands, it deafened the Spirits of destruction, along with all their creatures and servants, Spirits born of envy and hate. This powerful call to the Love of Creation anchored an eternal pillar of divine Light onto Mother Earth. With its purifying power, it consumed the heaviness which lay across Earth like wet blanket of sorrow. This brought Peace to a place which contained so much heartache.

"I'm really glad you and your dad came, Emma," he said glancing in her direction. It wasn't long after Leroy started working for Roy, that Hal invited them both to pray in the Inipi. The first time Emma sat in the lodge, she felt like she'd come home.

"What? Miss out on all this?" Emma smiled as they hiked a little further. "Not a chance."

There was a long moment of silence, as Leroy tried to work through things in his mind. For the whole time he was in California, she was constantly in his thoughts. Which wasn't unusual for two people who worked together, side by side most every day, for the last few years. But sitting in her childhood room that day, looking at all her pictures, filled in a chunk of Emma's life he never knew. But until this moment, he hadn't thought to bring it up.

"I can't believe you'd name a horse Snowball!" he scolded her for a moment, his mind flashing back to Emma's bedroom.

"Oh, you saw that picture?" she asked, a little embarrassed. "He was pure white," she said in her defense. "I think I was only 11, maybe 12 when I started riding him."

"Your room was so… pink," he came back, trying to figure this girl out, who he'd known now for quite a few years.

"I like pink," she admitted sheepishly. "It's one of my favorite colors."

"It's just funny. I just never saw you that way," Leroy admitted. "Remember the first time we met, when I was cleaning out the horse stalls?"

"Yeah, my dad had just kidnapped me and brought me out to the prairie to save me from killing myself," Emma recalled. "That was a long time ago. Thanks to Hal, I've been going to AA meetings ever since. And my dad still goes to Al-anon." Emma chuckled. Hal was this well worn thread which wove itself through their family. Knowing him so long, she couldn't imagine Hal not being part of her life. Or Leroy either for that matter. They'd been friends now for such a long time. It seemed natural to her to be part of Hal's ceremonies.

"Seems like, thanks to Hal and Creator, we're both sober," Leroy put together. "I remember when Hal and Kyle found me in front of the Grocery Mart." Leroy shook his head. "And now, I'm here, putting together ceremony and training horses for a living. Life can sure turn on a dime."

"You're good at it too," Emma confessed. "Not quite as good as

Hal, but a close second."

"Hal's a natural. I think he was born a horse in his last life," Leroy chuckled. "He's just got this way of understanding animals, and it don't matter what kind."

"He's got a big heart," Emma suggested. "It's what makes him a good man, in any situation, because he always comes from his heart."

Before he placed the towel down on the tall buffalo grasses, he stomped them down with his moccasins. As they sat down on the small bluff, looking at the ceremonial site and the expansive prairie, Emma saw something speckled poking up through the grass. It was a hawk feather.

"Oh, look at this," Emma exclaimed as she leaned over to pick it up. "A hawk feather. I had a dream that someone handed me a hawk feather this morning." But then she got quiet because she felt shy about telling him the rest of her dream.

"That's a nice one too," Leroy said as Emma showed it to him. Gazing at the cloud covered sky, over in the distance, one cloud looked like it was boiling. As she looked at it more closely, it took on the shape of a bear's head. It distinctly had two ears and a bear's snout.

"There's a bear in the sky," Emma mused for a moment.

"Where?" Leroy leaned his head towards her as he followed Emma's pointing finger with his eyes. The scent of wild flowers came from her hair. There were other good things he noticed too.

"See that cloud that looks like it's boiling? It has two ears and a bear's snout. And it looks like its mouth is moving, like it's saying something," Emma filled in. Leroy scouted the heavens and found the cloud she was pointing to. Seeing the snout move, he started to laugh.

"I think it's saying "Wau, WAU, WAU," Leroy laughed. Sitting on the bluff, they gazed out at the land in a comfortable silence for a long time. There was a gentle ease between them.

In his training to become a warrior, he always managed to have guts of steel. But there was a feeling down inside him that he couldn't ignore anymore. He'd been fighting it for a long time. Just like a buffalo, he knew he had to face this storm head-on. Otherwise, it'd get the better of him. But it seemed to be impossible, because of all the looming obstacles. Like a brick wall, he could barely muster up the courage to scale, it stared him down, gnawing at his insides. Then he looked deep into her forest green eyes. In that instant, he realized that he'd never even kissed her. But all the weeks when he was gone, he had truly missed her.

"Shh," Emma whispered as she listen to something. "Do you hear that?" Off in the distance, Leroy heard the sound of an animal crying. It sounded like a baby bear. Standing up, the wind blew his long brown hair from his strong, bronze face, revealing his soft earth-toned eyes. Like an hunting eagle, his sharp eyes scouted the surrounding rolling grasslands. Out from the underbrush, he saw the tall grasses shaking back and forth.

"There!" Leroy pointed towards some bushes about a half a football field way. Shuffling through the underbrush, was a mother black bear and her two baby cubs. Running and tumbling through the buffalo grasses, making a joyful raucous, were two brown, carefree fur balls. While the mother bear searched for food, her two toddlers chased and played.

"Look, way over there," Leroy pointed to the mama bear combing through the shrubs for berries. "You never see bears out here anymore."

"Oh," Emma squealed. "That is so sweet. The last time I saw baby bears was up in the Sequoias! Have you ever been to see the Redwoods?"

"Naw, not yet," he admitted. "Hal talked about them, when we traveled out west. But it would have been too far out of the way."

"Oh, you've got to see them sometime," Emma stated. "They are so magical."

"Maybe I'll go there with you one day," Leroy edged forth to confront that bigger than life brick wall. And then it happened. The words pushed themselves right out of his mouth as he moved her curls away from her mystical green eyes.

Spreading his brilliant, protective heavenly wings around Emma and Leroy, Micah whispered to Dakotah. "He's going to say it!"

"Oh, is that the plan?" asked Dakotah while his light filled eyes beamed. With his powerful wings, he shielded these two good people from interference.

"Part of the Great Mystery, I'd say," responded Micah, knowing the true Divine Mystery was Love.

With a humble heart and piercing eyes of soft, moist earth, Leroy reached his powerful, muscled, copper-colored arms across the space between them. His long, flowing dark brown hair fell forward as he pushed away the fear caught in his throat. Gently, he cupped her small hands in his. "I love you Emma," Leroy paused as her surprised eyes got very big. "I want you to be my wife."

The holiest waters on Earth streamed from her eyes, but she could not speak. The curls on her blonde head bobbed up and down. When she finally found her voice, she uttered a resounding 'YES!' That's when Leroy leaned his head towards hers and gently touched her lips with his.

Overcome with joy at this human love, which is so rare on Earth these days, Micah, the holy Warrior, shot through the skies like a flaming comet, leaving a trail of sparkling white fire behind him. Soaring and dashing over the rolling farmland speckled across the Great Plains, his heart roared with the Spirit of Love. This one lone holy Warrior trumpeted through the celestial sea of love, which held the stars in place. While gathering sparkling stardust on his brilliant wings, he called to the heavenly Host with his trumpet. They cascaded down like snowflakes from the Higher Realms. In a flash, they burst through the heavens with the Light of a thousand suns. Above every hotspot on the battlefield, the sky was lit with sacred fire love. This light washed the sky, shrinking the clouds of darkness until they evaporated from sight.

After a few moments, Leroy had the agonizing courage to admit something else. "I've felt that way for a long time now," he started. "But, I didn't want to lose my best friend, if you didn't feel the same way. And I couldn't see my way around the fact that most of my family hate white people," he laughed.

"I can't say I blame them, after all that's happened," Emma responded compassionately. "I mean, this whole ceremony came about because white Christian soldiers slaughtered Native woman and children."

"It's not only that," Leroy offered. "My mom's been trying to marry me off to a girl on the rez for a long time."

"Oh? What happened there?" Emma had the courage to ask.

"I don't know," Leroy admitted. "I just never felt that way about any of them. The one girl I thought I'd marry before I went to boot camp, found someone else after I left. So I just never looked back." Emma's gaze drifted to the mama bear and her cubs. There was a long silence as the holy Thunders rolled overhead.

Turning towards him, Emma looked across the prairie. It was so far away from the world she grew up in. "You know I grew up in California. Every kind of person under the sun lives there. I don't really see color. Not like they do out here. But I can tell when someone hates me," Emma responded. "And my dad's not very easy either."

"I'm not afraid of your dad," Leroy shot back. "I don't know.

Maybe it's a crazy idea. But I can't imagine not having you in my life."

"I thought about you everyday that you were gone," Emma admitted shyly holding the hawk feather in her hand.

"I know, me too," Leroy said as he held her hand.

"Well yeah, you think about yourself all the time!" Emma laughed, poking fun at him.

"You know what I mean," Leroy chuckled, nudging into her. "Seeing your pink room only made it worse. I thought about how much you gave up to live out here."

"It saved my life," Emma started. "Well, when Hal showed up in WalMart, that is when things got better. Before that, my dad had me locked up in a prison." Wrapping their arms around each other, they lay back down on the towel, watching the Thunders roll across the Big Sky.

Not long afterward, the Big Drum started pounding as the singers sang Medicine Songs to the Bear. On the wings of the wind, the music was carried across the prairie, into the Great Beyond. Someone else had spotted the mama bear and her cubs. A sign of healing for those who crossed over through the West Gate.

In high spirits, Leroy and Emma walked arm in arm, down the hill with shiny, bright smiles on their faces. From above, a gentle, loving rain began to fall. The Spirit of the Rain, these living waters cleared away the unworldly debris after centuries of war and destruction. Washed with Heaven's holy Light, the air was pure and fresh. The once blood-stained Earth was cleansed and reclaimed by the holy Warriors. Peace was restored. After more than a century, this patch of earth, riddled with violent spiritual storms, a place where, in one heartless act blood stained the soil, was now finally free. Through a vision of two bold men, ceremony and ceaseless prayer brought healing and love. Once again, allowing Spirit to touch ground making it sacred forevermore.

And so it was. In the land where the Eagle flies, that hatred was turned to Love. High above the mountain passes, this free bird rode the currents of the wind with its wings reaching out in opposite directions. Soaring above the summer clouds, this powerful raptor saw the People below and taught them freedom. Freedom from their lower natures. Freedom that is found in forgiveness. With every cycle of the moon, the Sacred Fire found its way back into the hearts of the People. With every season of Earth, the sacred spark within them slowly awakened. For the road Home lies within. It mattered not their creed or color of their skin. For they came from all over. Those roaring flames of the Sacred Fire gave them a place to get warm, after suffering so long in the cold.

With a humble heart, a skillful fisher of souls bumped along the back roads across a vast countryside in a beat-up pickup truck. On the way, he met lots of people who walked a razor's edge between two worlds; the world of Spirit and the world of flesh. Many were slaves to that flesh, as he once was himself. From experience he knew, it was never easy waking a man's spirit out of its deepest midnight slumber. Haunted by the hoot owls of the past, most had forgotten their eternal origins. There was an emptiness behind their searching, lonely eyes. But with tender words, he gently guided them back to the inner song of their soul.

Many a night, this peace-loving Earth Spirit slept under a glimmering canopy of stars. Sitting by a fireside, he was often guided by the Elders from Venus, Jupiter and Mars. Beyond the edges of time, all of humanity shared a common Spirit. It was around the Sacred Fire, where people gathered together, that the seeds of greatness began to stir. Here, they listened to the Spirit of the Stars which awakened their passion for Truth.

Before dawn's early light, under the sky's deep blue dome, speckled with twinkling morning stars, this humble fisher of souls stood in front of his camp stove waiting for his cowboy coffee to brew. Small sounds, birds chirping, Earth music from the world around him made his soul sing as he looked out across the prairie. Pouring a bunch of sugar into his tin mug, he counted the many teepees which dotted the land. There was so much to do. On her wings, the wind playfully carried the smoke from the blazing, crackling Sacred Fire across the rolling grasslands. Watching the flames lick towards the sky, he knew he had to cast a wide net in order to finish the mission at hand. There were spirits to cross over, battlegrounds to clear and souls to enlighten. And that was all before breakfast.

Stirring a little milk into his morning brew, he could hear that pounding sacred drumbeat along with song-filled voices starting at the outer edge of camp, the ceremonial morning alarm clock. On top of everything else, there was a wedding to plan and some horse whispering to do. The cycle of life kept going. As he put that tin mug to his mouth, he felt the hot liquid brew wet his lips, going down his throat to warm his stomach. *"Time to get cracking,"* he thought to himself as a rosy glow slowly spilled over the low, rolling hillsides on the eastern horizon.

Following the cycle of the moon, these two wayfarers and their small caravan had traveled far and wide across this grand countryside; Wounded Knee, Little Big Horn, the Trail of Tears and other blood-stained, battle-torn, haunted regions. With every Sacred Fire these killing fields, territories once ruled by forces of the darkest night, were reclaimed by the heavenly Warriors, restoring the sacredness which was once lost and soiled. With the blessing of holy men, Sacred Fireplaces lit up the land calling all good people to gathered and to pray their brothers Home.

After taking the last sip of his morning brew, he put the tin mug into a soapy bowl of water and rinsed it out. There was a kink in his back as he stretched from side to side. Though he never intended on being a road man, nothing made his heart smile more. As Grandma Moon dipped below the western horizon, he turned towards the teepee. He knew what he had to do next.

Exploding from the East, a huge flaming orb, a celestial ball of blazing fire, peeked over the rolling hillsides, in a beautiful sunrise. Rays of sparkling sunlight were caught in the heavy dew drops which coated the buffalo grasses "COME ON LEROY! GET UP!" Across the open field, his voice bellowed at his Second in Command, still fast asleep after a long ride. "WE'RE BURNING DAYLIGHT!"

TRAVELER OF THE STARS

He was a seasoned traveler of the stars

Who walked with the Creator of Saturn, Jupiter and Mars

Dancing in Sacred Circles with the Spirit of the Rain

He laughed as the waters splashed on the window pane

With a bow of fire and flaming arrows

The Spirit Path he chose was quite narrow

Traversing far across the Milky Way

Never long in one place did he stay

Within his heart lived the Philosopher's Stone

A search for Truth ruled his bones

In the heavens, he is quite a good friend

Who again I long to meet at this journey's end

A spiritual warrior who fought the good fight
He met his adversaries with strong delight
To become a Master, one needs another to oppose
These jousts of battle is what he chose

On wings of fire, he traveled the Four Winds
With Holy Thunder he healed double-hearted men
A lightning rod as his walking stick
Few matched his sweet smile and fiery wit

Knowing soul hunger in his earthly life
He sought to help others to heal their strife
With eagle bone whistles and fire light
He knew Great Spirit would make it right

Healing the Earth Mother is no small task
"Will you join me?" He would ask
Many hands make the work light
Heart-felt prayers keep the stars bright

When you chance to meet a traveler of the stars
Who walks with the Creator of Saturn, Jupiter and Mars
Your life, my friend, will forever change
And you will dance with the Spirit of the Rain

In puddles, your feet will move to the beat of the drum
In bright flowered meadows, your spirit will run

Around Sacred Fires, you will find your way
With heart-felt words, you will finally pray

AUTHOR'S NOTE

FOREST GREEN EYES

Looking into the deep of her forest green eyes
You could hear the Redwoods reaching up to the sky
The joy of Wonder followed her each and every step
Near the hollow of the woods, where the Creatures slept

Following her heart, skipping into another time
Where Children still laugh at nursery rhymes
Stillness enfolded her deep in the woods
Where only the whispers of Spirits understood

The longing of her heart, the desire of her soul
For the courage, the dauntless love to be bold
The Wind came upon her and blew her a kiss
"Come here, my Woodland Fairy Princess."

In the Faraway of the Meadow, there was a knoll
With a lonesome Oak Tree, where stories were told
Of Gallant Knights who rode their fierce steeds
To rescue Fair Maidens and fulfill grand, Heroic deeds

No mortal men gathered in the grove of knotty pine
To hear the wild and wooly tales of that faraway time
But every hoof print of Truth could be heard
Carried by the Wind on the wing of a bird

Up on the knoll of that Lonesome Oak Tree
Is a place where Creatures, Gnomes and Fairies long to be
To listen to the tales of a time yet to come
A time when All will remember the ONE

She leaned in as they whispered their stories of Old
Of sorcerers and dragons, and castles they told
The stars, they twinkled as the twilight came on
The moon was adorned in a shimmering saffron

Her eyes grew weary by the coming of the night
Cuddling with Creatures by the glowing firelight
In the morning when the sun made everything new
Amidst the meadow, with the Creatures, greeted a lovely Sky Blue

Hearkening Angels awaited in the hush of the morn
As a new glorious day of Life was about to be born
The Meadow Lark sang its love song to the dawn
Waiting for the skittering fairies to come along

As the Creature beside the Woodland Fairy stirred
Awakening each other without a single word
Her eyes slowly opened, hearing just in Time
The Universal Clock let out its Morning Chime

"Go My Children and make Thy Way
With this Blessing of a brand new day
For all that I AM, I have given Thee
Right Here under this lonesome Oak Tree"

So the skittering Fairies and the Creatures arose
Greeting each other in Loving Repose
Soon to retreat to the Hundred Acre Wood
Where only the Whispers of Spirits Understood

The longing of the Heart, the Need to be Free
A Life to be lived with Courage and Love, endlessly
Go forth while your heart is beating and live fully this day
Rejoice! For Love is leading, while you make Your Way

In the midst of all the Sun Dances and ceremonies, Ohiya and I found the time to visit the towering evergreens, the Redwoods, which are the Record Keepers and the Guardians of the West. It's magical there. But to enjoy it, the analytical mind has to be left behind. For the Redwoods are a mystical experience of the soul and the senses.

It was around that time, Ohiya told me a story about a Sun Dance he put together in Northern California. Loggers were threatening to clear cut Virgin Forest, the Old Ones who'd never been touched in a harmful way. For mere dollars, these thoughtless men were willing to destroy a kingdom of flora and fauna. So, to counteract that, Ohiya made a prayer and backed it with a Sun Dance. By the second year of the dance, the logging company went bankrupt. By the forth year of the dance, a new logging company bought the old one. With a conscious mind, this new logging company promised the people that they wouldn't cut down this Virgin Forest. It was a victory for creatures and redwoods, alike.

One autumn day, sitting on the floor of my room, Ohiya began to talk in his slow, methodical voice. "Before White Buffalo Calf Woman, there were many Spirits that made up the Great Mystery. They governed all of Creation." This is how my instruction began.

"During this time, the Eagle Nation was struggling, on the verge of extinction," Ohiya went on. "They prayed for assistance, guidance and health. The Great Mystery assisted. It answered by sending the Star Nation to assist the Eagle Nation. The Star Nation carried the Medicine

Bundles (external and internal) to the Eagle Nation. Accepting these Medicine Bundles, the Eagle Nation was healed through the teachings, ritual and ceremony."

While I listened to his every word, I took great notes. So many times now, I wish we'd bought a recorder. That way I'd have a recording of his voice and his teachings. "Shall I go on," he asked impatiently.

"The time is unknown, how long the Medicine Bundles were with the Eagle Nation," Ohiya continued. "But when the Buffalo Nation was struggling, on the verge of extinction, they asked the Great Mystery what to do. They didn't know what to do. The Great Mystery answered their prayer, by asking the Eagle Nation to pass on the Medicine Bundles to the Buffalo Nation."

By 2009, I'd been going to ceremony to Lakota Ceremonies for about 16 years, since 1993. But on the West Coast, no one really taught the Old Ways, Native ceremony. Perhaps they didn't know themselves. So, with my piecemeal knowledge, I admit, it was hard for me to comprehend this teaching at the time. I'd never heard it told, quite like this. 'Aho Mitakuye Oyasin' means for "All My Relations." And through this story, I learned what that meant. "Shall I go on?" Ohiya patiently waited for me to finish.

"And so, the Buffalo Nation received instructions on how this Medicine was going to be brought," Ohiya waited for my writing to catch up. "They were told to bring four strong muddy bulls, and put them in the Four Directions, facing inwards. They were given instructions and songs to sing. When they saw the Spirits bringing the Medicine to them, the leader of the Buffalo Nation made special preparations, a sacred circle."

"The leader of the Eagle Nation was instructed on how to take the Medicine to the Buffalo Nation. They were given songs and a formation. As the Eagle Nation came down, to bring their donation, they circled high above the Buffalo Nation, singing as they came down. When the buffalo heard the eagles singing, they started to dance and sing."

"The Eagle landed in the center of the Great Circle of Buffalo. The leader of the Buffalo accepted the Medicine. The four muddy bulls began to dance and sing in acceptance of the Medicine. Then, they went running out in the Four Directions to heal the Buffalo Nation."

He'd always give me this look as I was furiously trying to write it all down. I knew we should have gotten a recorder. I'd see him out of the corner of my eye, tapping the end of his pencil on the heel of his bare foot.

"Okay, okay! Give me a second," I'd say exasperated.

"And so that's how the Medicine came down, from the Star Nation to the Eagle Nation, to the Buffalo Nation. But then the Two-leggeds were out of balance, starving and asking for help. And that's when the Great Mystery instructed the Buffalo Nation to bring the two Medicine Bundles to the Two-leggeds," Ohiya sat there for a moment, in silence, allowing me, the pencil pusher, to scribble this all down.

How could I know, that he'd be gone a few months later? And that these memories (and my scribbled notes) of that afternoon, would be one of the cherished ones, all that I had left. "Shall we go on?" Over his glasses, Ohiya caught my eye.

"This Medicine," he began. "Came through to balance the External and the Internal, so that we could live in Harmony and Peace. The Buffalo Nation were instructed to choose the prettiest young maiden, a woman. They sent this young woman, Pte San Win, to bring the two Medicine Bundles (external and internal), to the Two-leggeds. But the Two-leggeds weren't ready for the Internal Medicine. So they only chose one, the External, which was the Sacred Pipe."

Later on, Ohiya explained to me, that the External Medicine Bundle was Ceremony. Which was a way for the Two-leggeds to communicate to their Creator. Through the Sacred Pipe, brought by White Buffalo Calf Woman, Pte San Win, healing would come to the Two-leggeds.

"Okay, good," Ohiya said, as he pushed himself off the floor and stretched his legs. We were done for that part of the afternoon. But the teachings continued. That same afternoon, I noticed so many similarities between Lakota Ceremony and the 12 Steps of Alcoholics Anonymous. Each, in their own way, brings the student to a working relationship with their Creator, where 'being of service' is the Highest Calling possible.

"I can only take you as far as you've been," Ohiya said to me, as we started this learning. "I can teach you about ceremony, just like teaching you about a car," Ohiya went on. "I'll show you how the car works, the brakes, the engine, the transmission," he paused. "But I won't give you the keys."

"WHY NOT?!" I asked a little indignantly. But he stayed silent, which was aggravating. Then, it dawned on me. "Oh, because the keys come from Spirit." And that's what we did. From scratch, we built Sun Dance Arbors, an Inipi (sweat lodge), did drug and alcohol counseling, and he threatened to put me in a pit, to do a Vision Quest. Some years before, I had done a Vision Quest, where you go up on the hill for four days to pray and fast. It was and is, a great experience, where I learned much about myself.

Ohiya had asked me to sun dance. It wasn't the first time I'd been asked to dance. Nor was it the last. But I was never 'called' to the Sun Dance Arbor to dance. Though it called me in other ways. And to give that commitment and sacrifice, it had to come from within me.

This story is inspired by real people and powerful dreams, visions. Though none of the characters in this story resemble them. So many people go through hardship on Mother Earth, mainly because they make wrong choices. Yet, Creator is always willing to guide the way out of the darkness, if we have the courage to ask. I wish you peace on your journey. I thank you for being willing to share this stretch of road with me. Peace and blessings... Aho Mitakuye Oyasin.

December 24, 2009 12:55 am; Ohiya's funeral was done and I was back in California. His spirit was around me all the time. He got pretty good at turning on and off certain lights. When I made him a spirit plate, sometimes he'd move the bowl across the table. Often he came into my dreams. There were times, I just longed to sleep, and we'd be together again. But morning always came. But on this one particular night, I was just going to turn out the light to go to sleep, when something compelled me to grab a pen. And this is what it wrote.

Rose, when I come back, you'll see
I'll have a strong body
One whose knees are good
With strong arms to chop wood

We'll ride horse down by the river
I'll keep my arrows in their quiver
We'll spend nights by fireside
Counting shooting stars 'til morning light

You'll fall asleep in my loving arms
I will keep you safe from harm

You'll be my woman, I'll be your man
Together, we will forever stand

For the love that brought us here together
Is among the stars now and forever

Rose, when I come back, you'll see
I will have a strong body
Wait until the morning light
Forever could begin tonight

    I waited for him for months, to ring the doorbell and be standing right outside the front door. People weave themselves into the blankets of our lives. When their thread is cut short, it leaves a hole, a stop. Sometimes the Weaver just seems to stop weaving. But that's not really true. It just feels like it, as we wade through pools of agonizing grief. Grief is like a waiting room, or a long, dimly lit hallway. It's a disbelief that someone is really gone. It's a grasping for things, which can't be reached. It's holding on. No matter what, it's holding on.

    Late one night, maybe 2 am, I felt his foot steps walking across my bed. They were heavy foot steps. I could feel the impressions on the foam mattress, the futon we shared lying on the floor. My eyes were still closed, but I could feel him there. "Don't spoke me!" I said sternly. He stopped. It was comforting to know his spirit was close by.

    One afternoon, I was sitting in the den watching TV, when I saw the light go on in my room. After a moment, I went and turned it off. His picture was in front of the light. I went back in the den to watch TV, when the light went on again. So I went back in the room. No one was there, no cats, nothing. And I looked deeply into his eyes, on the picture. With my hands on my hips, I gazed at his face, in the picture. Then, in all earnestness, I said. "You're getting really good at turning on and off the LIGHT! Why don't you just MATERIALIZE!"

    I could feel his energy, like lightning bolts, charging through the room. Then, after a long moment, the Light turned off. I felt his Spirit turn and stomp away. I laughed. You see, every morning I made his tea in the cup we bought at the Pendleton Store and shared a small plate of food with him. When we went out to eat, I made him a plate. One night, at a Vietnamese restaurant, I set him a place next to me. The soup called Pho, was set in the middle of the table. All of a sudden, it started moving towards Ohiya's place. No one was touching it. I guess he liked that soup.

    A few months back, Ohiya came into my dream. He was alive, he told me. I was so happy in the dream. We were driving the old Buick, lovingly called the "Rez Car" which drove to ceremony all over the West Coast. In the dream, we drove south on the interstate, towards San Francisco. We stopped in a small diner. There he was, talking to people he knew about ceremony. What I learned from all of this is, we don't die. We just change form.

www.ingramcontent.com/pod-product-compliance
Lightning Source LLC
Chambersburg PA
CBHW050747100426
42744CB00012BA/1927